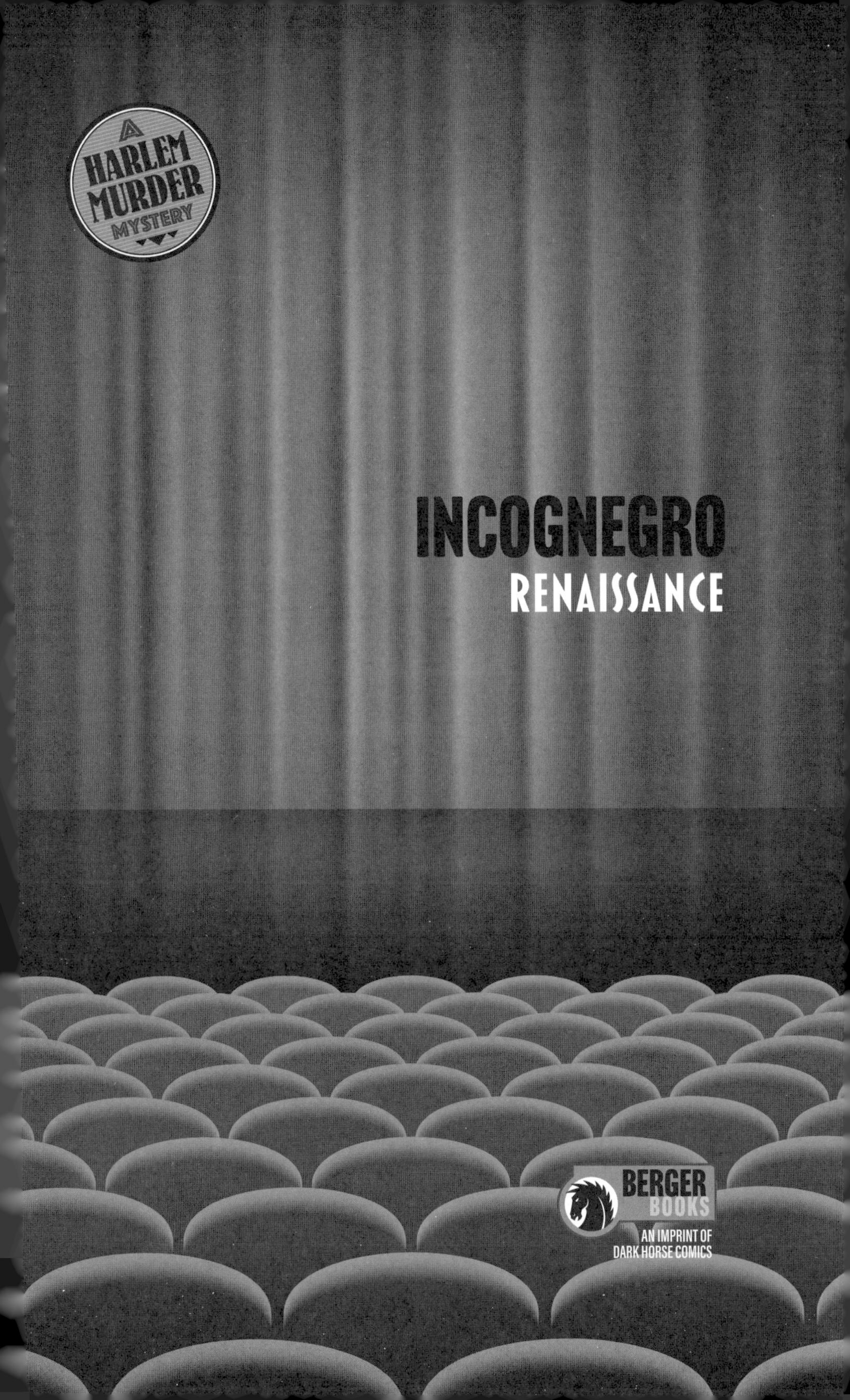
A HARLEM MURDER MYSTERY
INCOGNEGRO
RENAISSANCE
BERGER BOOKS
AN IMPRINT OF DARK HORSE COMICS

Story
MAT JOHNSON

Art
WARREN PLEECE

Letters
CLEM ROBINS

INCOG

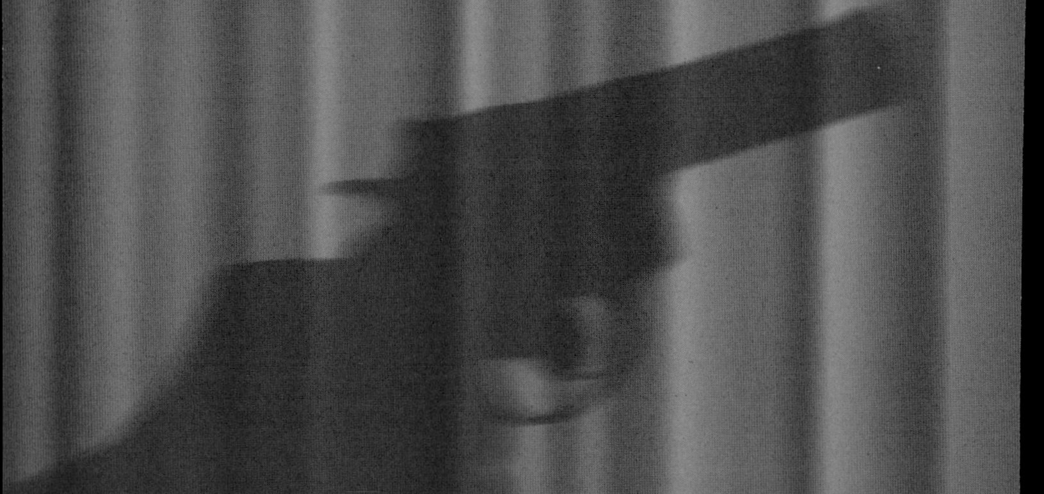

Logo & Book Design
RICHARD BRUNING

NEGRO
RENAISSANCE

Editor
KAREN BERGER

Associate Editor
RACHEL ROBERTS

Digital Art Technician
ADAM PRUETT

Publisher
MIKE RICHARDSON

CHAPTER I

"SOAKED"

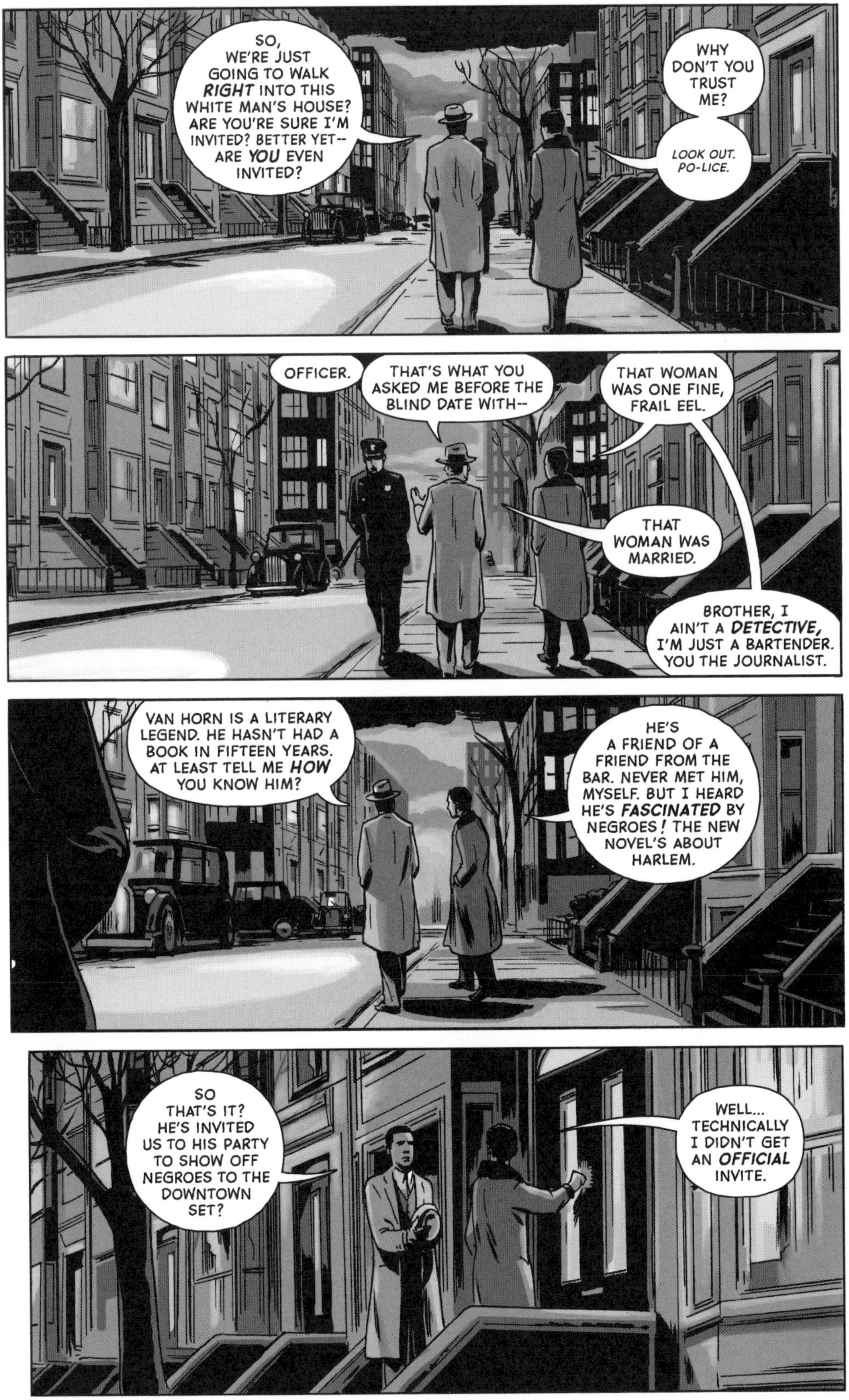
SO, WE'RE JUST GOING TO WALK *RIGHT* INTO THIS WHITE MAN'S HOUSE? ARE YOU'RE SURE I'M INVITED? BETTER YET-- ARE *YOU* EVEN INVITED?
WHY DON'T YOU TRUST ME?
LOOK OUT. PO-LICE.
OFFICER.
THAT'S WHAT YOU ASKED ME BEFORE THE BLIND DATE WITH--
THAT WOMAN WAS ONE FINE, FRAIL EEL.
THAT WOMAN WAS MARRIED.
BROTHER, I AIN'T A *DETECTIVE,* I'M JUST A BARTENDER. YOU THE JOURNALIST.
VAN HORN IS A LITERARY LEGEND. HE HASN'T HAD A BOOK IN FIFTEEN YEARS. AT LEAST TELL ME *HOW* YOU KNOW HIM?
HE'S A FRIEND OF A FRIEND FROM THE BAR. NEVER MET HIM, MYSELF. BUT I HEARD HE'S *FASCINATED* BY NEGROES*!* THE NEW NOVEL'S ABOUT HARLEM.
SO THAT'S IT? HE'S INVITED US TO HIS PARTY TO SHOW OFF NEGROES TO THE DOWNTOWN SET?
WELL... TECHNICALLY I DIDN'T GET AN *OFFICIAL* INVITE.

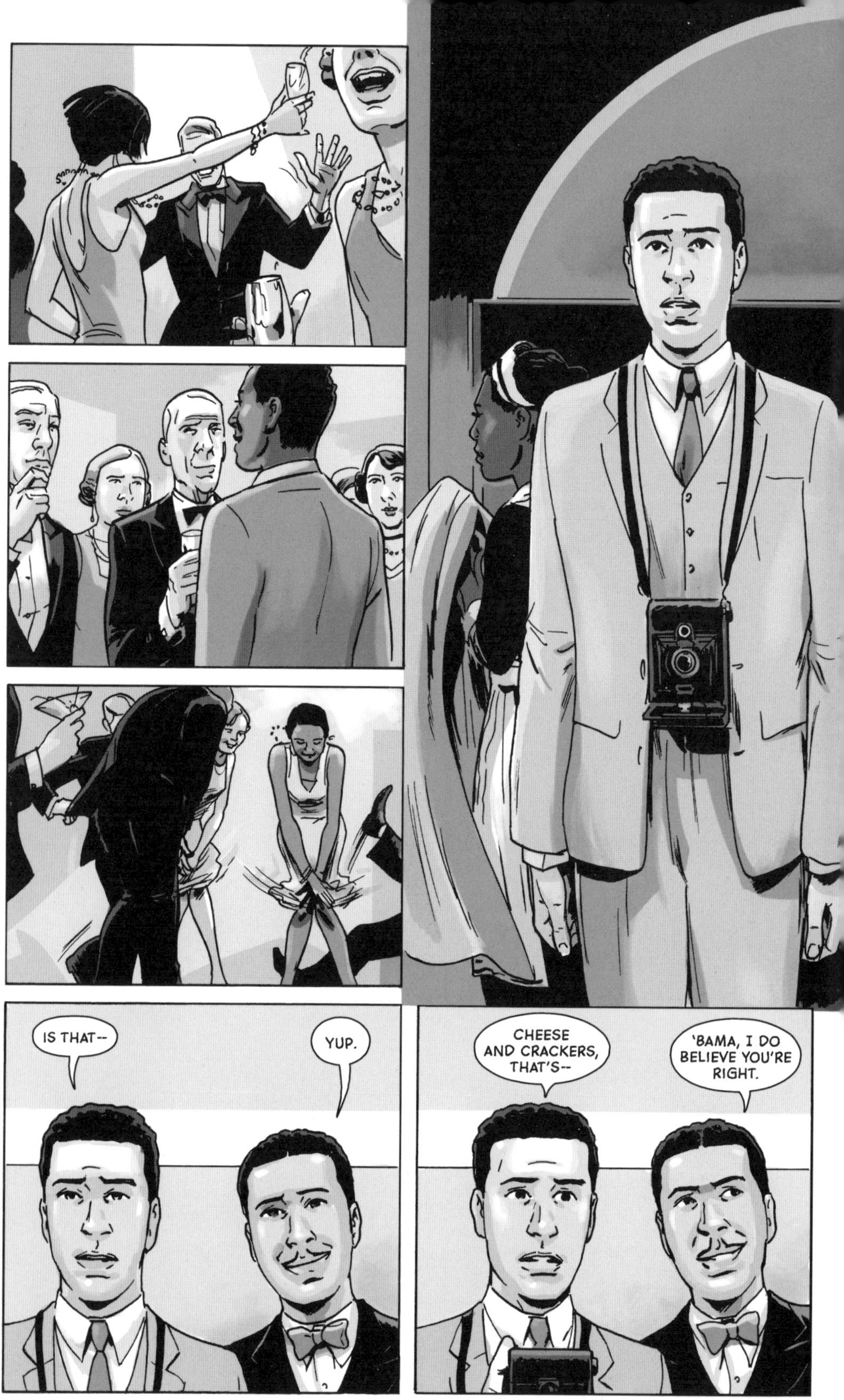
IS THAT--
YUP.
CHEESE AND CRACKERS, THAT'S--
'BAMA, I DO BELIEVE YOU'RE RIGHT.

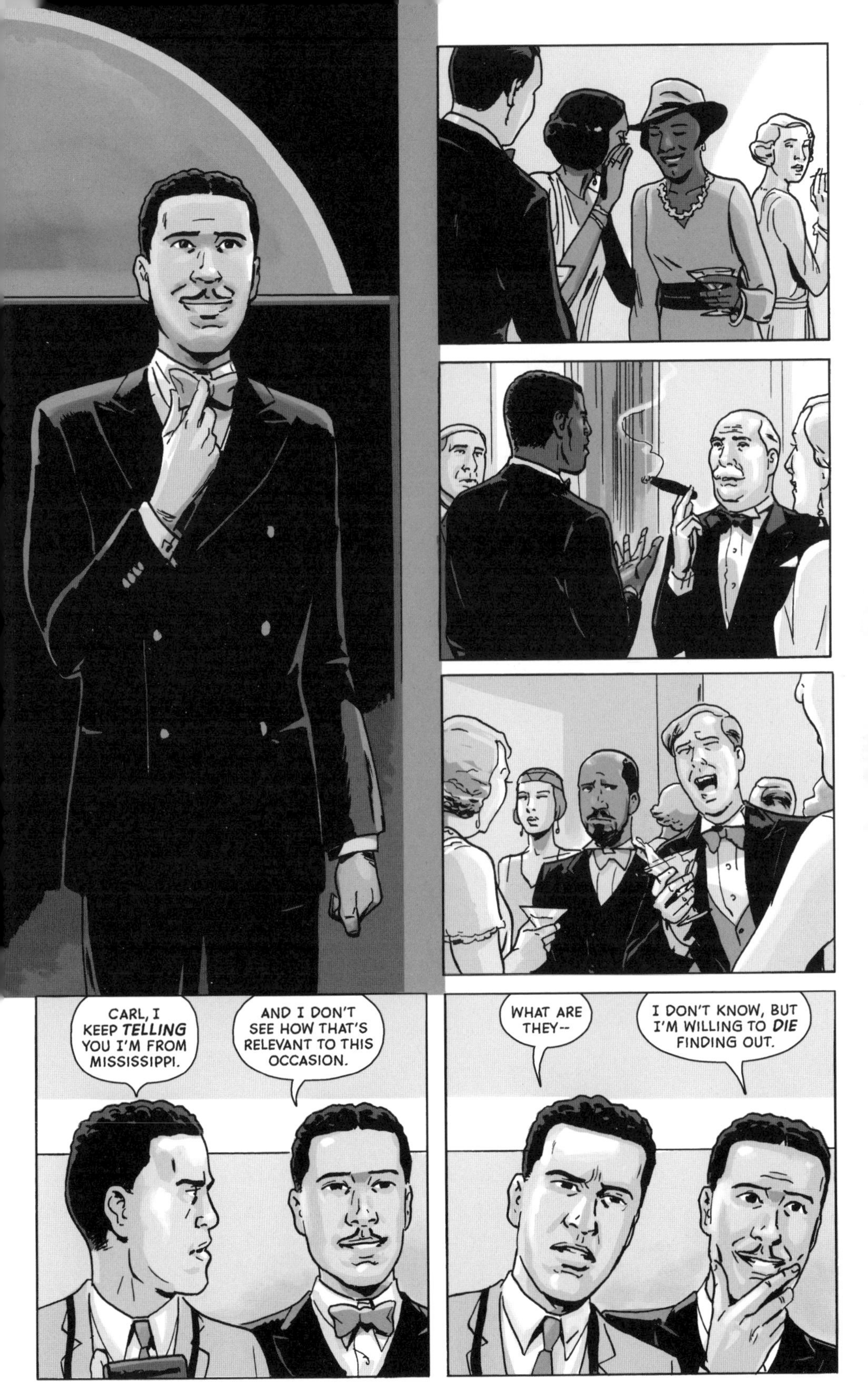
CARL, I KEEP TELLING YOU I'M FROM MISSISSIPPI.
AND I DON'T SEE HOW THAT'S RELEVANT TO THIS OCCASION.
WHAT ARE THEY--
I DON'T KNOW, BUT I'M WILLING TO DIE FINDING OUT.

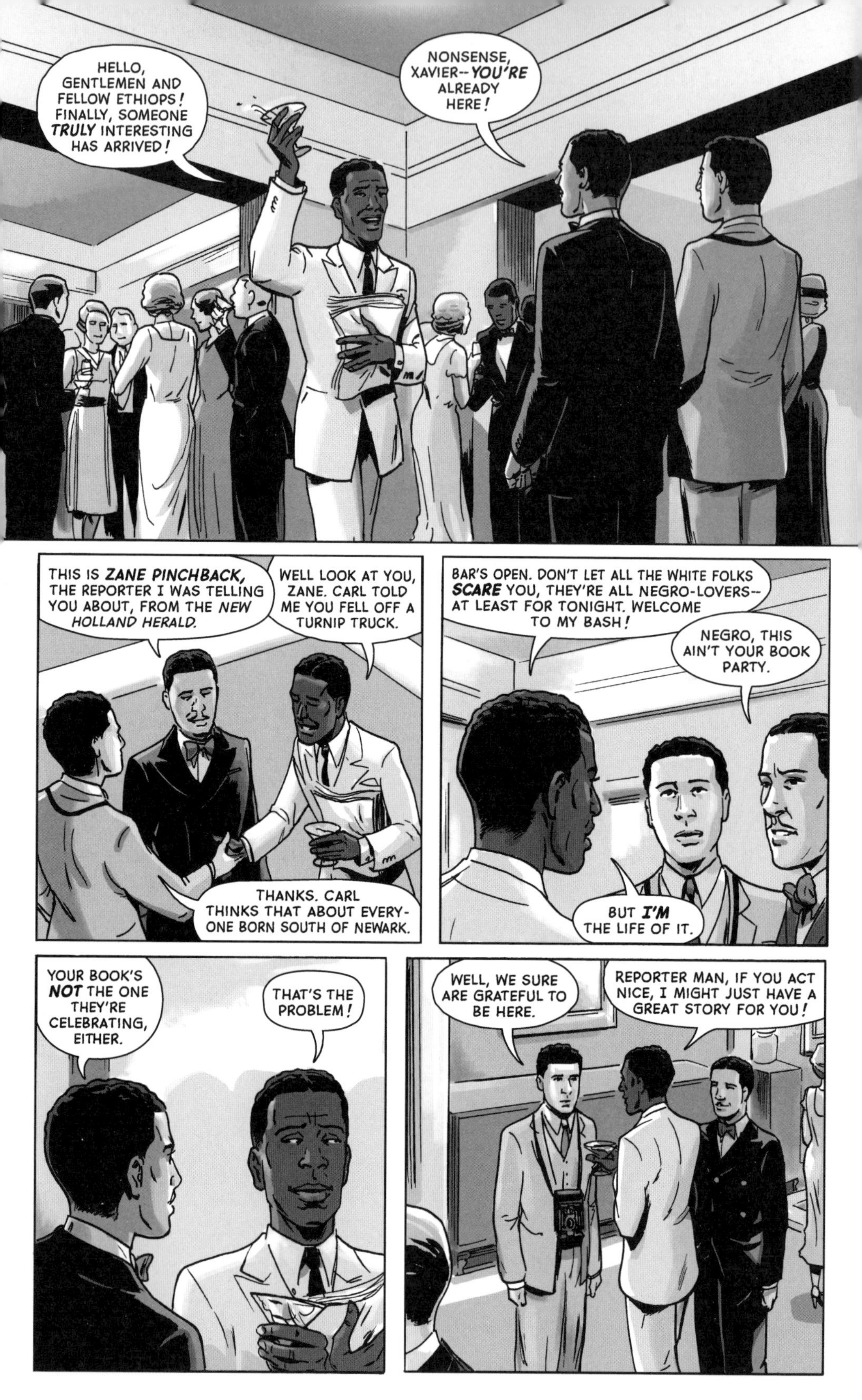
HELLO, GENTLEMEN AND FELLOW ETHIOPS! FINALLY, SOMEONE TRULY INTERESTING HAS ARRIVED!
NONSENSE, XAVIER--YOU'RE ALREADY HERE!
THIS IS ZANE PINCHBACK, THE REPORTER I WAS TELLING YOU ABOUT, FROM THE NEW HOLLAND HERALD.
WELL LOOK AT YOU, ZANE. CARL TOLD ME YOU FELL OFF A TURNIP TRUCK.
THANKS. CARL THINKS THAT ABOUT EVERY-ONE BORN SOUTH OF NEWARK.
BAR'S OPEN. DON'T LET ALL THE WHITE FOLKS SCARE YOU, THEY'RE ALL NEGRO-LOVERS-- AT LEAST FOR TONIGHT. WELCOME TO MY BASH!
NEGRO, THIS AIN'T YOUR BOOK PARTY.
BUT I'M THE LIFE OF IT.
YOUR BOOK'S NOT THE ONE THEY'RE CELEBRATING, EITHER.
THAT'S THE PROBLEM!
WELL, WE SURE ARE GRATEFUL TO BE HERE.
REPORTER MAN, IF YOU ACT NICE, I MIGHT JUST HAVE A GREAT STORY FOR YOU!

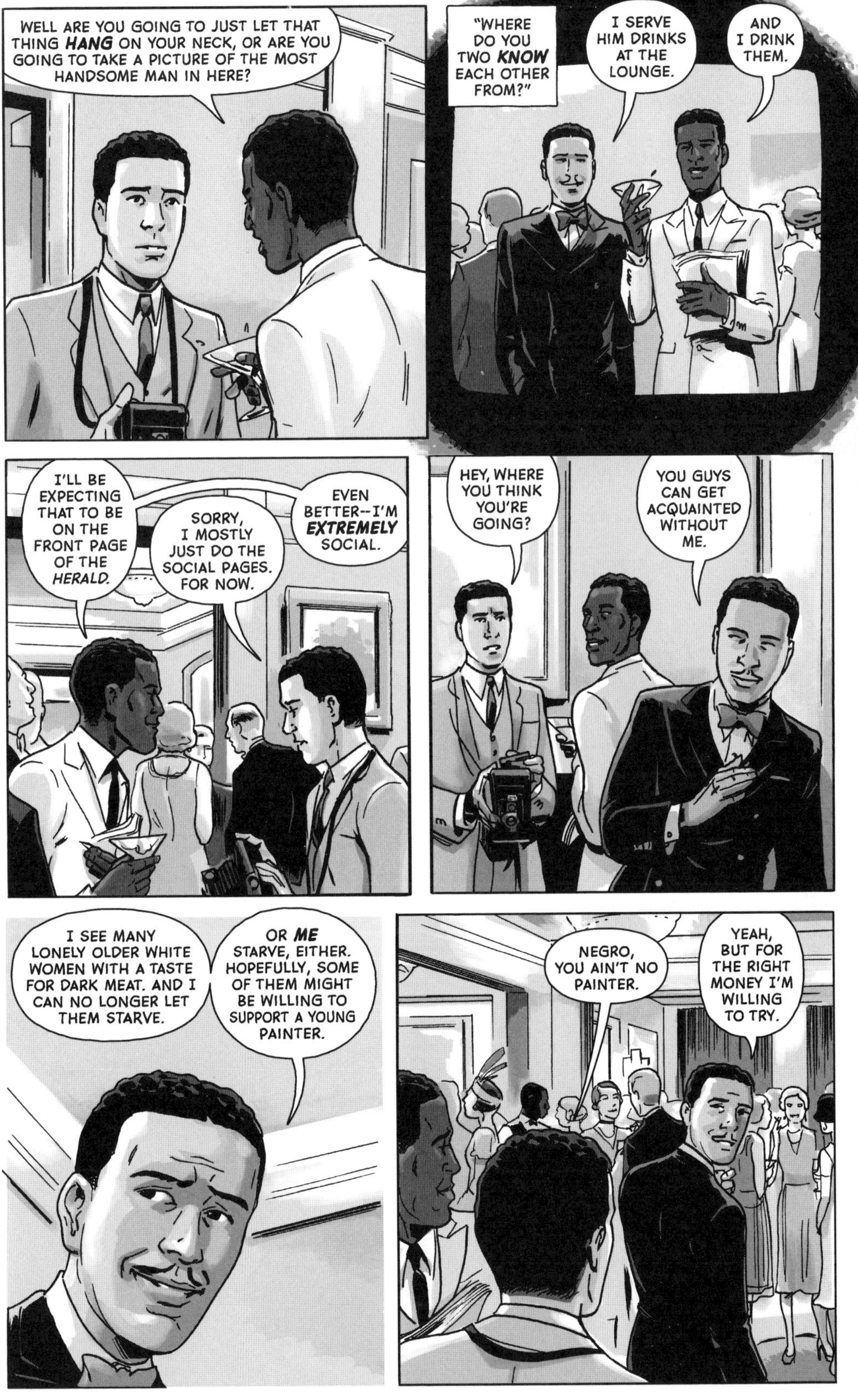
WELL ARE YOU GOING TO JUST LET THAT THING HANG ON YOUR NECK, OR ARE YOU GOING TO TAKE A PICTURE OF THE MOST HANDSOME MAN IN HERE?
"WHERE DO YOU TWO KNOW EACH OTHER FROM?"
I SERVE HIM DRINKS AT THE LOUNGE.
AND I DRINK THEM.
I'LL BE EXPECTING THAT TO BE ON THE FRONT PAGE OF THE HERALD.
SORRY, I MOSTLY JUST DO THE SOCIAL PAGES. FOR NOW.
EVEN BETTER--I'M EXTREMELY SOCIAL.
HEY, WHERE YOU THINK YOU'RE GOING?
YOU GUYS CAN GET ACQUAINTED WITHOUT ME.
I SEE MANY LONELY OLDER WHITE WOMEN WITH A TASTE FOR DARK MEAT. AND I CAN NO LONGER LET THEM STARVE.
OR ME STARVE, EITHER. HOPEFULLY, SOME OF THEM MIGHT BE WILLING TO SUPPORT A YOUNG PAINTER.
NEGRO, YOU AIN'T NO PAINTER.
YEAH, BUT FOR THE RIGHT MONEY I'M WILLING TO TRY.

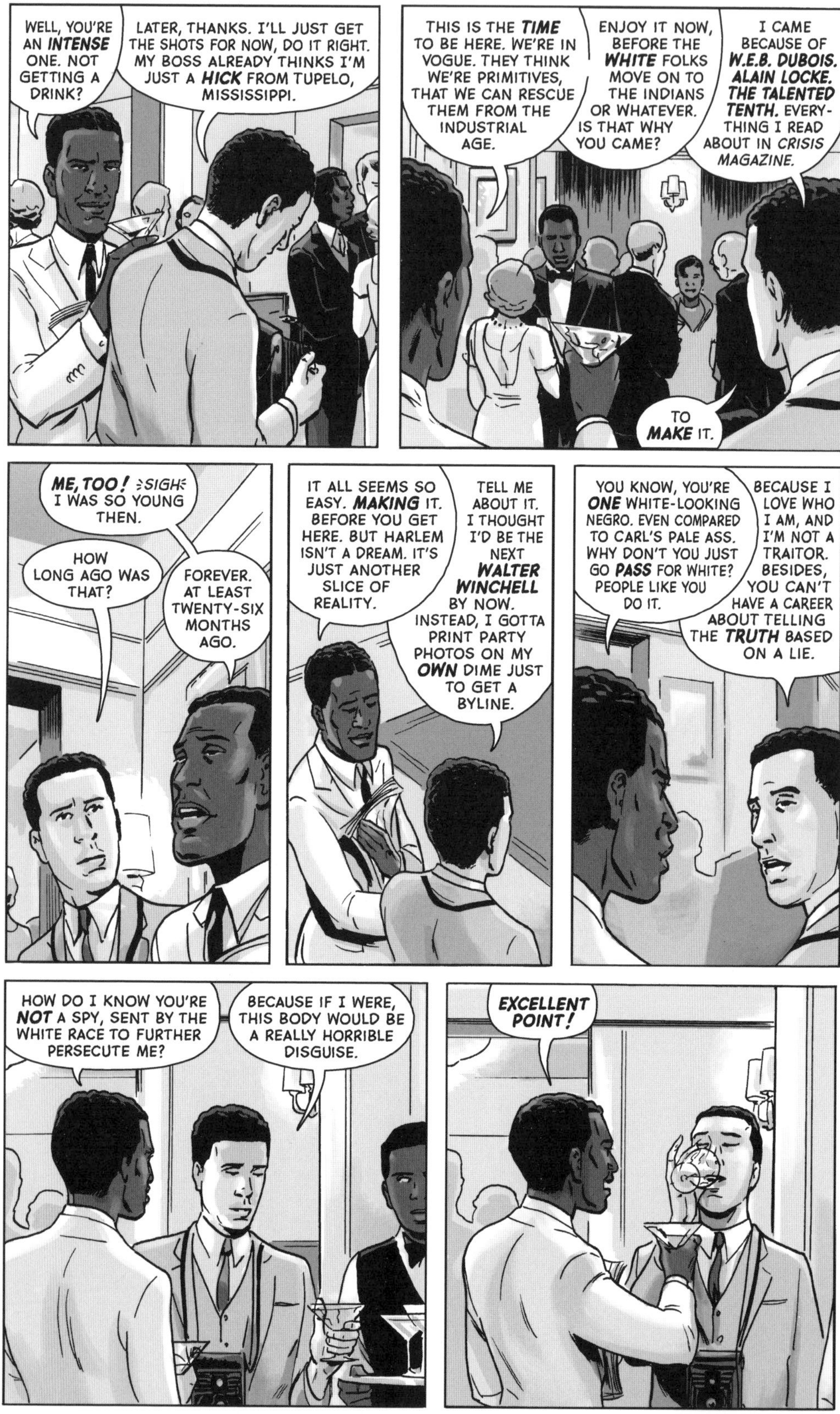
WELL, YOU'RE AN INTENSE ONE. NOT GETTING A DRINK?
LATER, THANKS. I'LL JUST GET THE SHOTS FOR NOW, DO IT RIGHT. MY BOSS ALREADY THINKS I'M JUST A HICK FROM TUPELO, MISSISSIPPI.
THIS IS THE TIME TO BE HERE. WE'RE IN VOGUE. THEY THINK WE'RE PRIMITIVES, THAT WE CAN RESCUE THEM FROM THE INDUSTRIAL AGE.
ENJOY IT NOW, BEFORE THE WHITE FOLKS MOVE ON TO THE INDIANS OR WHATEVER. IS THAT WHY YOU CAME?
I CAME BECAUSE OF W.E.B. DUBOIS. ALAIN LOCKE. THE TALENTED TENTH. EVERY-THING I READ ABOUT IN CRISIS MAGAZINE.
TO MAKE IT.
ME, TOO! SIGH I WAS SO YOUNG THEN.
HOW LONG AGO WAS THAT?
FOREVER. AT LEAST TWENTY-SIX MONTHS AGO.
IT ALL SEEMS SO EASY. MAKING IT. BEFORE YOU GET HERE. BUT HARLEM ISN'T A DREAM. IT'S JUST ANOTHER SLICE OF REALITY.
TELL ME ABOUT IT. I THOUGHT I'D BE THE NEXT WALTER WINCHELL BY NOW. INSTEAD, I GOTTA PRINT PARTY PHOTOS ON MY OWN DIME JUST TO GET A BYLINE.
YOU KNOW, YOU'RE ONE WHITE-LOOKING NEGRO. EVEN COMPARED TO CARL'S PALE ASS. WHY DON'T YOU JUST GO PASS FOR WHITE? PEOPLE LIKE YOU DO IT.
BECAUSE I LOVE WHO I AM, AND I'M NOT A TRAITOR. BESIDES, YOU CAN'T HAVE A CAREER ABOUT TELLING THE TRUTH BASED ON A LIE.
HOW DO I KNOW YOU'RE NOT A SPY, SENT BY THE WHITE RACE TO FURTHER PERSECUTE ME?
BECAUSE IF I WERE, THIS BODY WOULD BE A REALLY HORRIBLE DISGUISE.
EXCELLENT POINT!

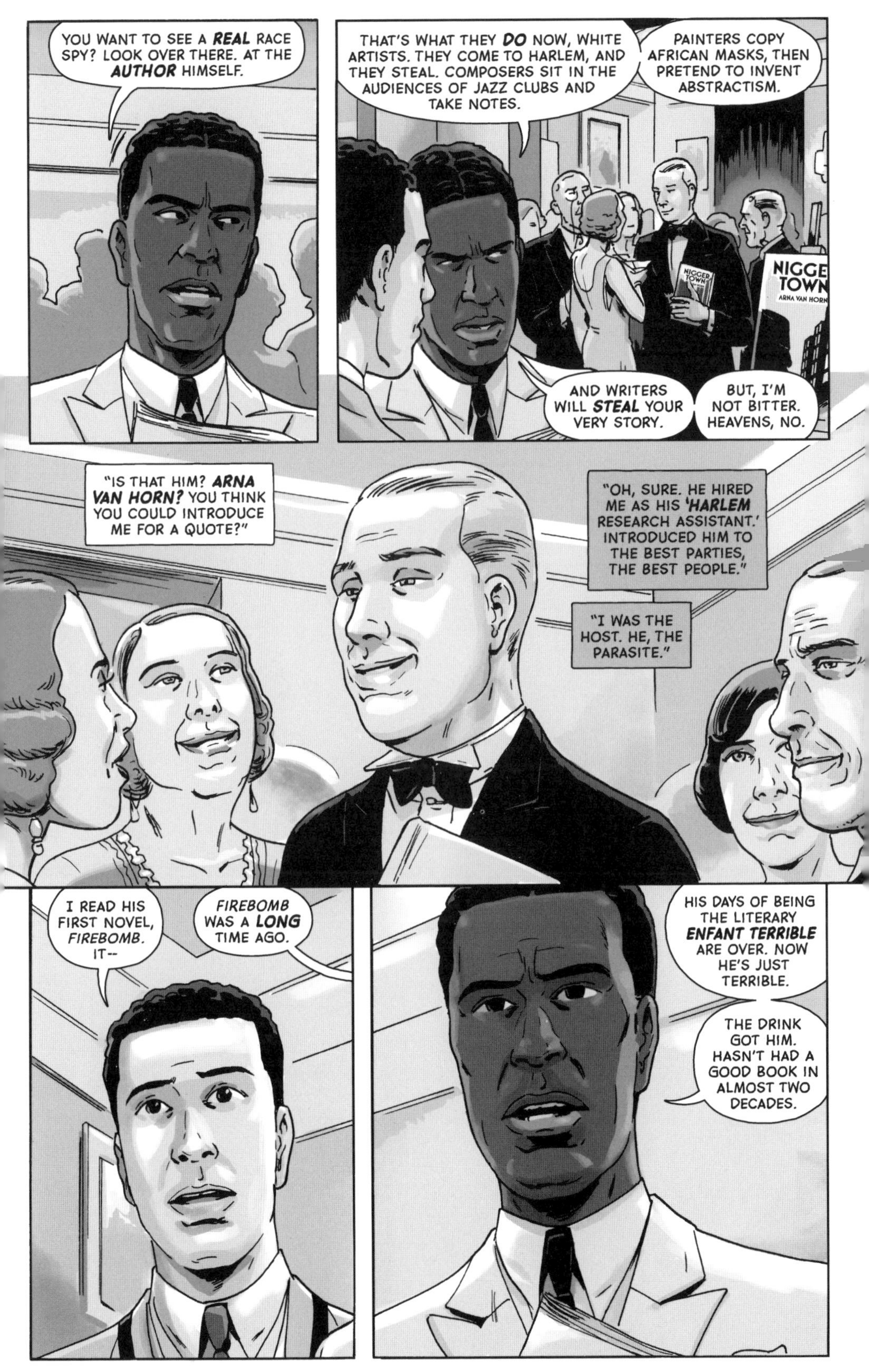

YOU WANT TO SEE A **REAL** RACE SPY? LOOK OVER THERE. AT THE **AUTHOR** HIMSELF.
THAT'S WHAT THEY **DO** NOW, WHITE ARTISTS. THEY COME TO HARLEM, AND THEY STEAL. COMPOSERS SIT IN THE AUDIENCES OF JAZZ CLUBS AND TAKE NOTES.
PAINTERS COPY AFRICAN MASKS, THEN PRETEND TO INVENT ABSTRACTISM.
NIGGER TOWN
NIGGE TOWN
ARNA VAN HORN
AND WRITERS WILL **STEAL** YOUR VERY STORY.
BUT, I'M NOT BITTER. HEAVENS, NO.
"IS THAT HIM? **ARNA VAN HORN?** YOU THINK YOU COULD INTRODUCE ME FOR A QUOTE?"
"OH, SURE. HE HIRED ME AS HIS '**HARLEM** RESEARCH ASSISTANT.' INTRODUCED HIM TO THE BEST PARTIES, THE BEST PEOPLE."
"I WAS THE HOST. HE, THE PARASITE."
I READ HIS FIRST NOVEL, *FIREBOMB.* IT--
FIREBOMB WAS A **LONG** TIME AGO.
HIS DAYS OF BEING THE LITERARY ***ENFANT TERRIBLE*** ARE OVER. NOW HE'S JUST TERRIBLE.
THE DRINK GOT HIM. HASN'T HAD A GOOD BOOK IN ALMOST TWO DECADES.

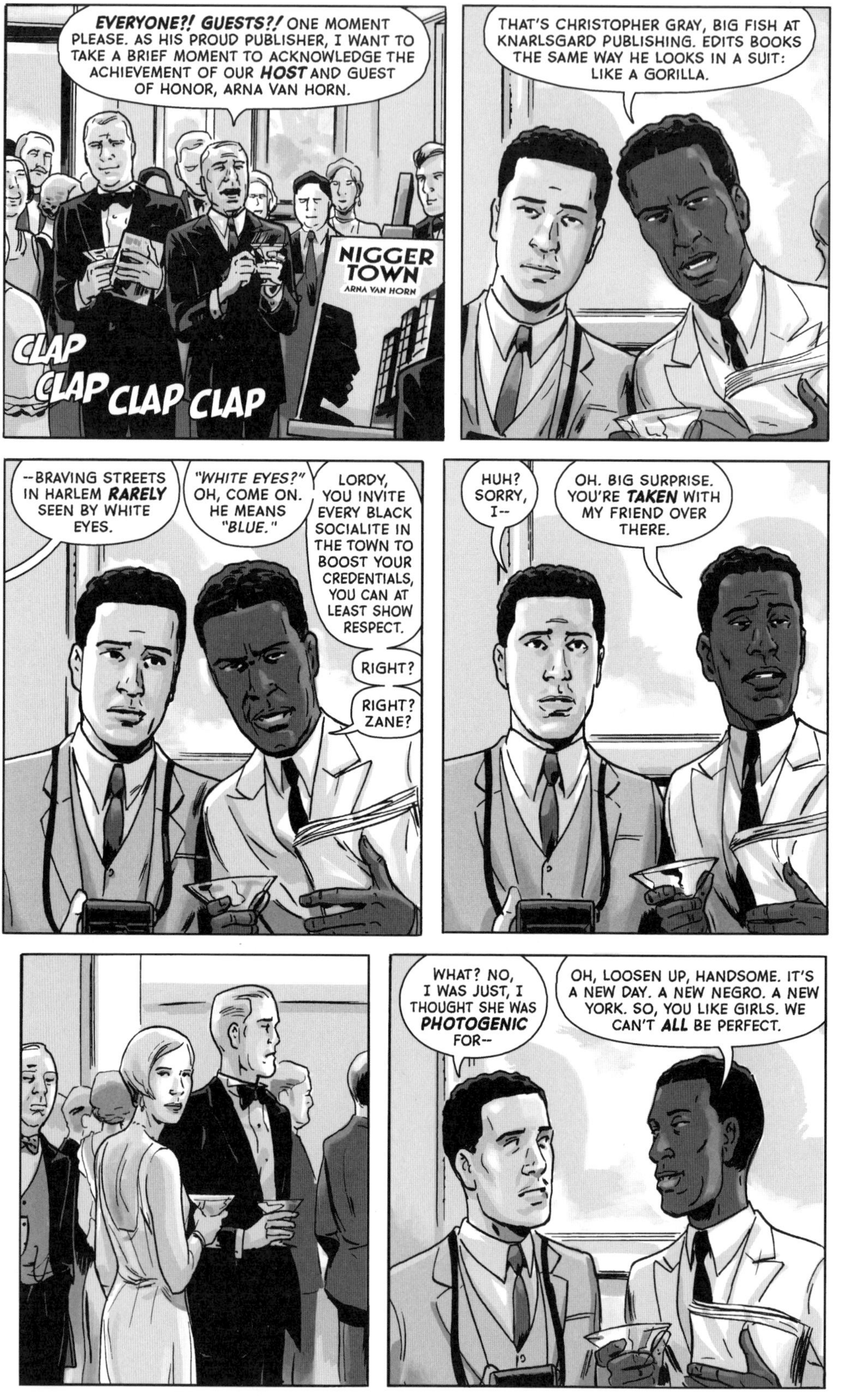
EVERYONE?! GUESTS?! ONE MOMENT PLEASE. AS HIS PROUD PUBLISHER, I WANT TO TAKE A BRIEF MOMENT TO ACKNOWLEDGE THE ACHIEVEMENT OF OUR HOST AND GUEST OF HONOR, ARNA VAN HORN.
NIGGER TOWN
ARNA VAN HORN
CLAP CLAP CLAP CLAP
THAT'S CHRISTOPHER GRAY, BIG FISH AT KNARLSGARD PUBLISHING. EDITS BOOKS THE SAME WAY HE LOOKS IN A SUIT: LIKE A GORILLA.
--BRAVING STREETS IN HARLEM RARELY SEEN BY WHITE EYES.
"WHITE EYES?" OH, COME ON. HE MEANS "BLUE."
LORDY, YOU INVITE EVERY BLACK SOCIALITE IN THE TOWN TO BOOST YOUR CREDENTIALS, YOU CAN AT LEAST SHOW RESPECT.
RIGHT?
RIGHT? ZANE?
HUH? SORRY, I--
OH. BIG SURPRISE. YOU'RE TAKEN WITH MY FRIEND OVER THERE.
WHAT? NO, I WAS JUST, I THOUGHT SHE WAS PHOTOGENIC FOR--
OH, LOOSEN UP, HANDSOME. IT'S A NEW DAY. A NEW NEGRO. A NEW YORK. SO, YOU LIKE GIRLS. WE CAN'T ALL BE PERFECT.

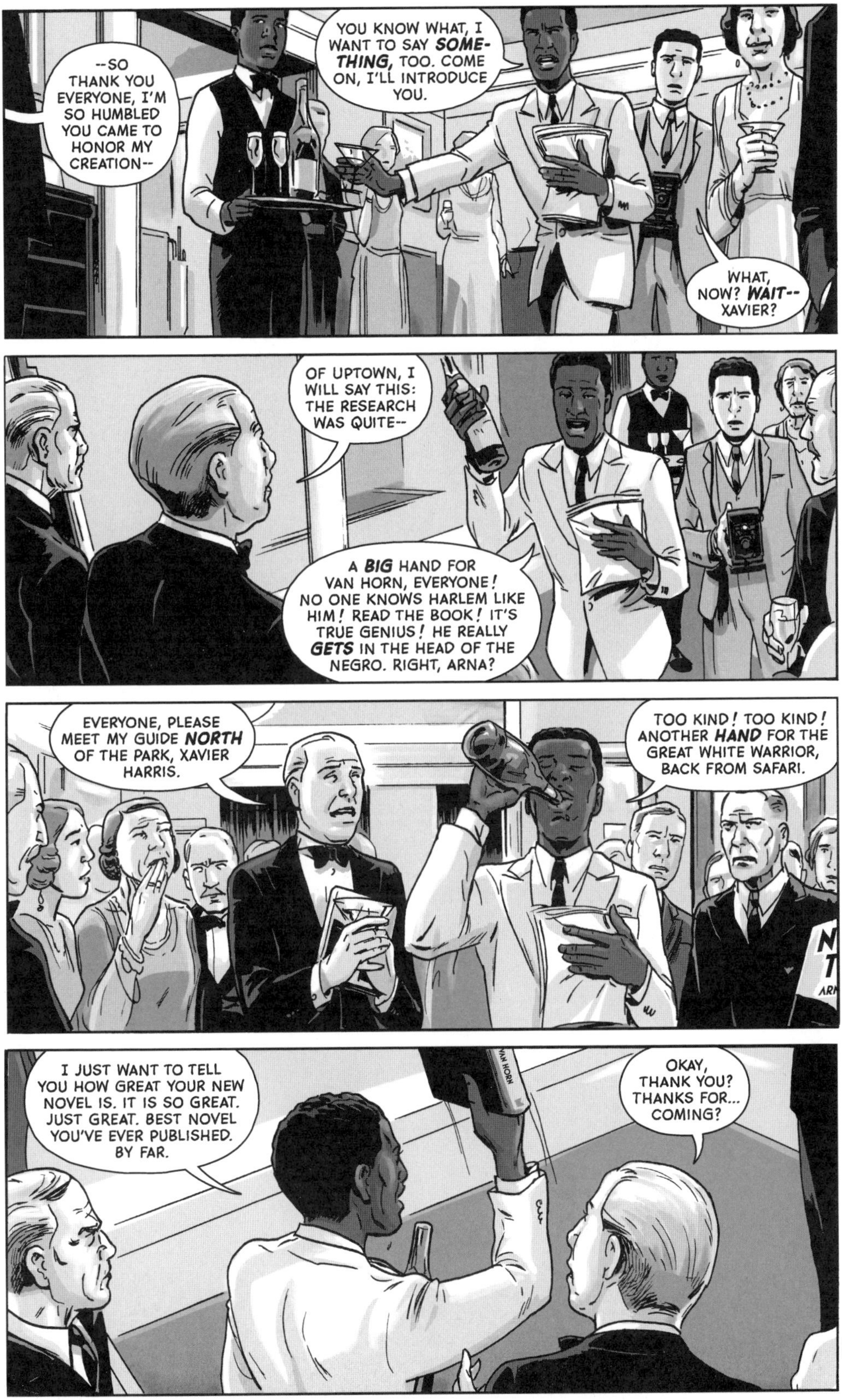
--SO THANK YOU EVERYONE, I'M SO HUMBLED YOU CAME TO HONOR MY CREATION--
YOU KNOW WHAT, I WANT TO SAY **SOMETHING,** TOO. COME ON, I'LL INTRODUCE YOU.
WHAT, NOW? **WAIT--** XAVIER?
OF UPTOWN, I WILL SAY THIS: THE RESEARCH WAS QUITE--
A **BIG** HAND FOR VAN HORN, EVERYONE! NO ONE KNOWS HARLEM LIKE HIM! READ THE BOOK! IT'S TRUE GENIUS! HE REALLY **GETS** IN THE HEAD OF THE NEGRO. RIGHT, ARNA?
EVERYONE, PLEASE MEET MY GUIDE **NORTH** OF THE PARK, XAVIER HARRIS.
TOO KIND! TOO KIND! ANOTHER **HAND** FOR THE GREAT WHITE WARRIOR, BACK FROM SAFARI.
I JUST WANT TO TELL YOU HOW GREAT YOUR NEW NOVEL IS. IT IS SO GREAT. JUST GREAT. BEST NOVEL YOU'VE EVER PUBLISHED. BY FAR.
VAN HORN
OKAY, THANK YOU? THANKS FOR... COMING?

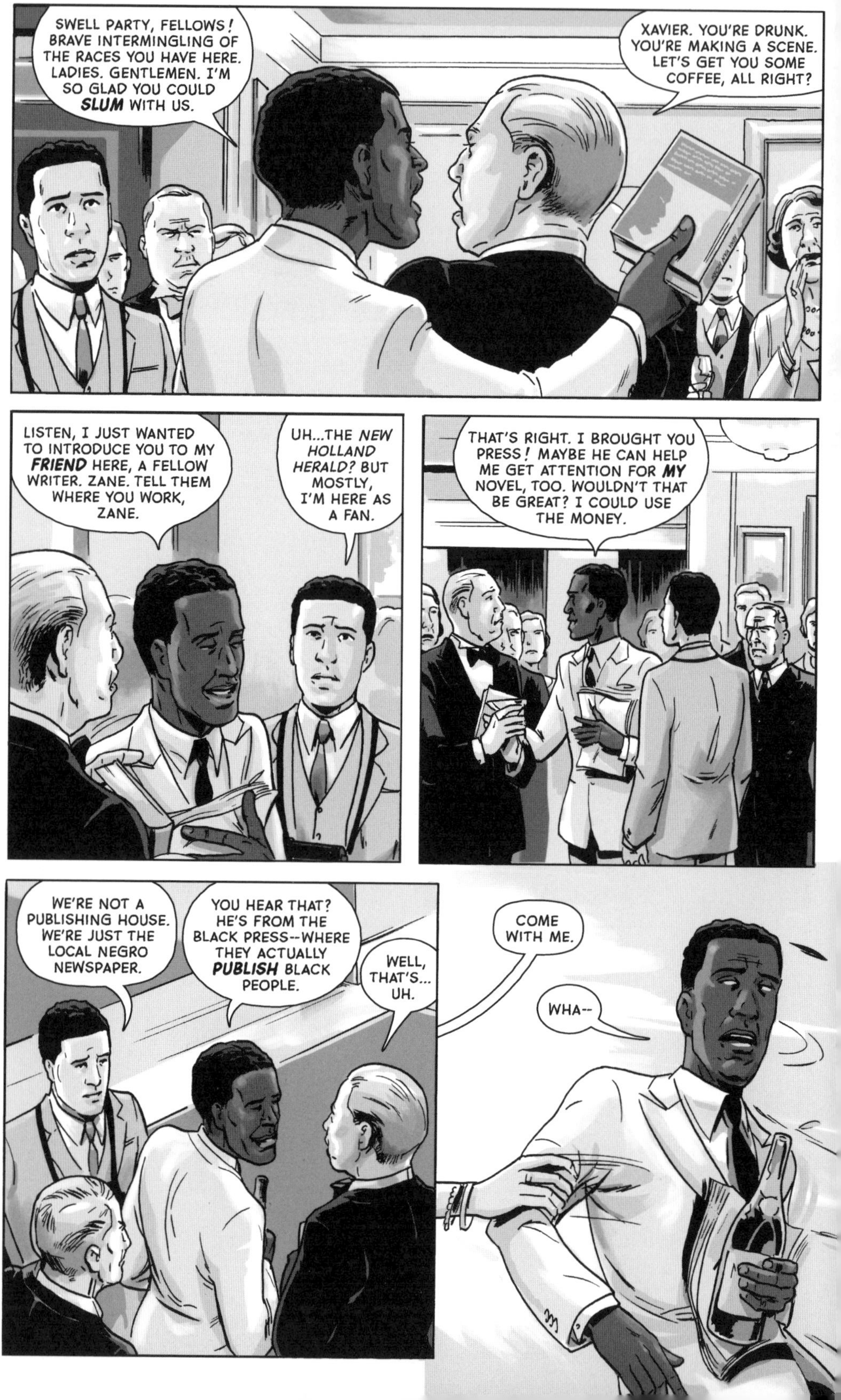
SWELL PARTY, FELLOWS! BRAVE INTERMINGLING OF THE RACES YOU HAVE HERE. LADIES. GENTLEMEN. I'M SO GLAD YOU COULD SLUM WITH US.
XAVIER. YOU'RE DRUNK. YOU'RE MAKING A SCENE. LET'S GET YOU SOME COFFEE, ALL RIGHT?
LISTEN, I JUST WANTED TO INTRODUCE YOU TO MY FRIEND HERE, A FELLOW WRITER. ZANE. TELL THEM WHERE YOU WORK, ZANE.
UH...THE NEW HOLLAND HERALD? BUT MOSTLY, I'M HERE AS A FAN.
THAT'S RIGHT. I BROUGHT YOU PRESS! MAYBE HE CAN HELP ME GET ATTENTION FOR MY NOVEL, TOO. WOULDN'T THAT BE GREAT? I COULD USE THE MONEY.
WE'RE NOT A PUBLISHING HOUSE. WE'RE JUST THE LOCAL NEGRO NEWSPAPER.
YOU HEAR THAT? HE'S FROM THE BLACK PRESS--WHERE THEY ACTUALLY PUBLISH BLACK PEOPLE.
WELL, THAT'S... UH.
COME WITH ME.
WHA--

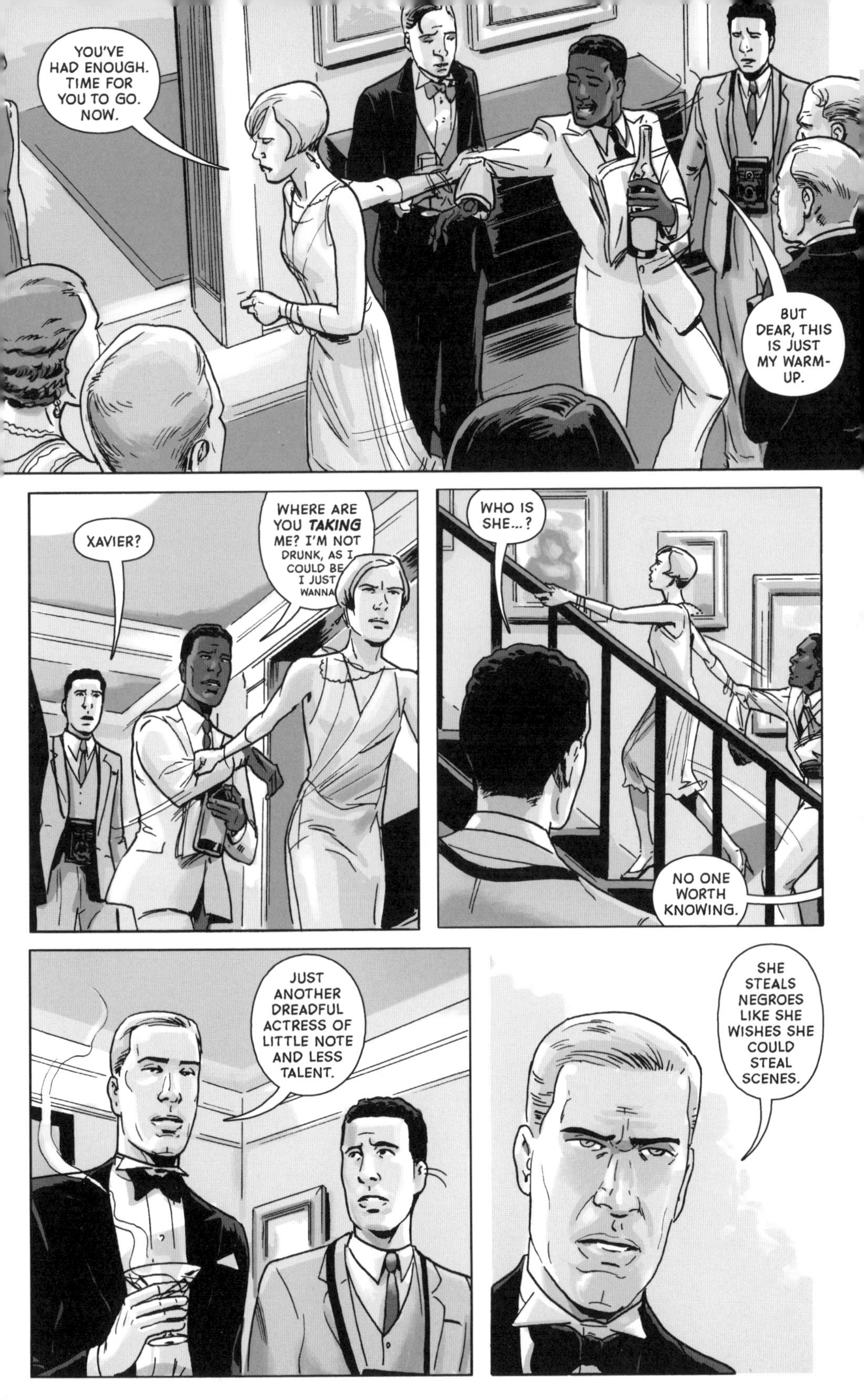
YOU'VE HAD ENOUGH. TIME FOR YOU TO GO. NOW.
BUT DEAR, THIS IS JUST MY WARM-UP.
XAVIER?
WHERE ARE YOU TAKING ME? I'M NOT DRUNK, AS I COULD BE. I JUST WANNA
WHO IS SHE...?
NO ONE WORTH KNOWING.
JUST ANOTHER DREADFUL ACTRESS OF LITTLE NOTE AND LESS TALENT.
SHE STEALS NEGROES LIKE SHE WISHES SHE COULD STEAL SCENES.

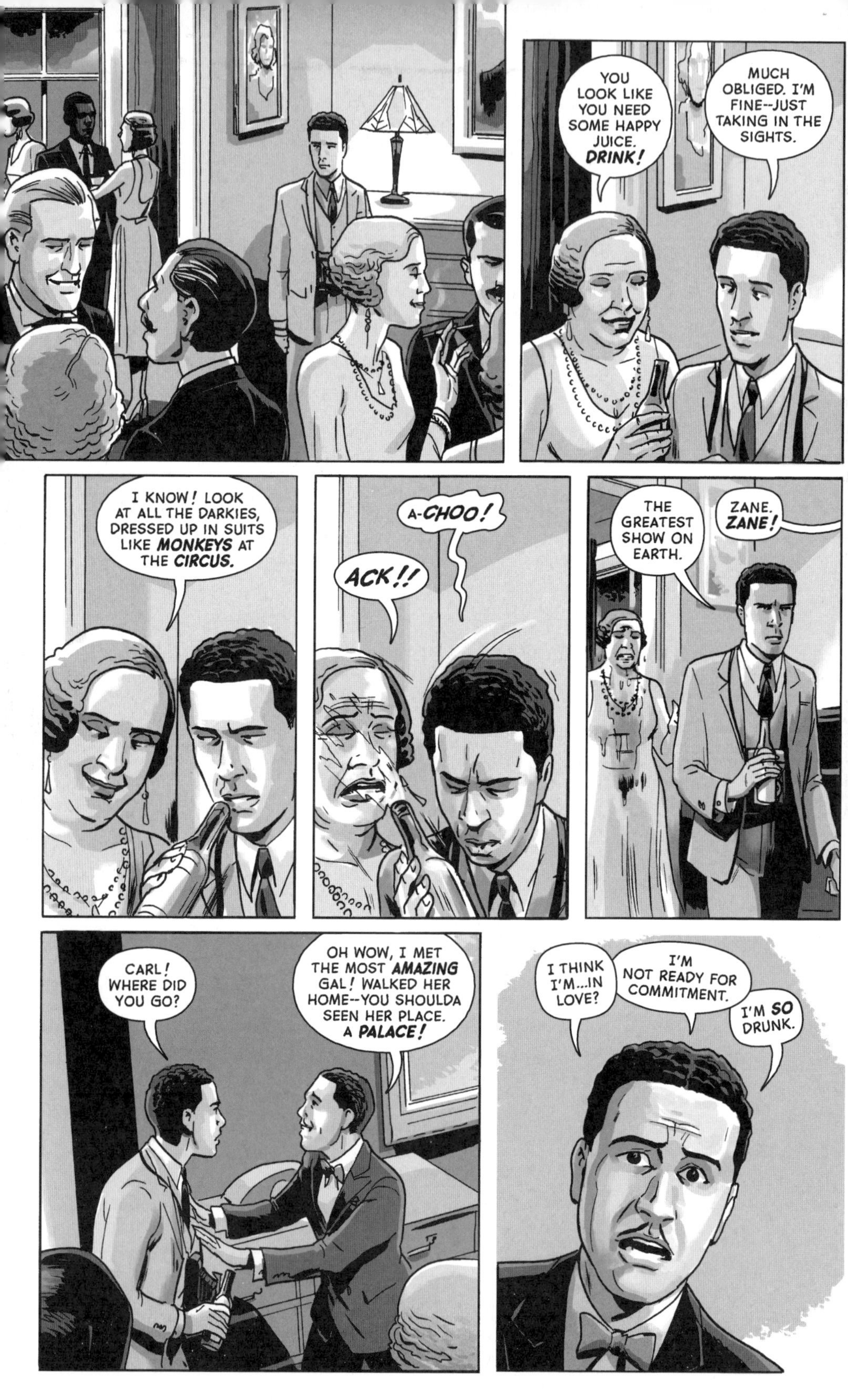
YOU LOOK LIKE YOU NEED SOME HAPPY JUICE. DRINK!
MUCH OBLIGED. I'M FINE--JUST TAKING IN THE SIGHTS.
I KNOW! LOOK AT ALL THE DARKIES, DRESSED UP IN SUITS LIKE MONKEYS AT THE CIRCUS.
A-CHOO!
ACK!!
THE GREATEST SHOW ON EARTH.
ZANE. ZANE!
CARL! WHERE DID YOU GO?
OH WOW, I MET THE MOST AMAZING GAL! WALKED HER HOME--YOU SHOULDA SEEN HER PLACE. A PALACE!
I THINK I'M...IN LOVE?
I'M NOT READY FOR COMMITMENT.
I'M SO DRUNK.

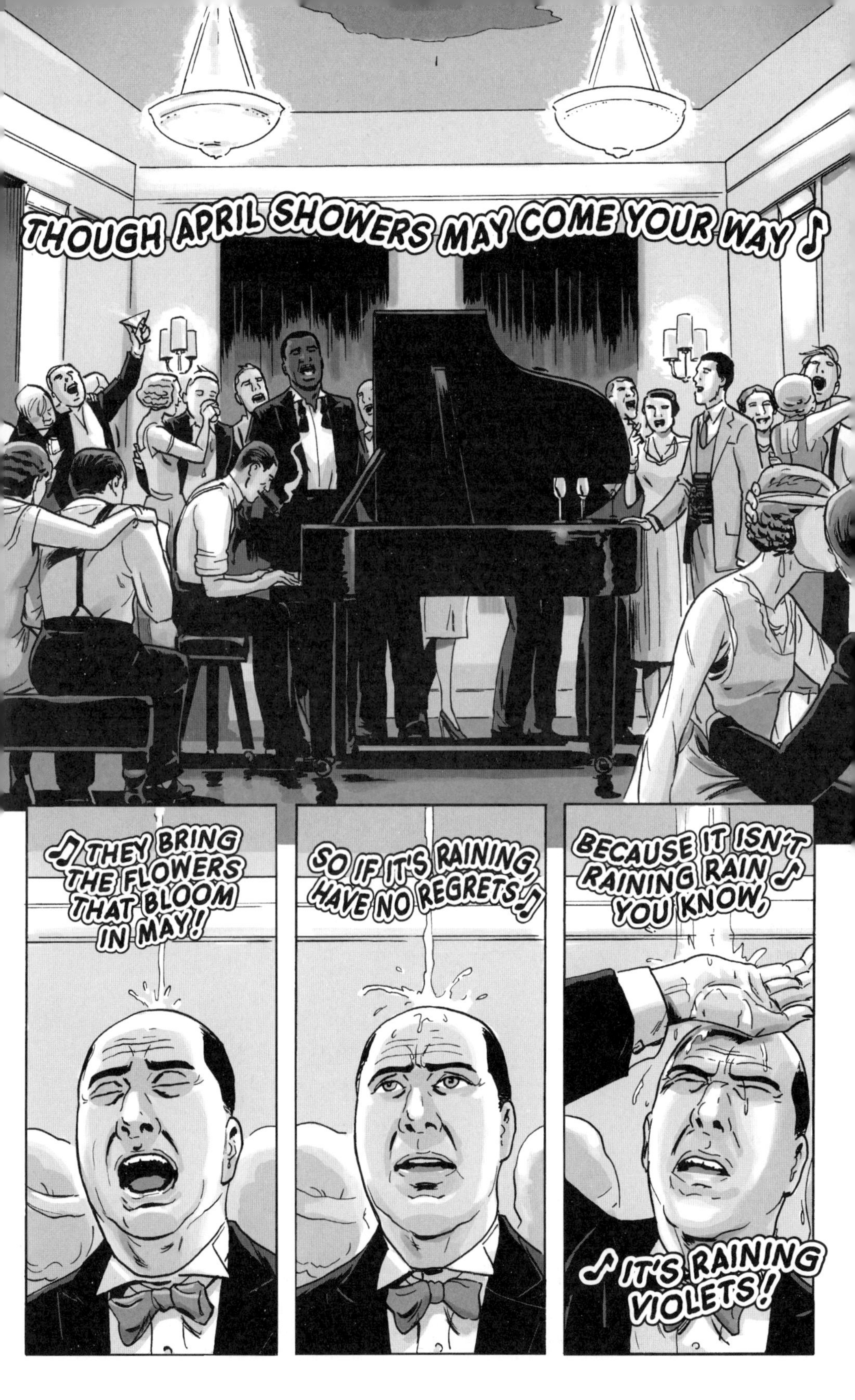
THOUGH APRIL SHOWERS MAY COME YOUR WAY ♪
♪ THEY BRING THE FLOWERS THAT BLOOM IN MAY!
SO IF IT'S RAINING, HAVE NO REGRETS ♪
BECAUSE IT ISN'T RAINING RAIN ♪ YOU KNOW,
♪ IT'S RAINING VIOLETS!

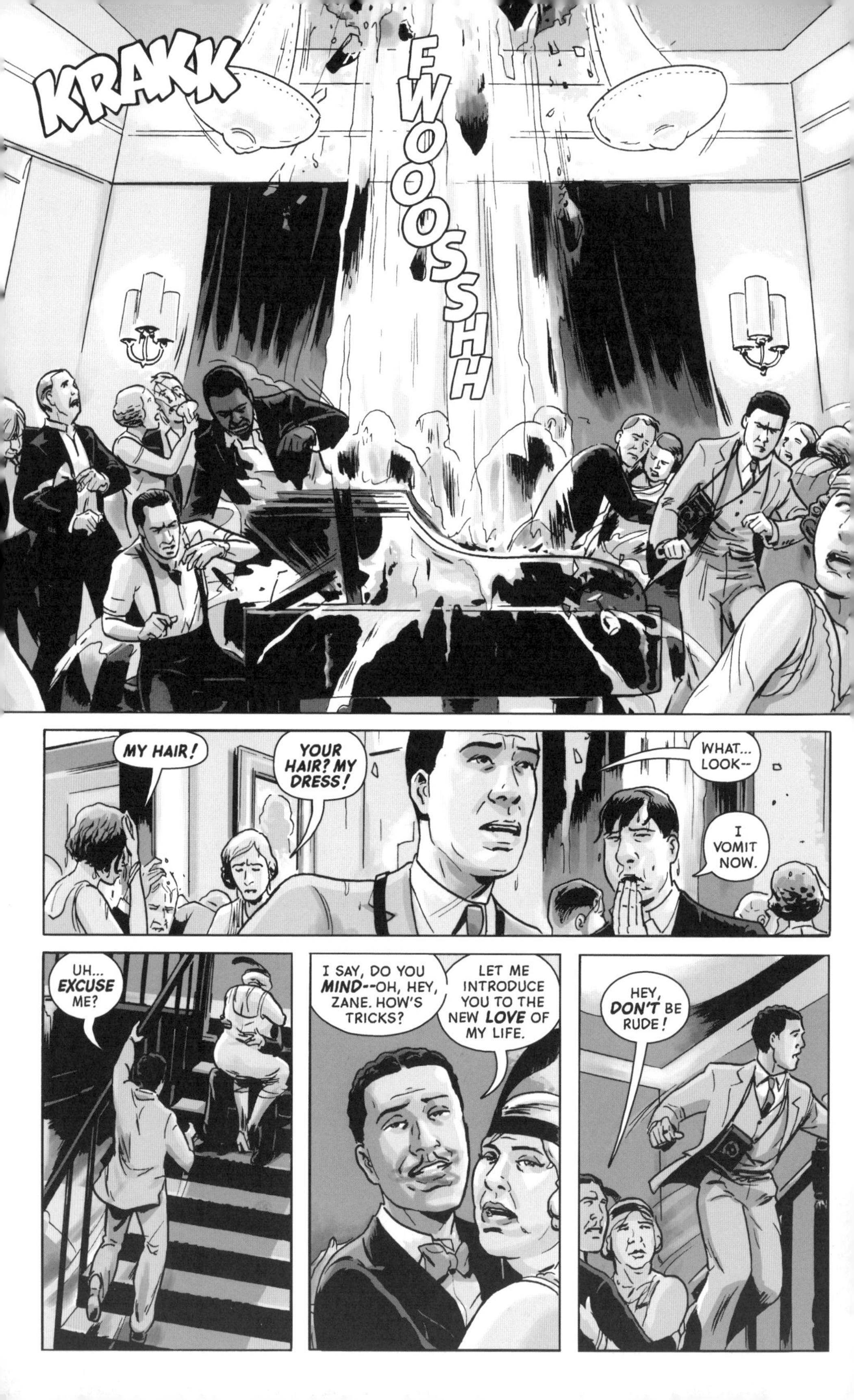
KRAKK
FWOOOSSHH
MY HAIR!
YOUR HAIR? MY DRESS!
WHAT... LOOK--
I VOMIT NOW.
UH... EXCUSE ME?
I SAY, DO YOU MIND--OH, HEY, ZANE. HOW'S TRICKS?
LET ME INTRODUCE YOU TO THE NEW LOVE OF MY LIFE.
HEY, DON'T BE RUDE!

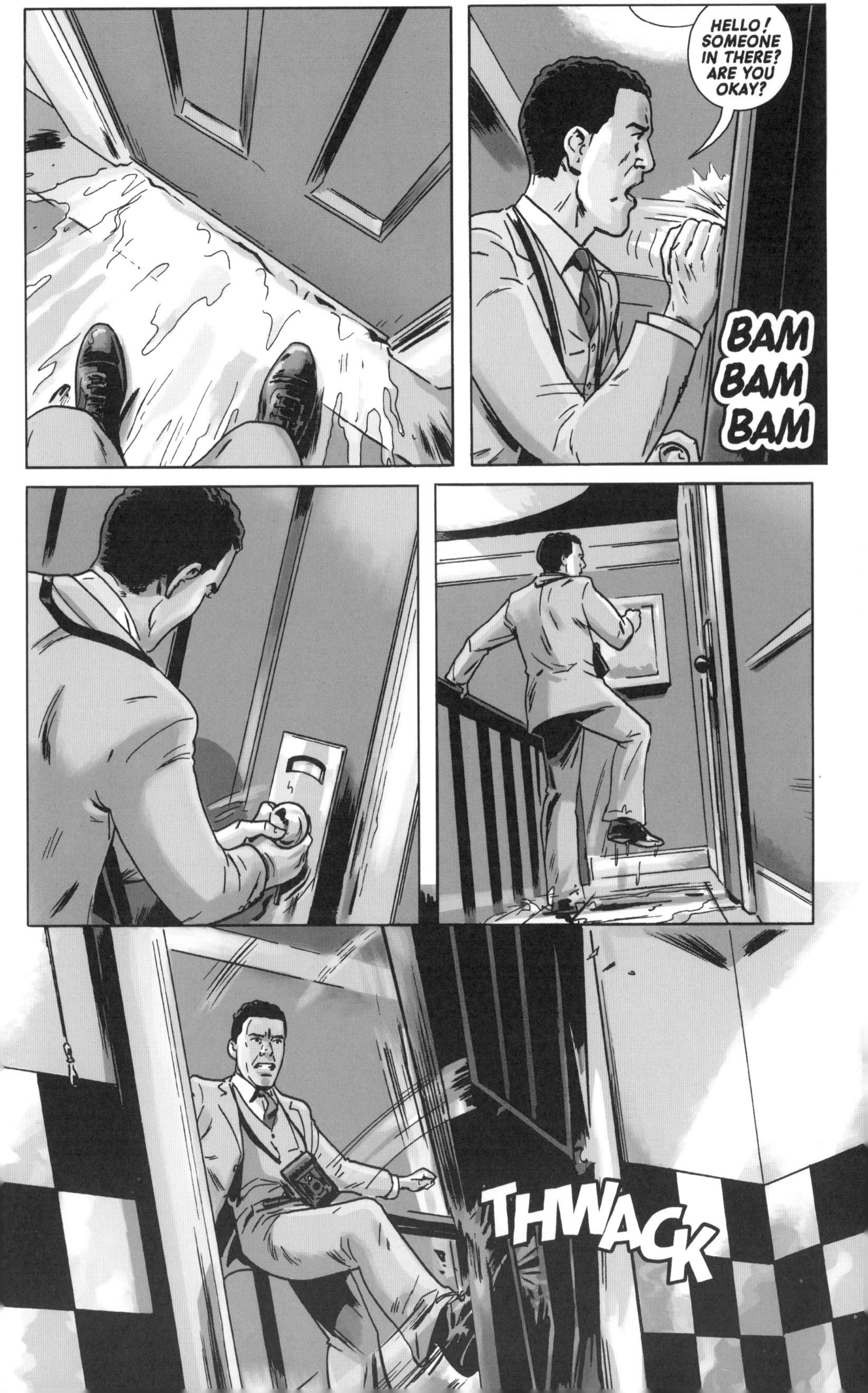
HELLO! SOMEONE IN THERE? ARE YOU OKAY?
BAM BAM BAM
THWACK

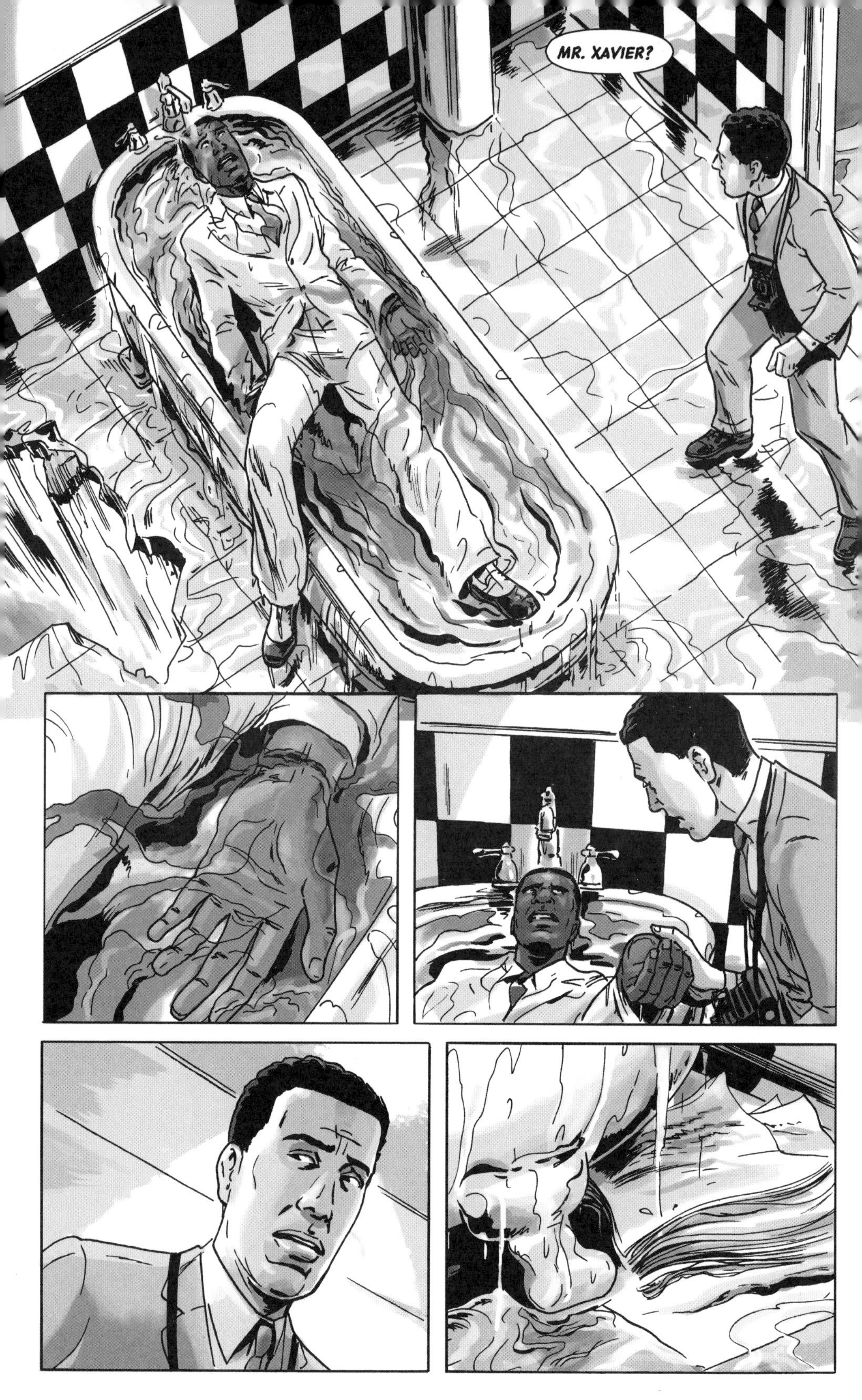
MR. XAVIER?

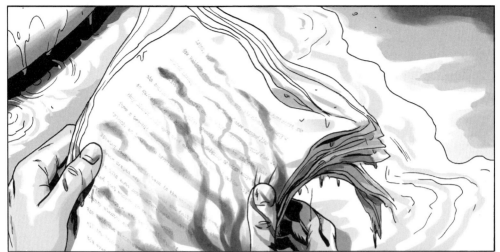

WHO **ARE** YOU?! WHAT DID YOU--?

I--HIS MANUSCRIPT-- I--I--

NO! **NO!**

MISS! LADY--WAIT! **PLEASE!**

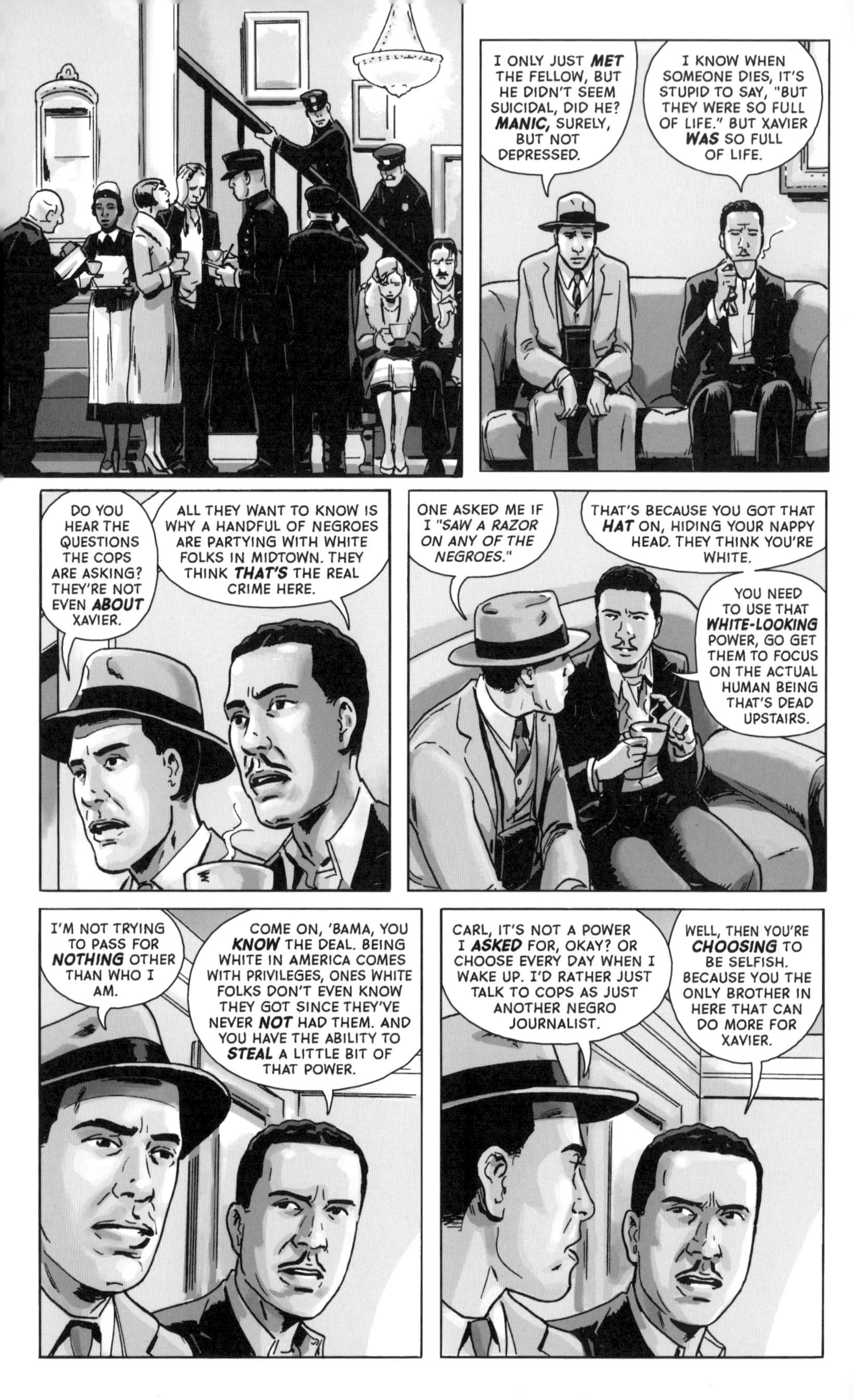
I ONLY JUST MET THE FELLOW, BUT HE DIDN'T SEEM SUICIDAL, DID HE? MANIC, SURELY, BUT NOT DEPRESSED.
I KNOW WHEN SOMEONE DIES, IT'S STUPID TO SAY, "BUT THEY WERE SO FULL OF LIFE." BUT XAVIER WAS SO FULL OF LIFE.
DO YOU HEAR THE QUESTIONS THE COPS ARE ASKING? THEY'RE NOT EVEN ABOUT XAVIER.
ALL THEY WANT TO KNOW IS WHY A HANDFUL OF NEGROES ARE PARTYING WITH WHITE FOLKS IN MIDTOWN. THEY THINK THAT'S THE REAL CRIME HERE.
ONE ASKED ME IF I "SAW A RAZOR ON ANY OF THE NEGROES."
THAT'S BECAUSE YOU GOT THAT HAT ON, HIDING YOUR NAPPY HEAD. THEY THINK YOU'RE WHITE.
YOU NEED TO USE THAT WHITE-LOOKING POWER, GO GET THEM TO FOCUS ON THE ACTUAL HUMAN BEING THAT'S DEAD UPSTAIRS.
I'M NOT TRYING TO PASS FOR NOTHING OTHER THAN WHO I AM.
COME ON, 'BAMA, YOU KNOW THE DEAL. BEING WHITE IN AMERICA COMES WITH PRIVILEGES, ONES WHITE FOLKS DON'T EVEN KNOW THEY GOT SINCE THEY'VE NEVER NOT HAD THEM. AND YOU HAVE THE ABILITY TO STEAL A LITTLE BIT OF THAT POWER.
CARL, IT'S NOT A POWER I ASKED FOR, OKAY? OR CHOOSE EVERY DAY WHEN I WAKE UP. I'D RATHER JUST TALK TO COPS AS JUST ANOTHER NEGRO JOURNALIST.
WELL, THEN YOU'RE CHOOSING TO BE SELFISH. BECAUSE YOU THE ONLY BROTHER IN HERE THAT CAN DO MORE FOR XAVIER.

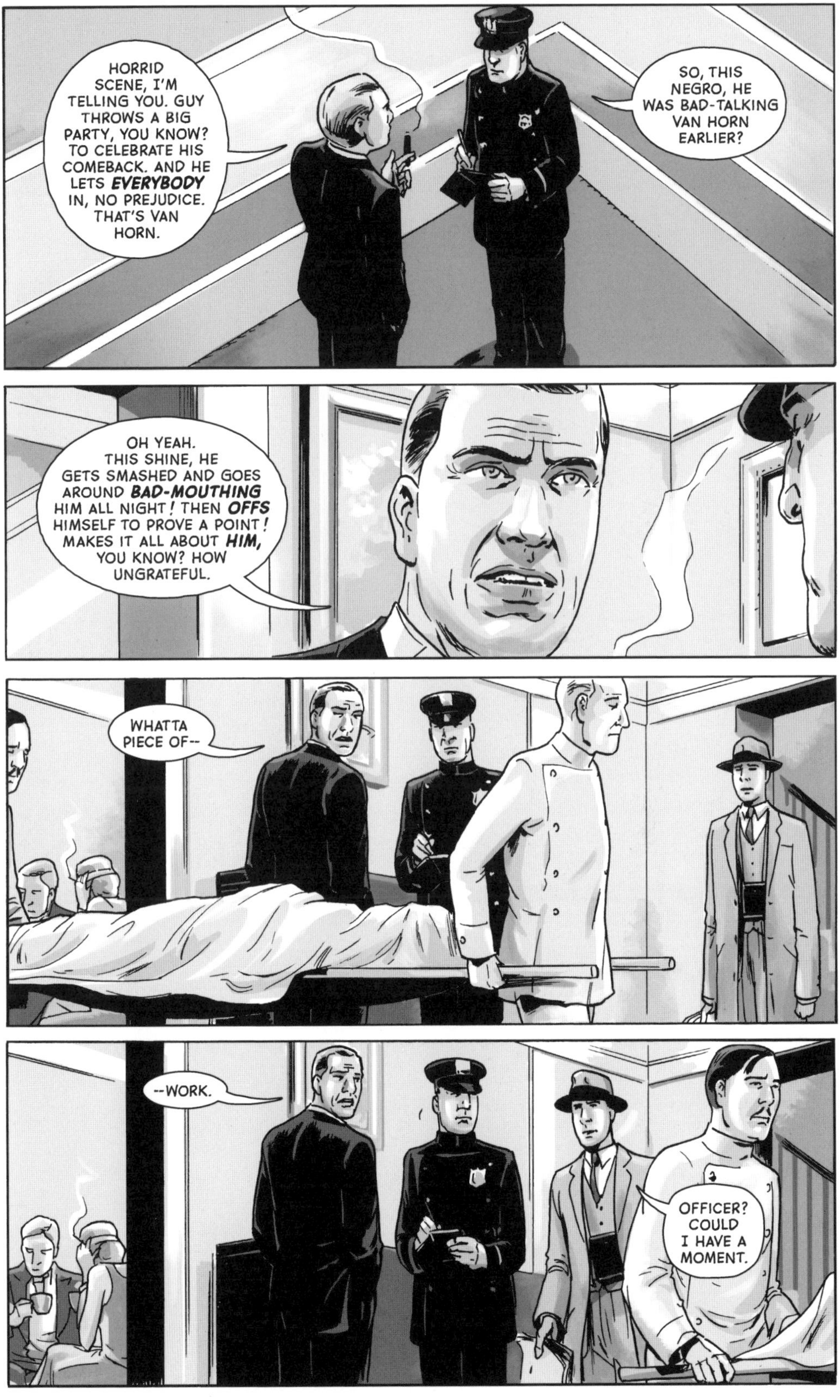
HORRID SCENE, I'M TELLING YOU. GUY THROWS A BIG PARTY, YOU KNOW? TO CELEBRATE HIS COMEBACK. AND HE LETS EVERYBODY IN, NO PREJUDICE. THAT'S VAN HORN.
SO, THIS NEGRO, HE WAS BAD-TALKING VAN HORN EARLIER?
OH YEAH. THIS SHINE, HE GETS SMASHED AND GOES AROUND BAD-MOUTHING HIM ALL NIGHT! THEN OFFS HIMSELF TO PROVE A POINT! MAKES IT ALL ABOUT HIM, YOU KNOW? HOW UNGRATEFUL.
WHATTA PIECE OF--
--WORK.
OFFICER? COULD I HAVE A MOMENT.

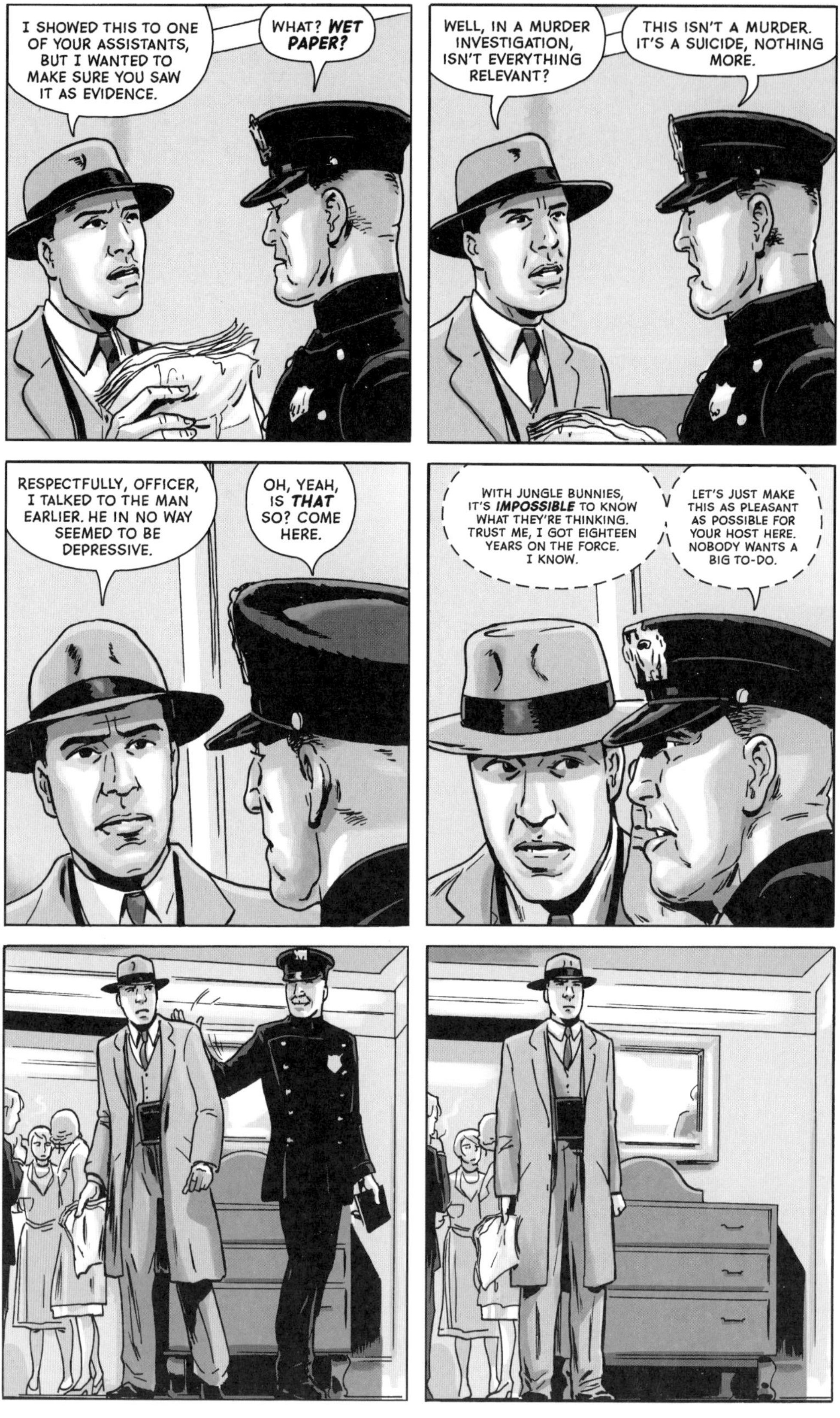

I SHOWED THIS TO ONE OF YOUR ASSISTANTS, BUT I WANTED TO MAKE SURE YOU SAW IT AS EVIDENCE.
WHAT? **WET PAPER?**
WELL, IN A MURDER INVESTIGATION, ISN'T EVERYTHING RELEVANT?
THIS ISN'T A MURDER. IT'S A SUICIDE, NOTHING MORE.
RESPECTFULLY, OFFICER, I TALKED TO THE MAN EARLIER. HE IN NO WAY SEEMED TO BE DEPRESSIVE.
OH, YEAH, IS **THAT** SO? COME HERE.
WITH JUNGLE BUNNIES, IT'S ***IMPOSSIBLE*** TO KNOW WHAT THEY'RE THINKING. TRUST ME, I GOT EIGHTEEN YEARS ON THE FORCE. I KNOW.
LET'S JUST MAKE THIS AS PLEASANT AS POSSIBLE FOR YOUR HOST HERE. NOBODY WANTS A BIG TO-DO.

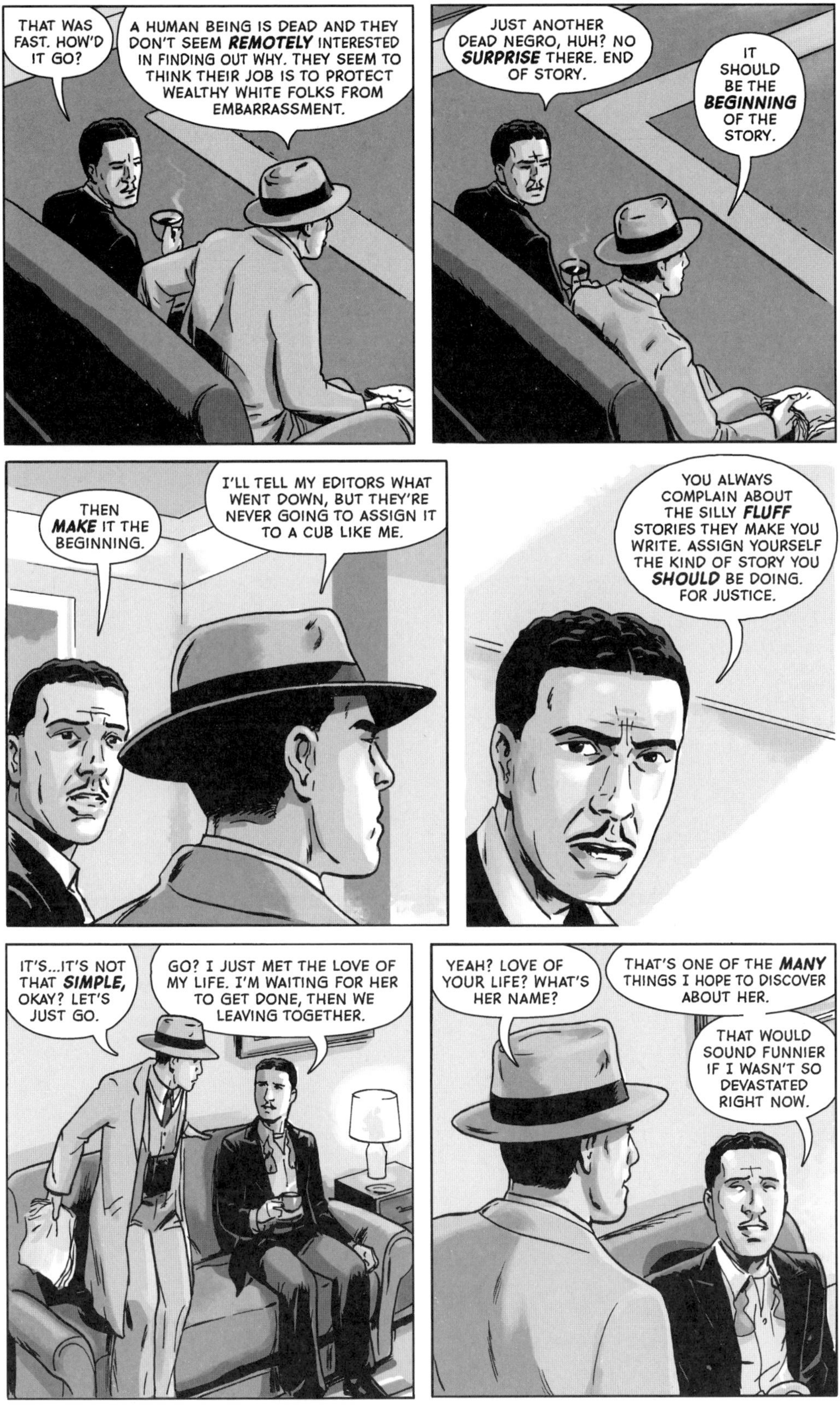
THAT WAS FAST. HOW'D IT GO?
A HUMAN BEING IS DEAD AND THEY DON'T SEEM **REMOTELY** INTERESTED IN FINDING OUT WHY. THEY SEEM TO THINK THEIR JOB IS TO PROTECT WEALTHY WHITE FOLKS FROM EMBARRASSMENT.
JUST ANOTHER DEAD NEGRO, HUH? NO **SURPRISE** THERE. END OF STORY.
IT SHOULD BE THE **BEGINNING** OF THE STORY.
THEN **MAKE** IT THE BEGINNING.
I'LL TELL MY EDITORS WHAT WENT DOWN, BUT THEY'RE NEVER GOING TO ASSIGN IT TO A CUB LIKE ME.
YOU ALWAYS COMPLAIN ABOUT THE SILLY **FLUFF** STORIES THEY MAKE YOU WRITE. ASSIGN YOURSELF THE KIND OF STORY YOU **SHOULD** BE DOING. FOR JUSTICE.
IT'S...IT'S NOT THAT **SIMPLE,** OKAY? LET'S JUST GO.
GO? I JUST MET THE LOVE OF MY LIFE. I'M WAITING FOR HER TO GET DONE, THEN WE LEAVING TOGETHER.
YEAH? LOVE OF YOUR LIFE? WHAT'S HER NAME?
THAT'S ONE OF THE **MANY** THINGS I HOPE TO DISCOVER ABOUT HER.
THAT WOULD SOUND FUNNIER IF I WASN'T SO DEVASTATED RIGHT NOW.

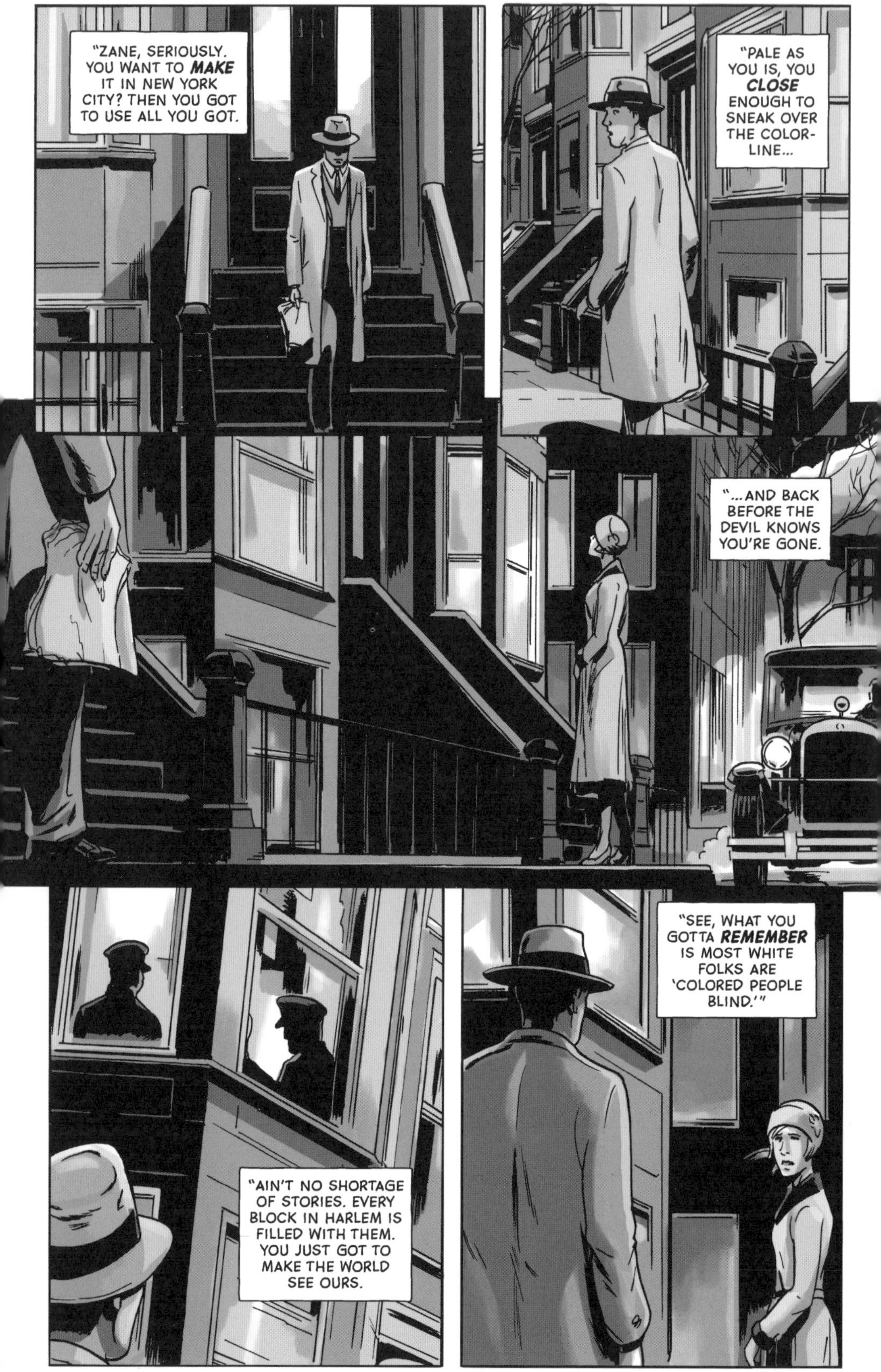
"ZANE, SERIOUSLY. YOU WANT TO MAKE IT IN NEW YORK CITY? THEN YOU GOT TO USE ALL YOU GOT.
"PALE AS YOU IS, YOU CLOSE ENOUGH TO SNEAK OVER THE COLOR-LINE...
"...AND BACK BEFORE THE DEVIL KNOWS YOU'RE GONE.
"AIN'T NO SHORTAGE OF STORIES. EVERY BLOCK IN HARLEM IS FILLED WITH THEM. YOU JUST GOT TO MAKE THE WORLD SEE OURS.
"SEE, WHAT YOU GOTTA REMEMBER IS MOST WHITE FOLKS ARE 'COLORED PEOPLE BLIND.'"

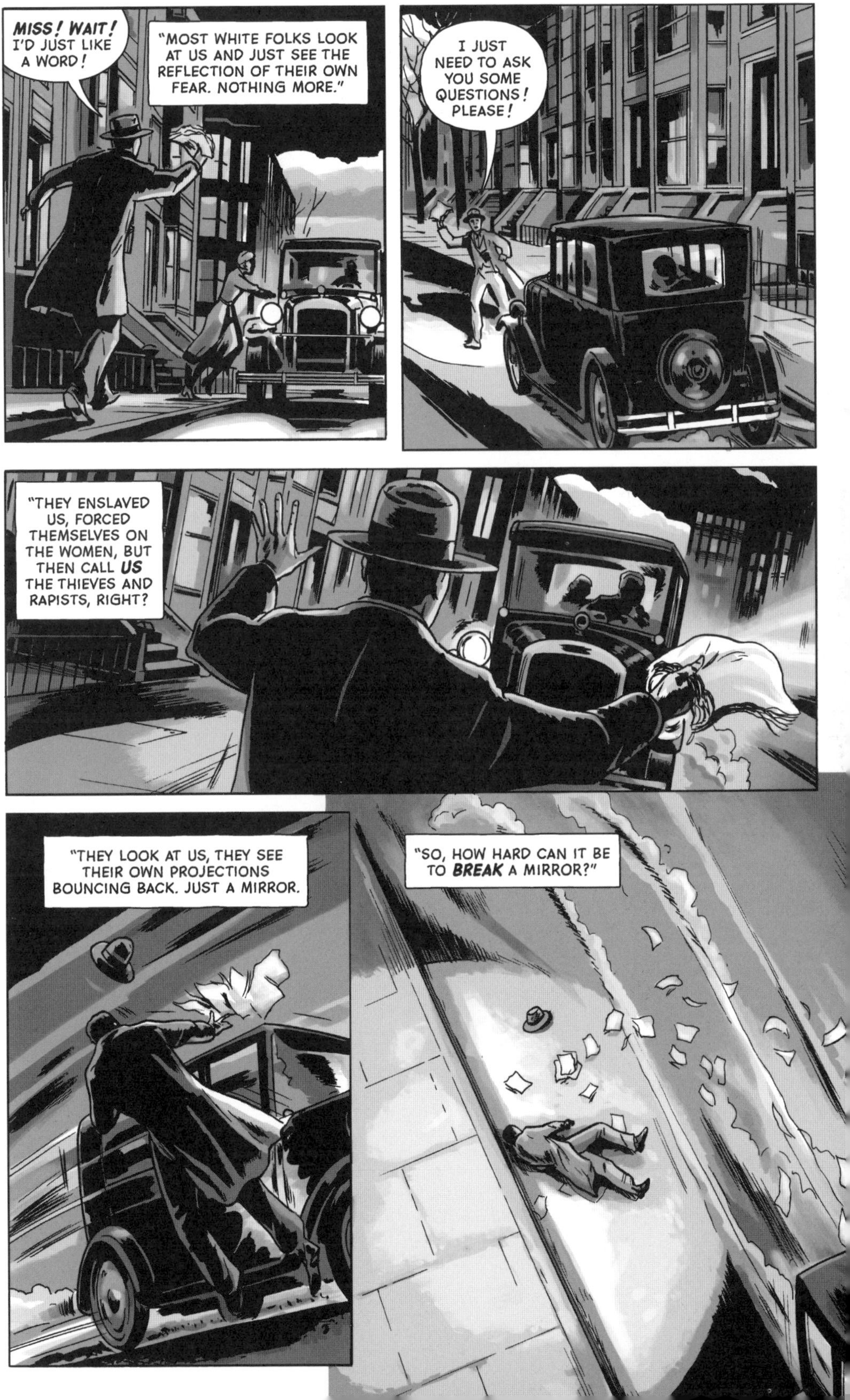
MISS! WAIT! I'D JUST LIKE A WORD!
"MOST WHITE FOLKS LOOK AT US AND JUST SEE THE REFLECTION OF THEIR OWN FEAR. NOTHING MORE."
I JUST NEED TO ASK YOU SOME QUESTIONS! PLEASE!
"THEY ENSLAVED US, FORCED THEMSELVES ON THE WOMEN, BUT THEN CALL US THE THIEVES AND RAPISTS, RIGHT?
"THEY LOOK AT US, THEY SEE THEIR OWN PROJECTIONS BOUNCING BACK. JUST A MIRROR.
"SO, HOW HARD CAN IT BE TO BREAK A MIRROR?"

CHAPTER II

"COTTON"

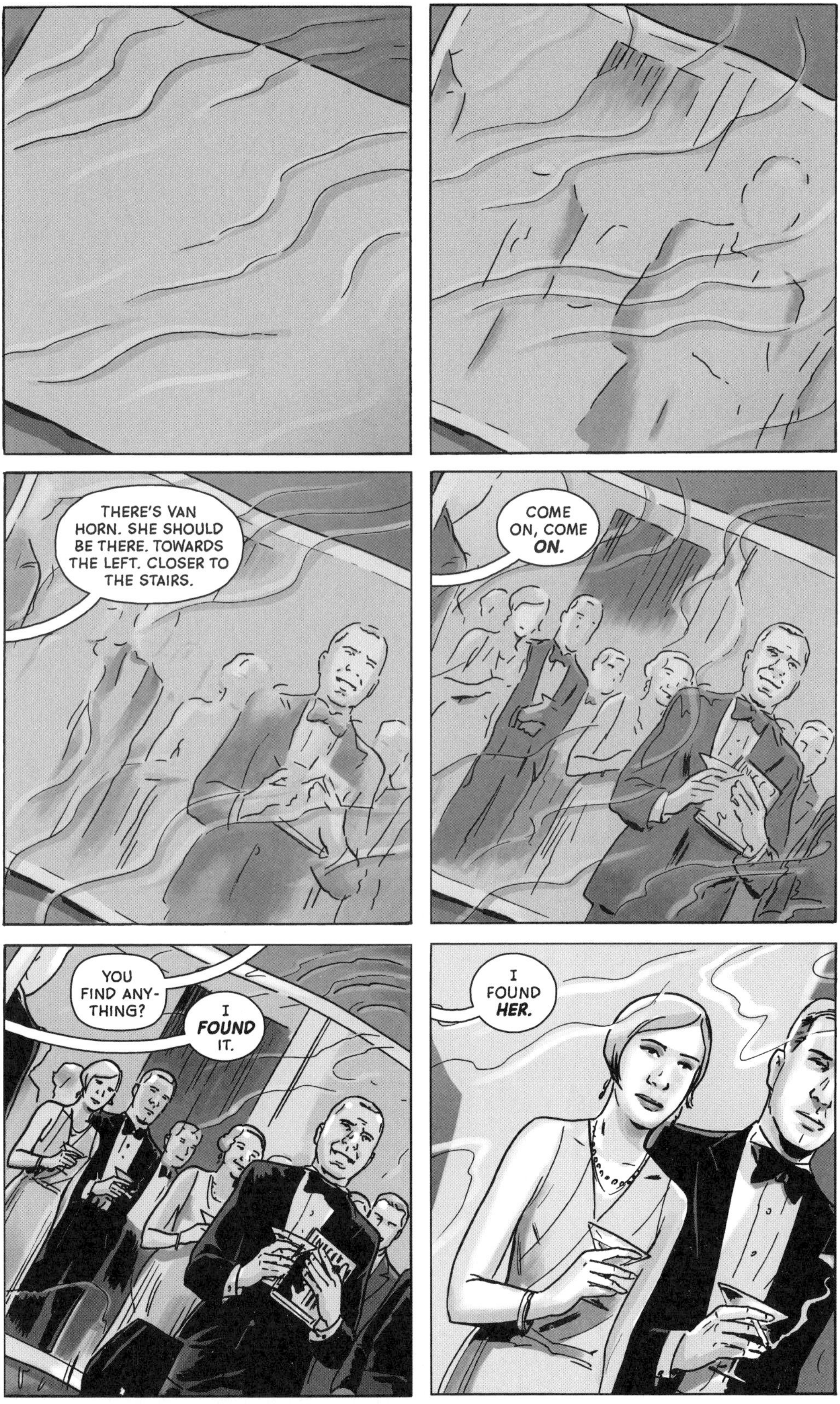
THERE'S VAN HORN. SHE SHOULD BE THERE. TOWARDS THE LEFT. CLOSER TO THE STAIRS.
COME ON, COME ***ON.***
YOU FIND ANY-THING?
I ***FOUND*** IT.
I FOUND ***HER.***

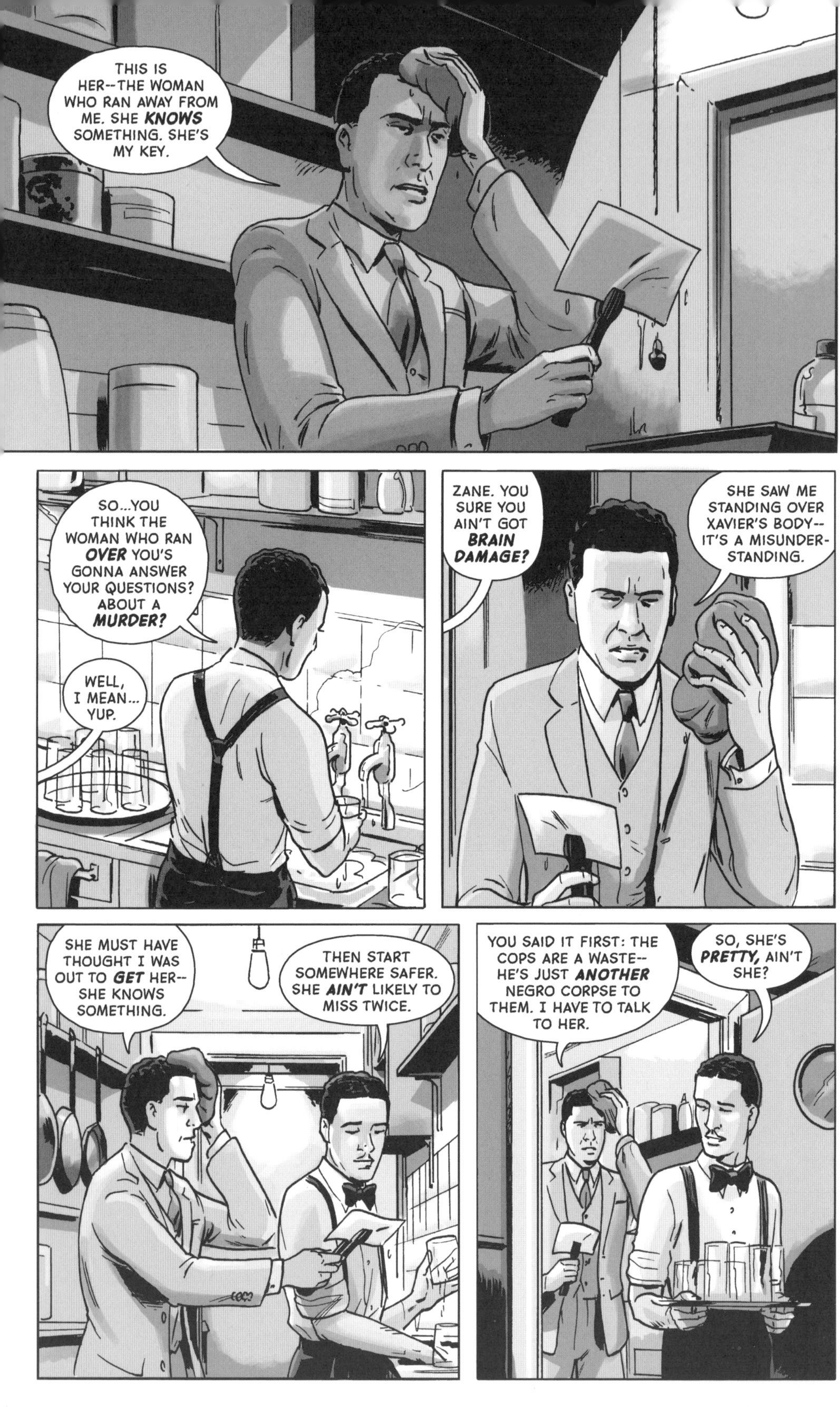
THIS IS HER--THE WOMAN WHO RAN AWAY FROM ME. SHE **KNOWS** SOMETHING. SHE'S MY KEY.
SO...YOU THINK THE WOMAN WHO RAN **OVER** YOU'S GONNA ANSWER YOUR QUESTIONS? ABOUT A **MURDER?**
WELL, I MEAN... YUP.
ZANE. YOU SURE YOU AIN'T GOT **BRAIN DAMAGE?**
SHE SAW ME STANDING OVER XAVIER'S BODY--IT'S A MISUNDERSTANDING.
SHE MUST HAVE THOUGHT I WAS OUT TO **GET** HER--SHE KNOWS SOMETHING.
THEN START SOMEWHERE SAFER. SHE **AIN'T** LIKELY TO MISS TWICE.
YOU SAID IT FIRST: THE COPS ARE A WASTE--HE'S JUST **ANOTHER** NEGRO CORPSE TO THEM. I HAVE TO TALK TO HER.
SO, SHE'S **PRETTY,** AIN'T SHE?

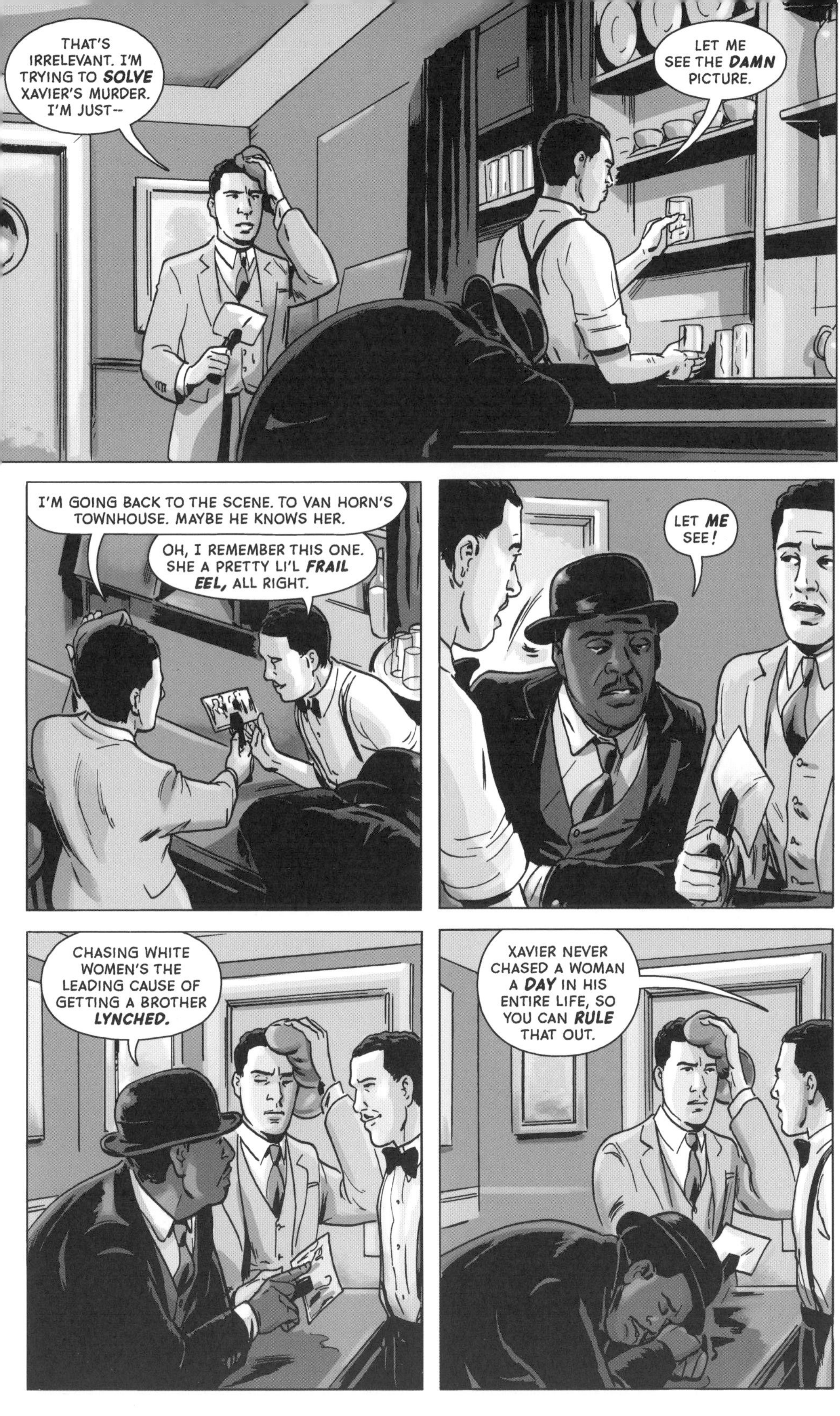
THAT'S IRRELEVANT. I'M TRYING TO SOLVE XAVIER'S MURDER. I'M JUST--
LET ME SEE THE DAMN PICTURE.
I'M GOING BACK TO THE SCENE. TO VAN HORN'S TOWNHOUSE. MAYBE HE KNOWS HER.
OH, I REMEMBER THIS ONE. SHE A PRETTY LI'L FRAIL EEL, ALL RIGHT.
LET ME SEE!
CHASING WHITE WOMEN'S THE LEADING CAUSE OF GETTING A BROTHER LYNCHED.
XAVIER NEVER CHASED A WOMAN A DAY IN HIS ENTIRE LIFE, SO YOU CAN RULE THAT OUT.

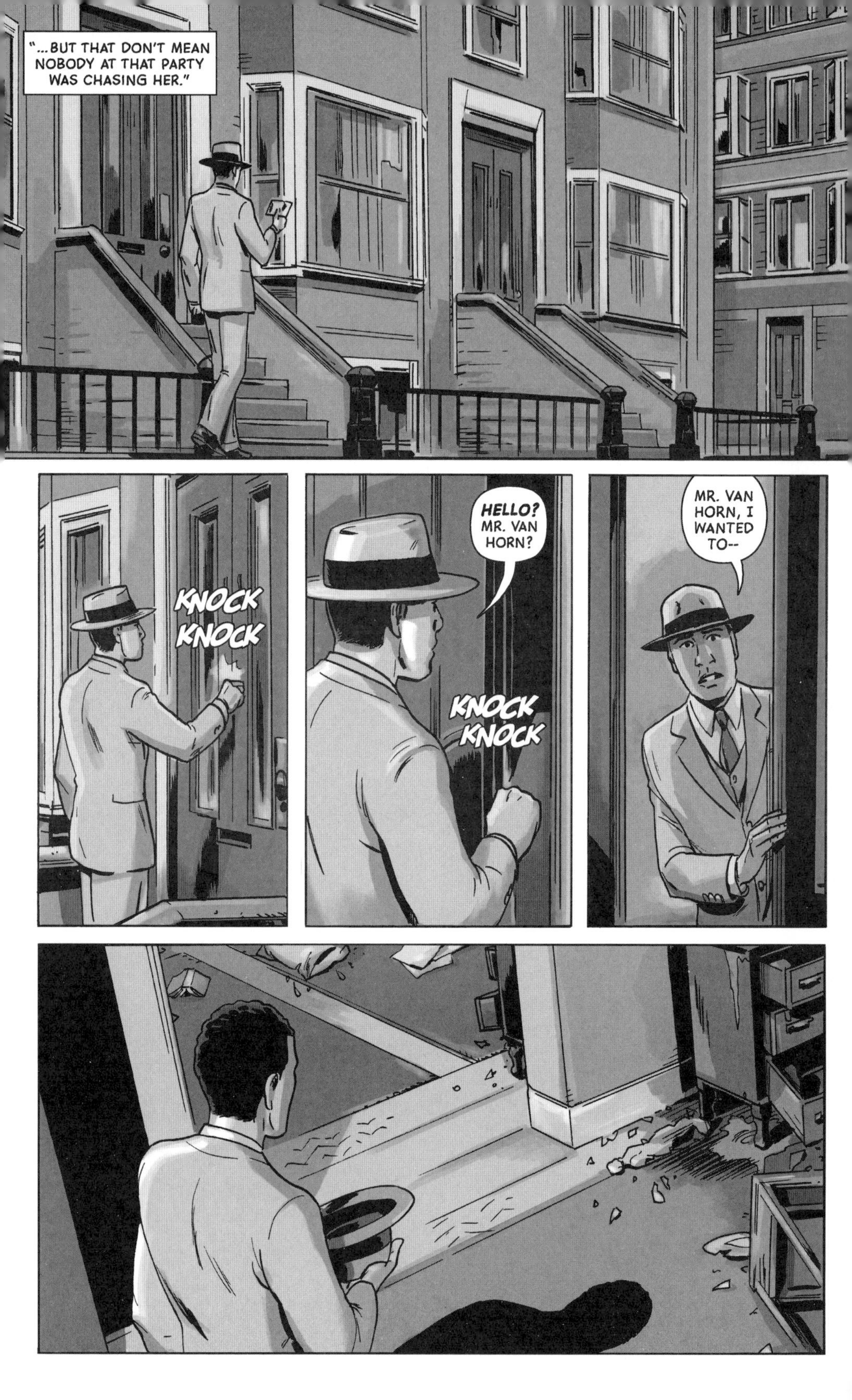
"...BUT THAT DON'T MEAN NOBODY AT THAT PARTY WAS CHASING HER."
KNOCK KNOCK
HELLO? MR. VAN HORN?
KNOCK KNOCK
MR. VAN HORN, I WANTED TO--

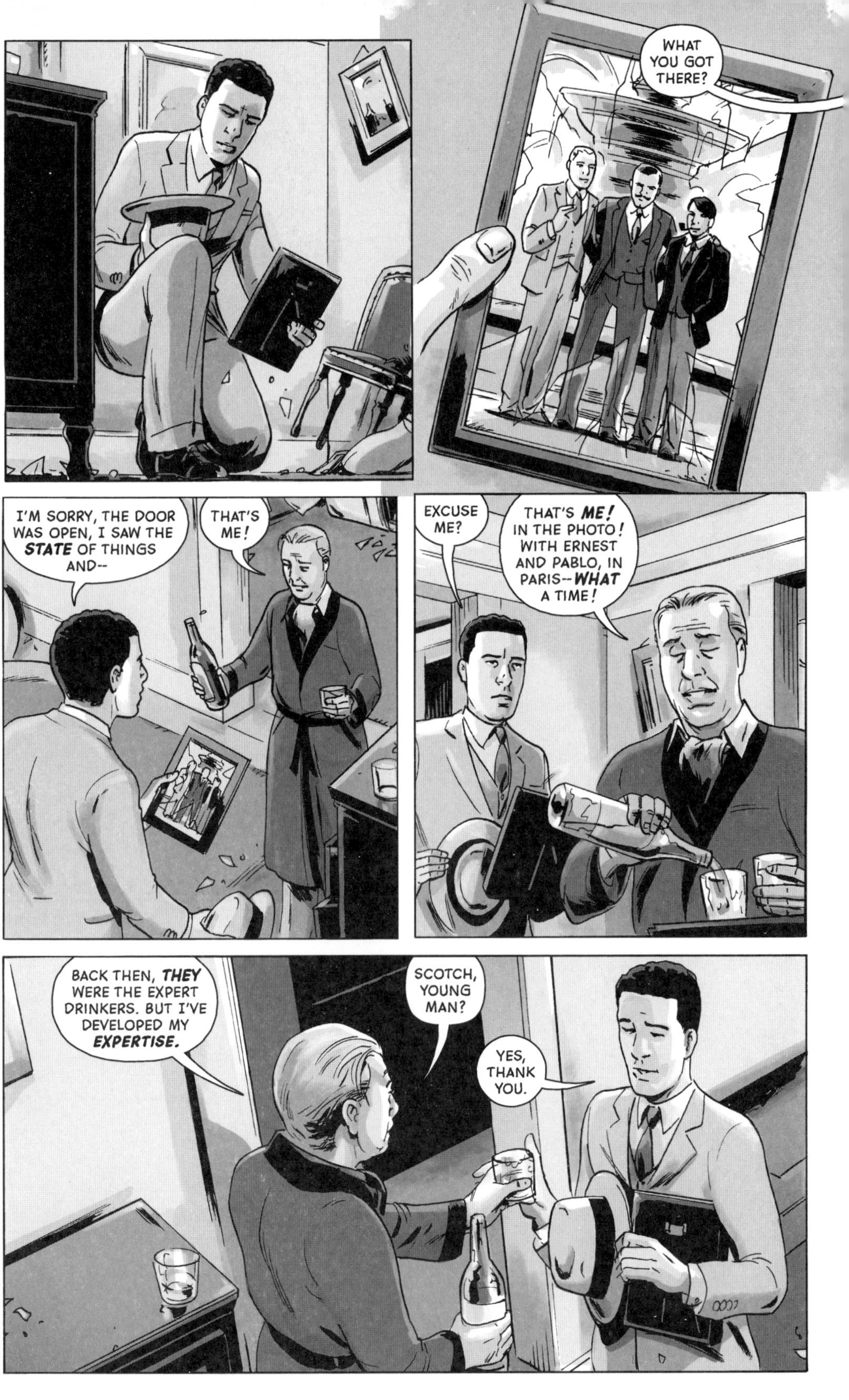

WHAT YOU GOT THERE?
I'M SORRY, THE DOOR WAS OPEN, I SAW THE **STATE** OF THINGS AND--
THAT'S ME!
EXCUSE ME?
THAT'S **ME!** IN THE PHOTO! WITH ERNEST AND PABLO, IN PARIS--**WHAT** A TIME!
BACK THEN, **THEY** WERE THE EXPERT DRINKERS. BUT I'VE DEVELOPED MY **EXPERTISE.**
SCOTCH, YOUNG MAN?
YES, THANK YOU.

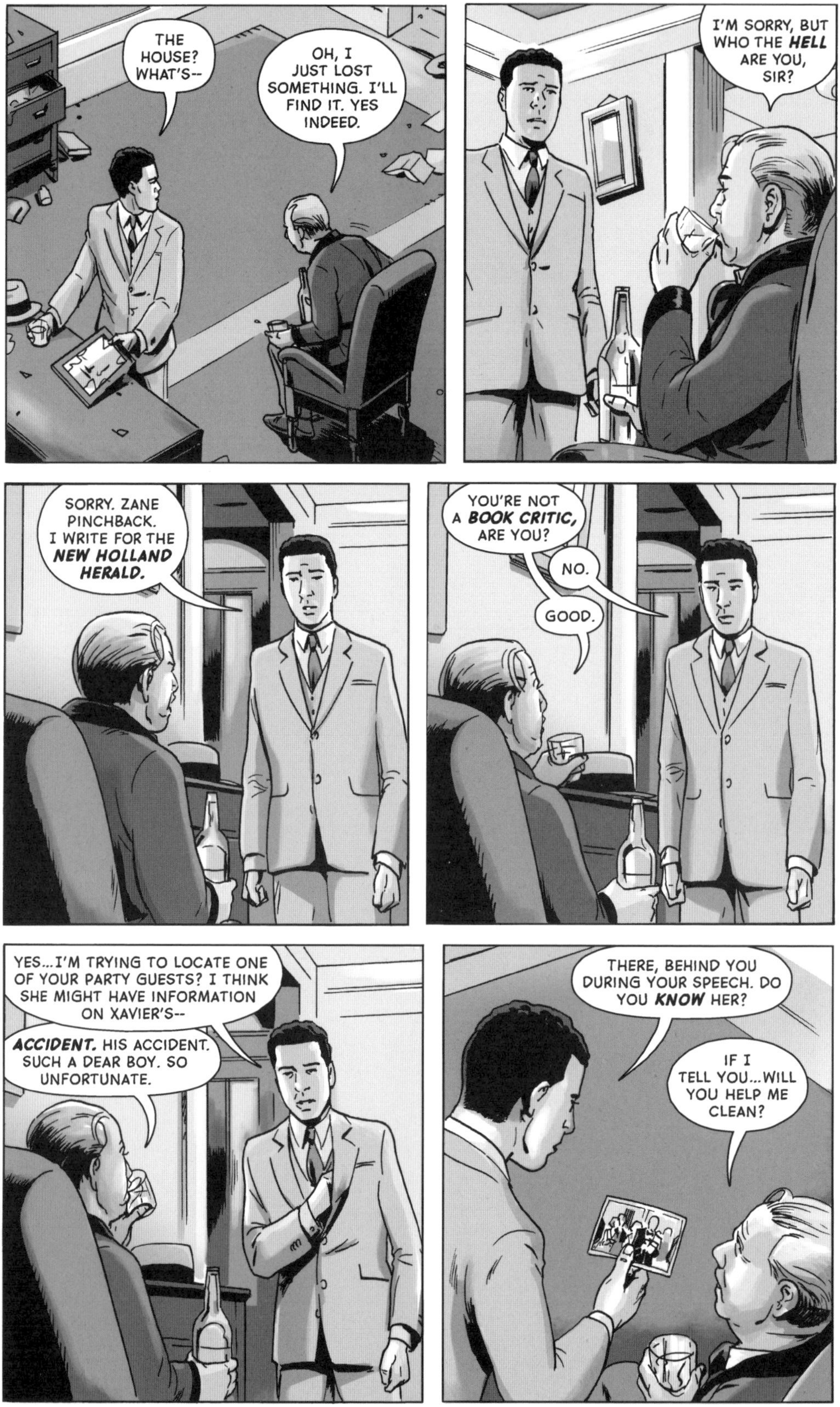
THE HOUSE? WHAT'S--
OH, I JUST LOST SOMETHING. I'LL FIND IT. YES INDEED.
I'M SORRY, BUT WHO THE **HELL** ARE YOU, SIR?
SORRY. ZANE PINCHBACK. I WRITE FOR THE ***NEW HOLLAND HERALD.***
YOU'RE NOT A ***BOOK CRITIC,*** ARE YOU?
NO.
GOOD.
YES...I'M TRYING TO LOCATE ONE OF YOUR PARTY GUESTS? I THINK SHE MIGHT HAVE INFORMATION ON XAVIER'S--
ACCIDENT. HIS ACCIDENT. SUCH A DEAR BOY. SO UNFORTUNATE.
THERE, BEHIND YOU DURING YOUR SPEECH. DO YOU ***KNOW*** HER?
IF I TELL YOU...WILL YOU HELP ME CLEAN?

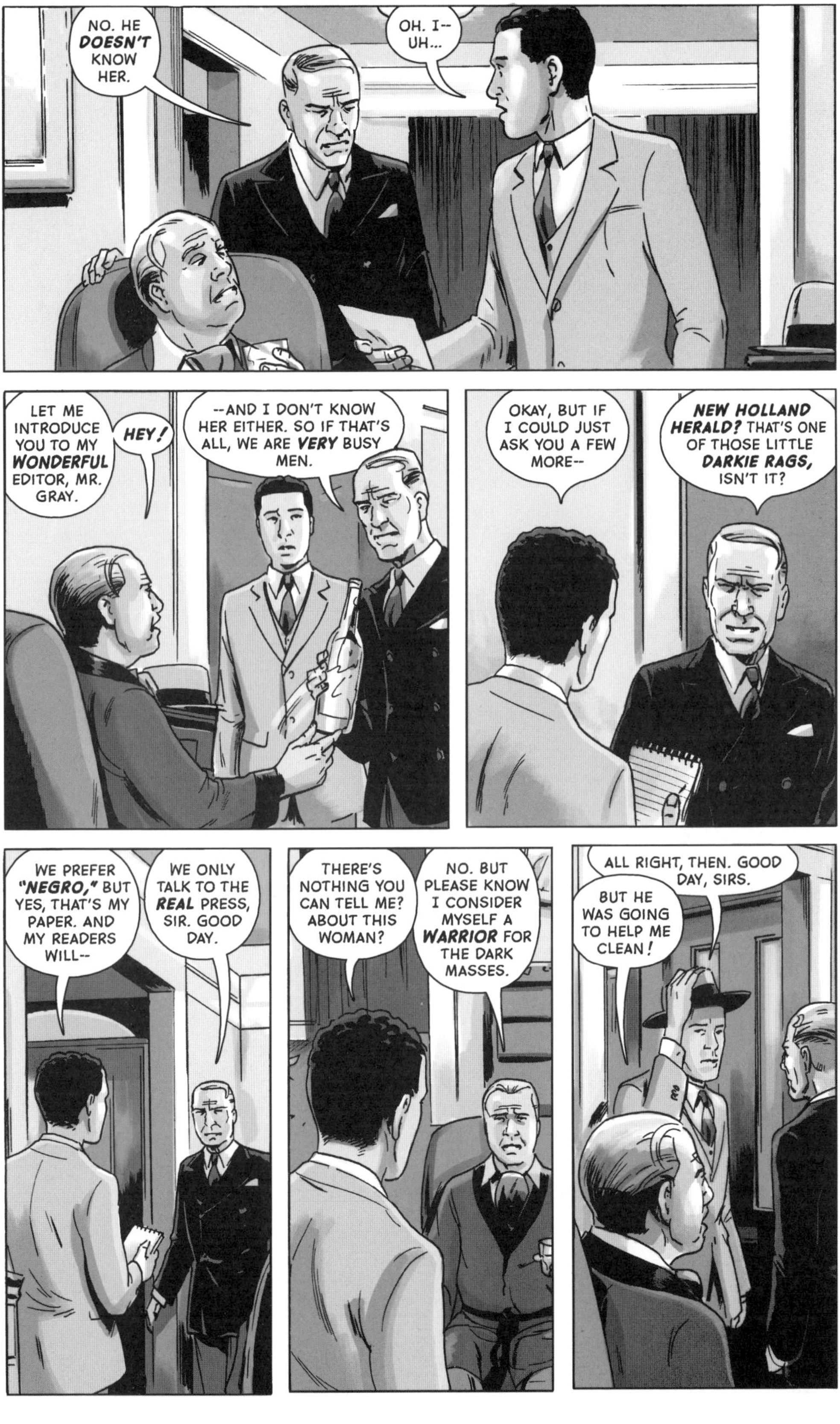
NO. HE DOESN'T KNOW HER.
OH. I-- UH...
LET ME INTRODUCE YOU TO MY WONDERFUL EDITOR, MR. GRAY.
HEY!
--AND I DON'T KNOW HER EITHER. SO IF THAT'S ALL, WE ARE VERY BUSY MEN.
OKAY, BUT IF I COULD JUST ASK YOU A FEW MORE--
NEW HOLLAND HERALD? THAT'S ONE OF THOSE LITTLE DARKIE RAGS, ISN'T IT?
WE PREFER "NEGRO," BUT YES, THAT'S MY PAPER. AND MY READERS WILL--
WE ONLY TALK TO THE REAL PRESS, SIR. GOOD DAY.
THERE'S NOTHING YOU CAN TELL ME? ABOUT THIS WOMAN?
NO. BUT PLEASE KNOW I CONSIDER MYSELF A WARRIOR FOR THE DARK MASSES.
ALL RIGHT, THEN. GOOD DAY, SIRS.
BUT HE WAS GOING TO HELP ME CLEAN!

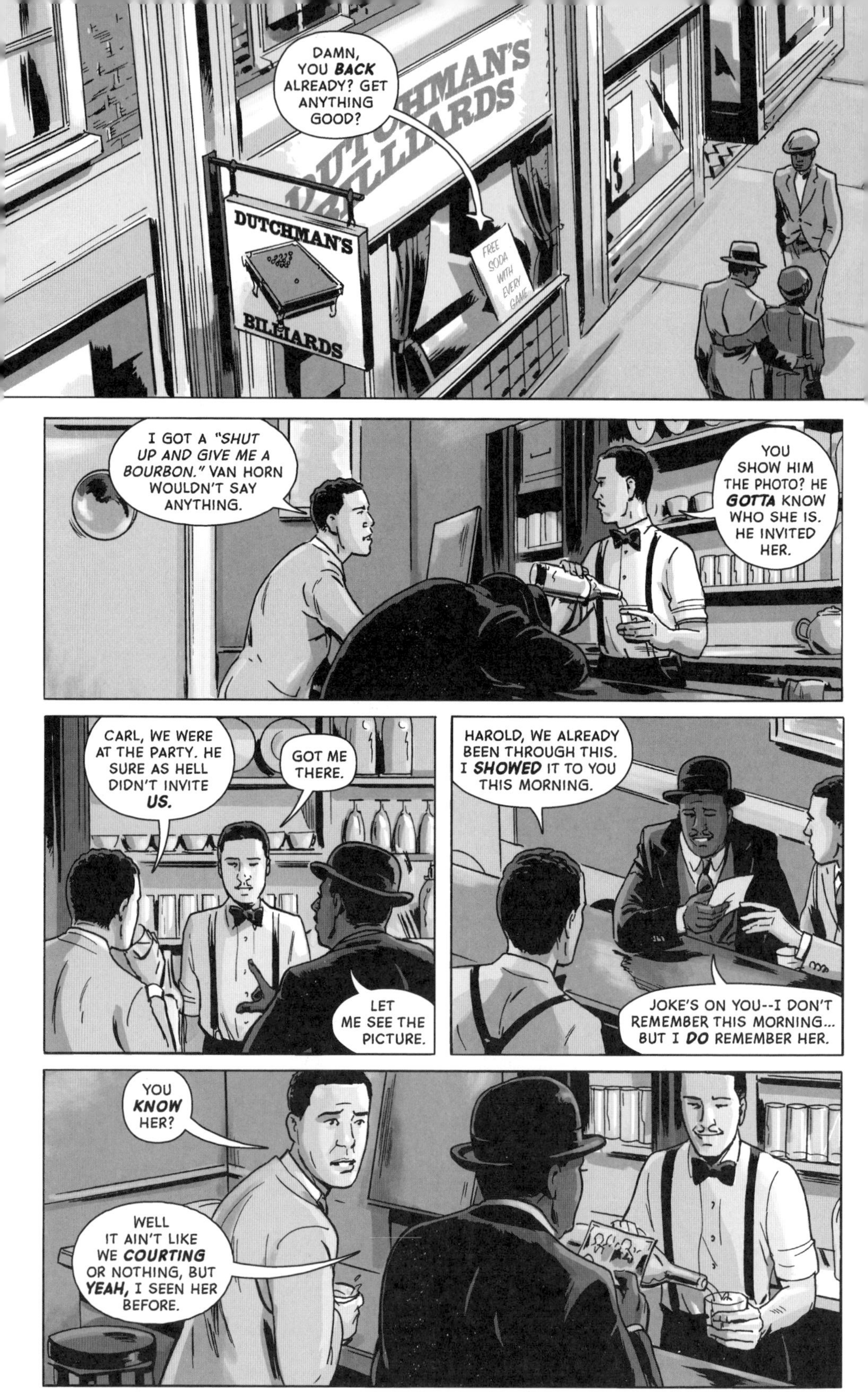
DUTCHMAN'S BILLIARDS
DUTCHMAN'S BILLIARDS
DAMN, YOU **BACK** ALREADY? GET ANYTHING GOOD?
FREE SODA WITH EVERY GAME
I GOT A *"SHUT UP AND GIVE ME A BOURBON."* VAN HORN WOULDN'T SAY ANYTHING.
YOU SHOW HIM THE PHOTO? HE **GOTTA** KNOW WHO SHE IS. HE INVITED HER.
CARL, WE WERE AT THE PARTY. HE SURE AS HELL DIDN'T INVITE ***US.***
GOT ME THERE.
LET ME SEE THE PICTURE.
HAROLD, WE ALREADY BEEN THROUGH THIS. I ***SHOWED*** IT TO YOU THIS MORNING.
JOKE'S ON YOU--I DON'T REMEMBER THIS MORNING... BUT I ***DO*** REMEMBER HER.
YOU ***KNOW*** HER?
WELL IT AIN'T LIKE WE ***COURTING*** OR NOTHING, BUT ***YEAH,*** I SEEN HER BEFORE.

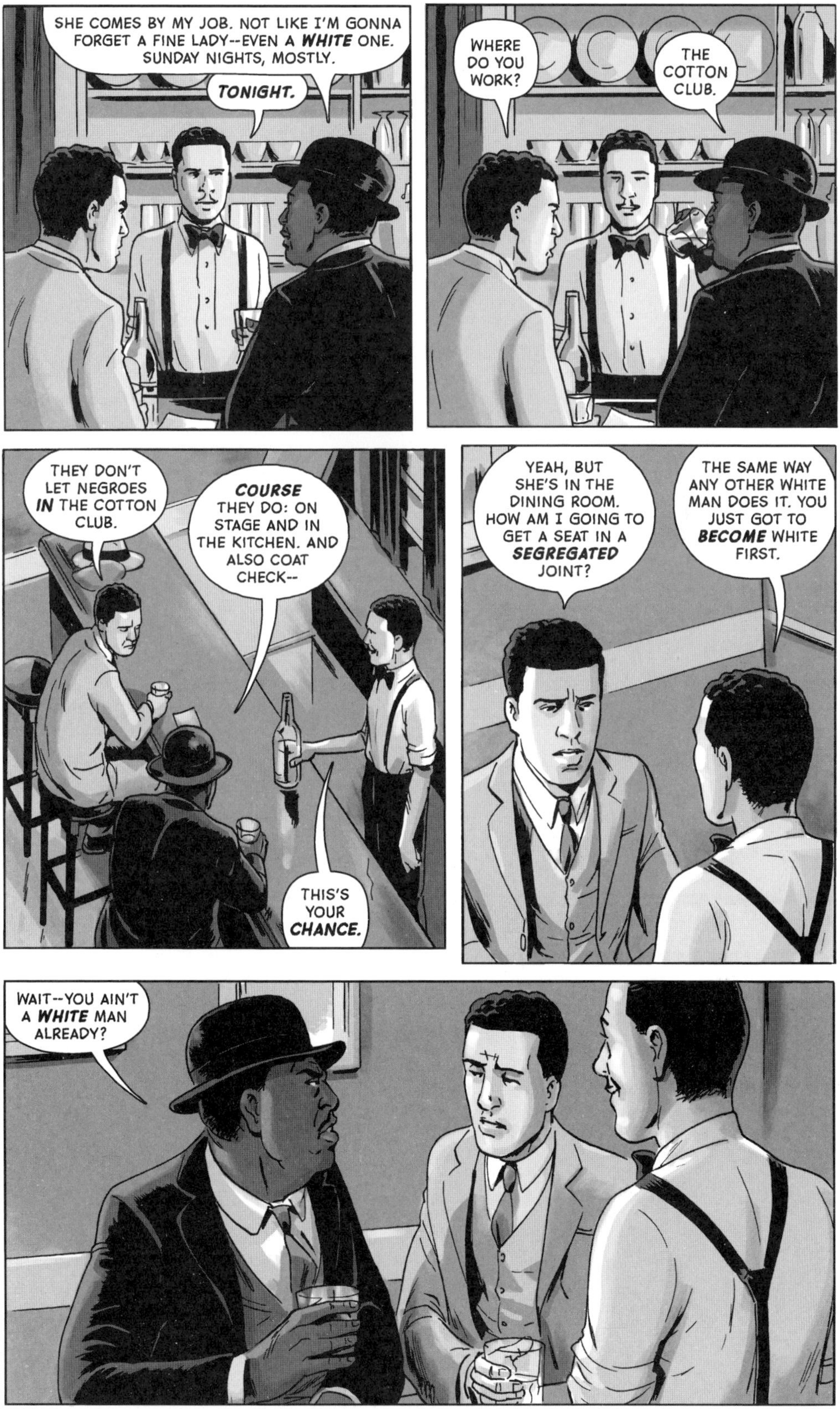
SHE COMES BY MY JOB. NOT LIKE I'M GONNA FORGET A FINE LADY--EVEN A *WHITE* ONE. SUNDAY NIGHTS, MOSTLY.
TONIGHT.
WHERE DO YOU WORK?
THE COTTON CLUB.
THEY DON'T LET NEGROES *IN* THE COTTON CLUB.
COURSE THEY DO: ON STAGE AND IN THE KITCHEN. AND ALSO COAT CHECK--
THIS'S YOUR *CHANCE.*
YEAH, BUT SHE'S IN THE DINING ROOM. HOW AM I GOING TO GET A SEAT IN A *SEGREGATED* JOINT?
THE SAME WAY ANY OTHER WHITE MAN DOES IT. YOU JUST GOT TO *BECOME* WHITE FIRST.
WAIT--YOU AIN'T A *WHITE* MAN ALREADY?

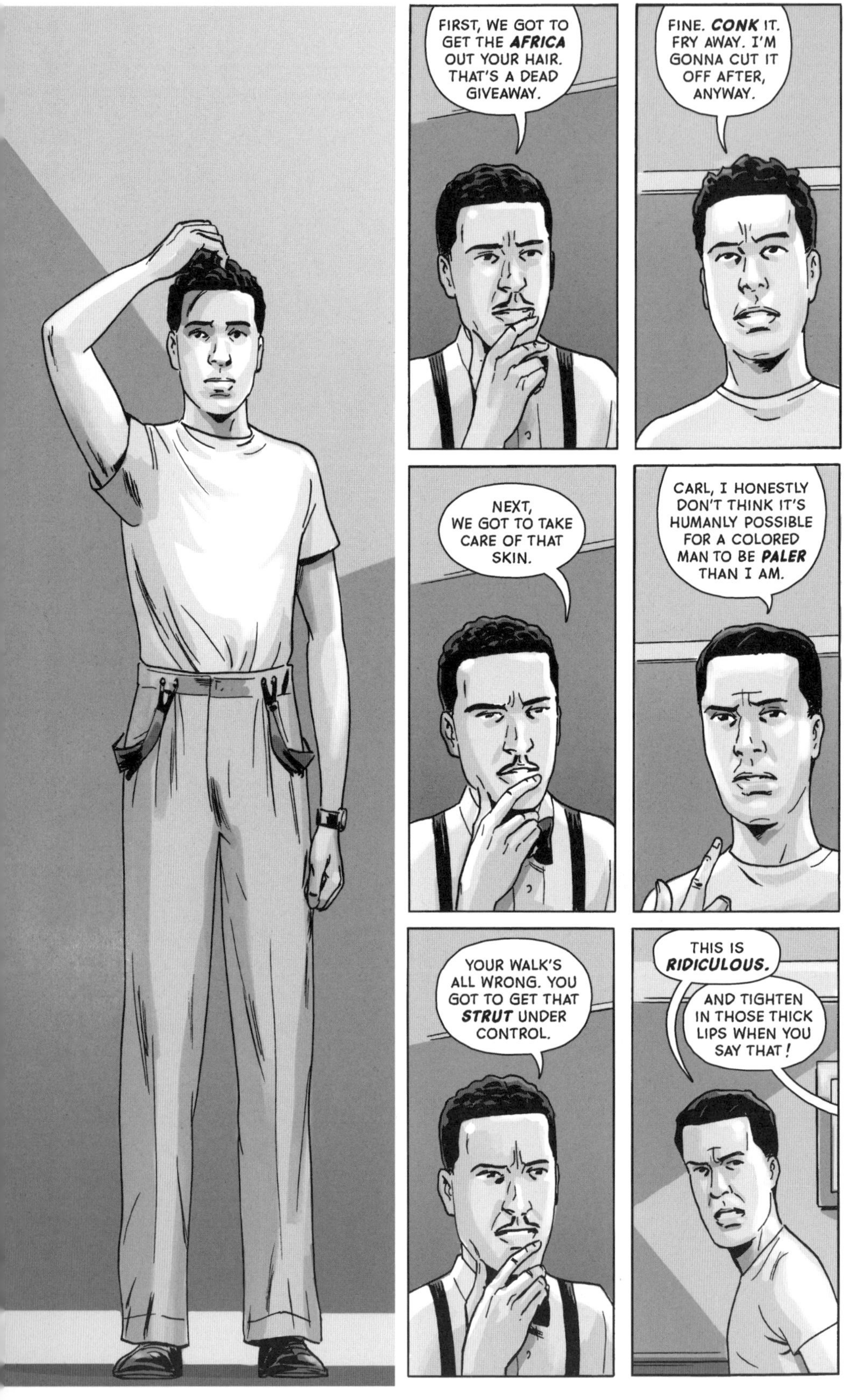

FIRST, WE GOT TO GET THE AFRICA OUT YOUR HAIR. THAT'S A DEAD GIVEAWAY.
FINE. CONK IT. FRY AWAY. I'M GONNA CUT IT OFF AFTER, ANYWAY.
NEXT, WE GOT TO TAKE CARE OF THAT SKIN.
CARL, I HONESTLY DON'T THINK IT'S HUMANLY POSSIBLE FOR A COLORED MAN TO BE PALER THAN I AM.
YOUR WALK'S ALL WRONG. YOU GOT TO GET THAT STRUT UNDER CONTROL.
THIS IS RIDICULOUS.
AND TIGHTEN IN THOSE THICK LIPS WHEN YOU SAY THAT!

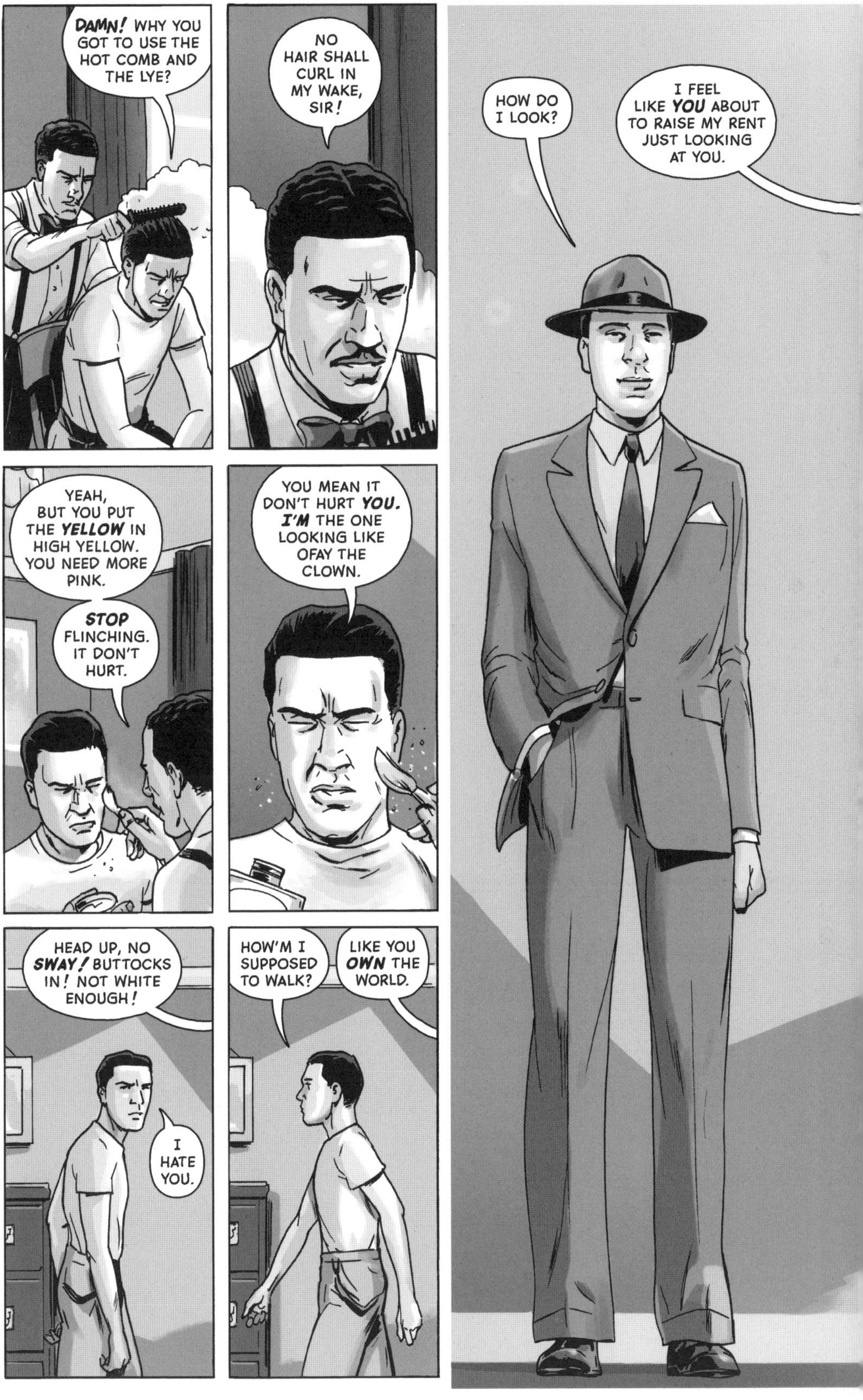
DAMN! WHY YOU GOT TO USE THE HOT COMB AND THE LYE?
NO HAIR SHALL CURL IN MY WAKE, SIR!
YEAH, BUT YOU PUT THE YELLOW IN HIGH YELLOW. YOU NEED MORE PINK.
STOP FLINCHING. IT DON'T HURT.
YOU MEAN IT DON'T HURT YOU. I'M THE ONE LOOKING LIKE OFAY THE CLOWN.
HEAD UP, NO SWAY! BUTTOCKS IN! NOT WHITE ENOUGH!
I HATE YOU.
HOW'M I SUPPOSED TO WALK?
LIKE YOU OWN THE WORLD.
HOW DO I LOOK?
I FEEL LIKE YOU ABOUT TO RAISE MY RENT JUST LOOKING AT YOU.

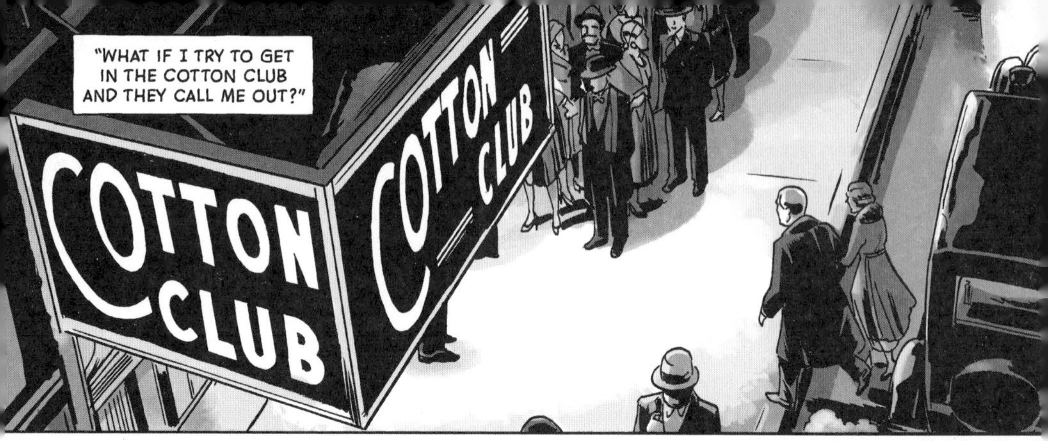
"WHAT IF I TRY TO GET IN THE COTTON CLUB AND THEY CALL ME OUT?"
COTTON CLUB
COTTON CLUB

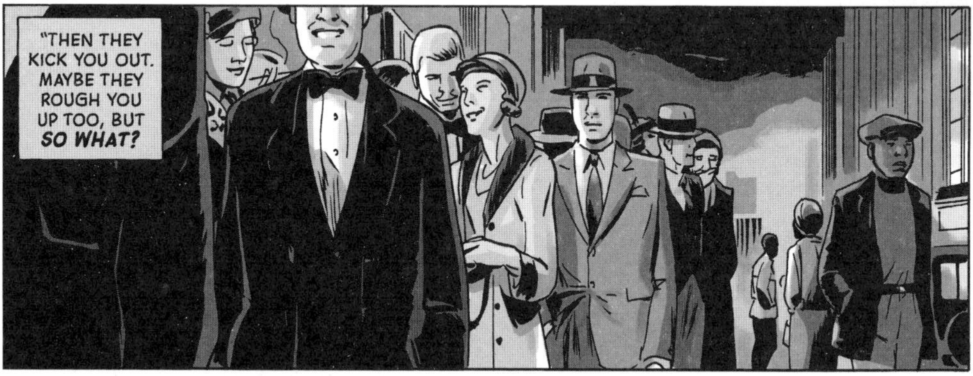
"THEN THEY KICK YOU OUT. MAYBE THEY ROUGH YOU UP TOO, BUT ***SO WHAT?***

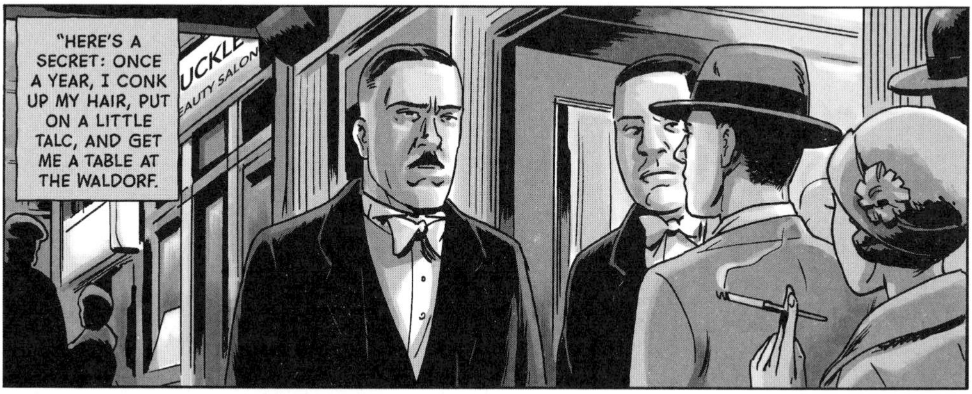
"HERE'S A SECRET: ONCE A YEAR, I CONK UP MY HAIR, PUT ON A LITTLE TALC, AND GET ME A TABLE AT THE WALDORF.
UCKLE
EAUTY SALON

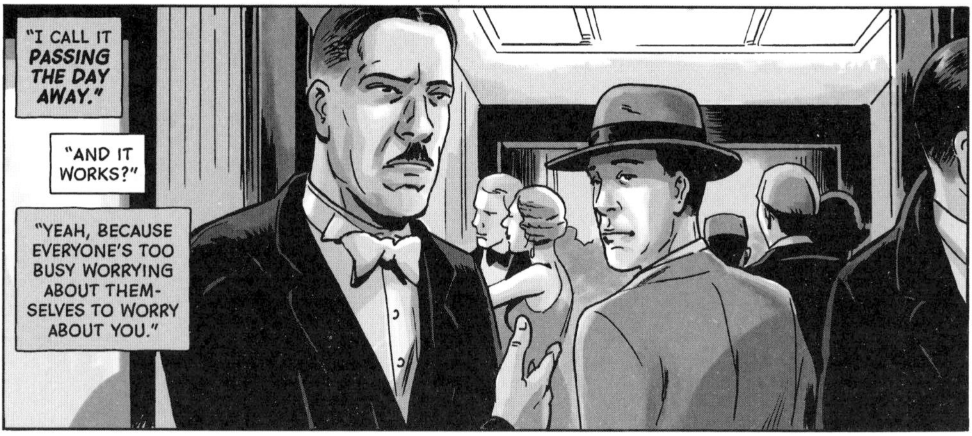
"I CALL IT ***PASSING THE DAY AWAY.***"
"AND IT WORKS?"
"YEAH, BECAUSE EVERYONE'S TOO BUSY WORRYING ABOUT THEM-SELVES TO WORRY ABOUT YOU."

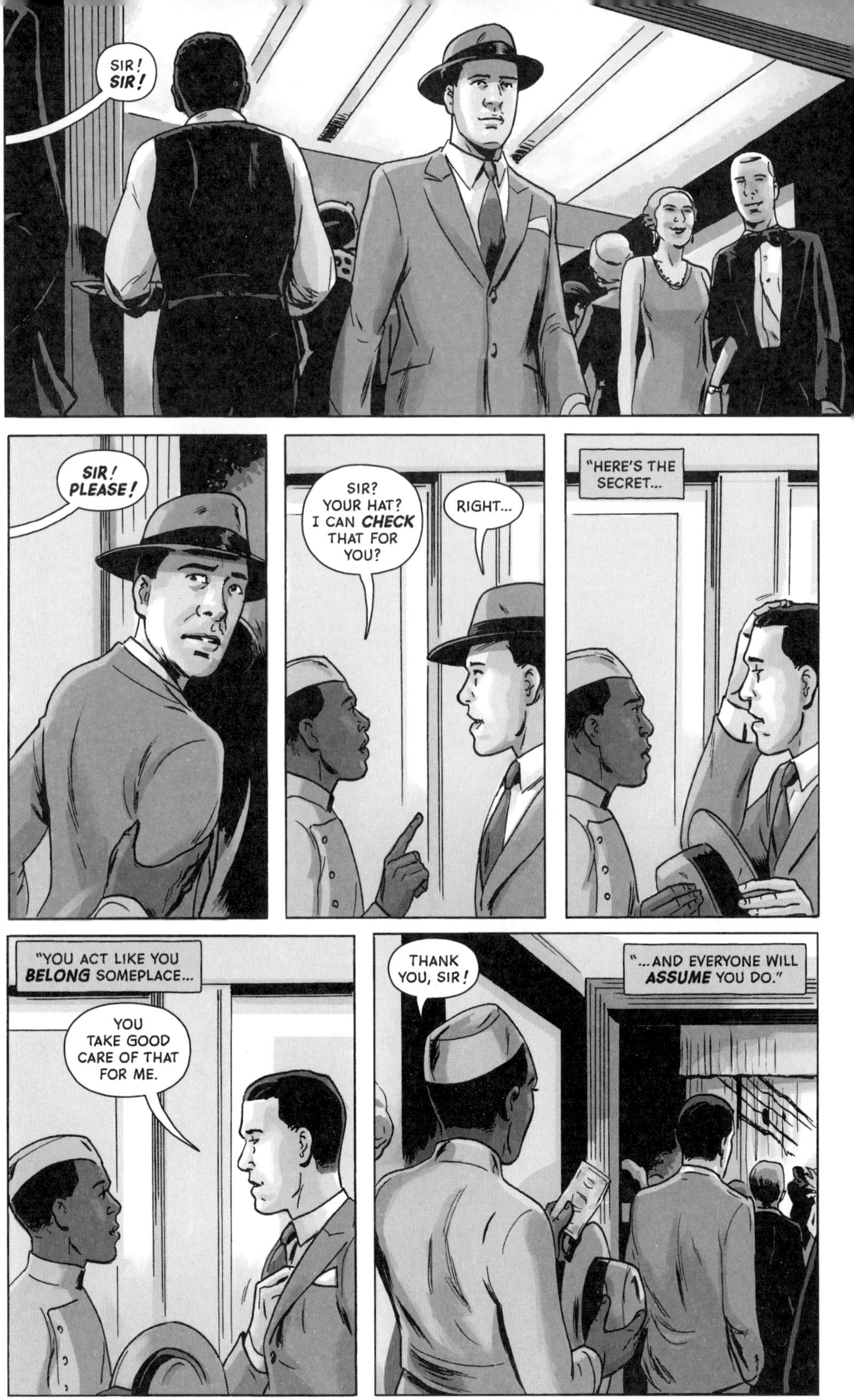
SIR! SIR!
SIR! PLEASE!
SIR? YOUR HAT? I CAN CHECK THAT FOR YOU?
RIGHT...
"HERE'S THE SECRET...
"YOU ACT LIKE YOU BELONG SOMEPLACE...
YOU TAKE GOOD CARE OF THAT FOR ME.
THANK YOU, SIR!
"...AND EVERYONE WILL ASSUME YOU DO."

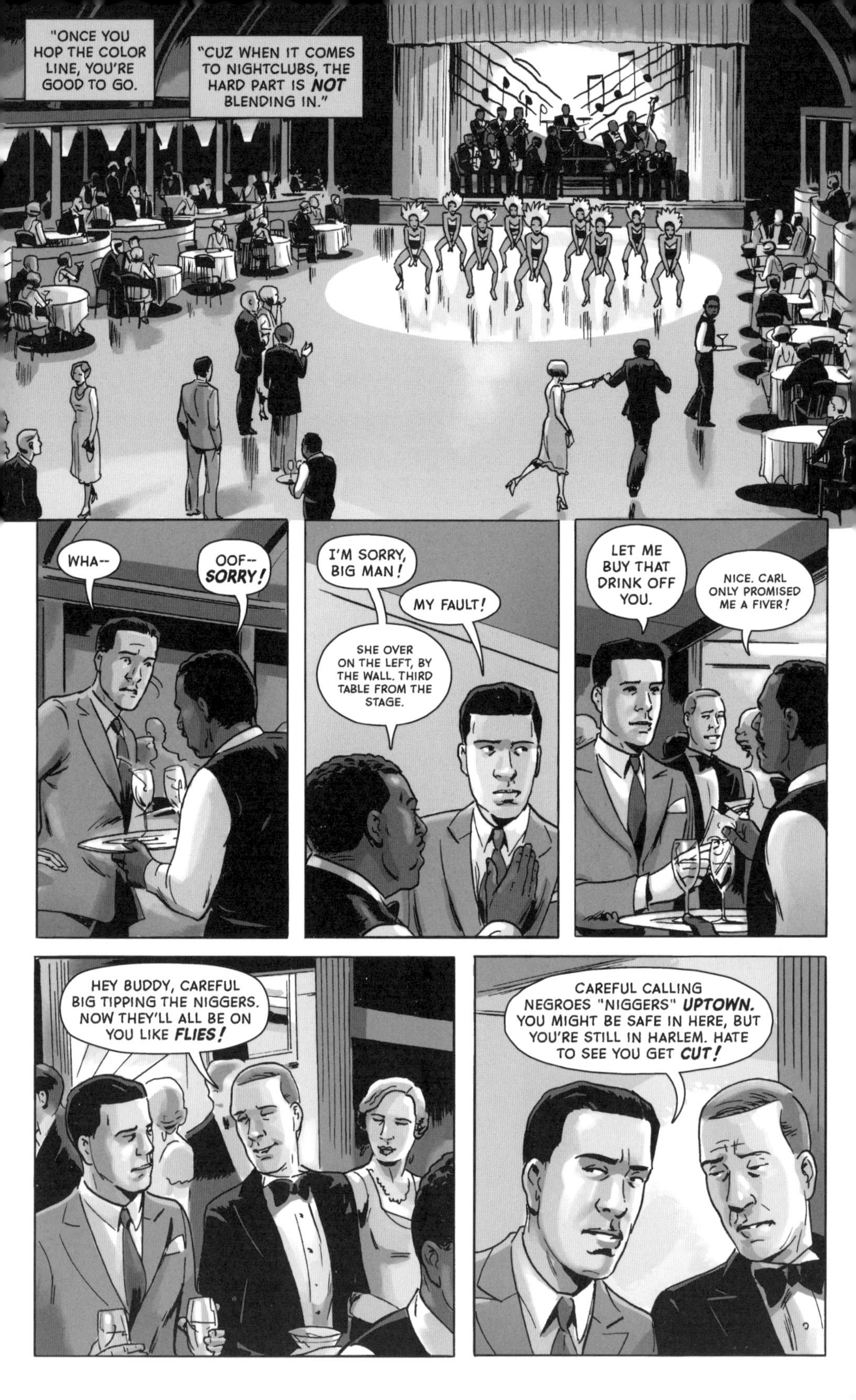
"ONCE YOU HOP THE COLOR LINE, YOU'RE GOOD TO GO.
"CUZ WHEN IT COMES TO NIGHTCLUBS, THE HARD PART IS NOT BLENDING IN."
WHA--
OOF-- SORRY!
I'M SORRY, BIG MAN!
MY FAULT!
SHE OVER ON THE LEFT, BY THE WALL. THIRD TABLE FROM THE STAGE.
LET ME BUY THAT DRINK OFF YOU.
NICE. CARL ONLY PROMISED ME A FIVER!
HEY BUDDY, CAREFUL BIG TIPPING THE NIGGERS. NOW THEY'LL ALL BE ON YOU LIKE FLIES!
CAREFUL CALLING NEGROES "NIGGERS" UPTOWN. YOU MIGHT BE SAFE IN HERE, BUT YOU'RE STILL IN HARLEM. HATE TO SEE YOU GET CUT!

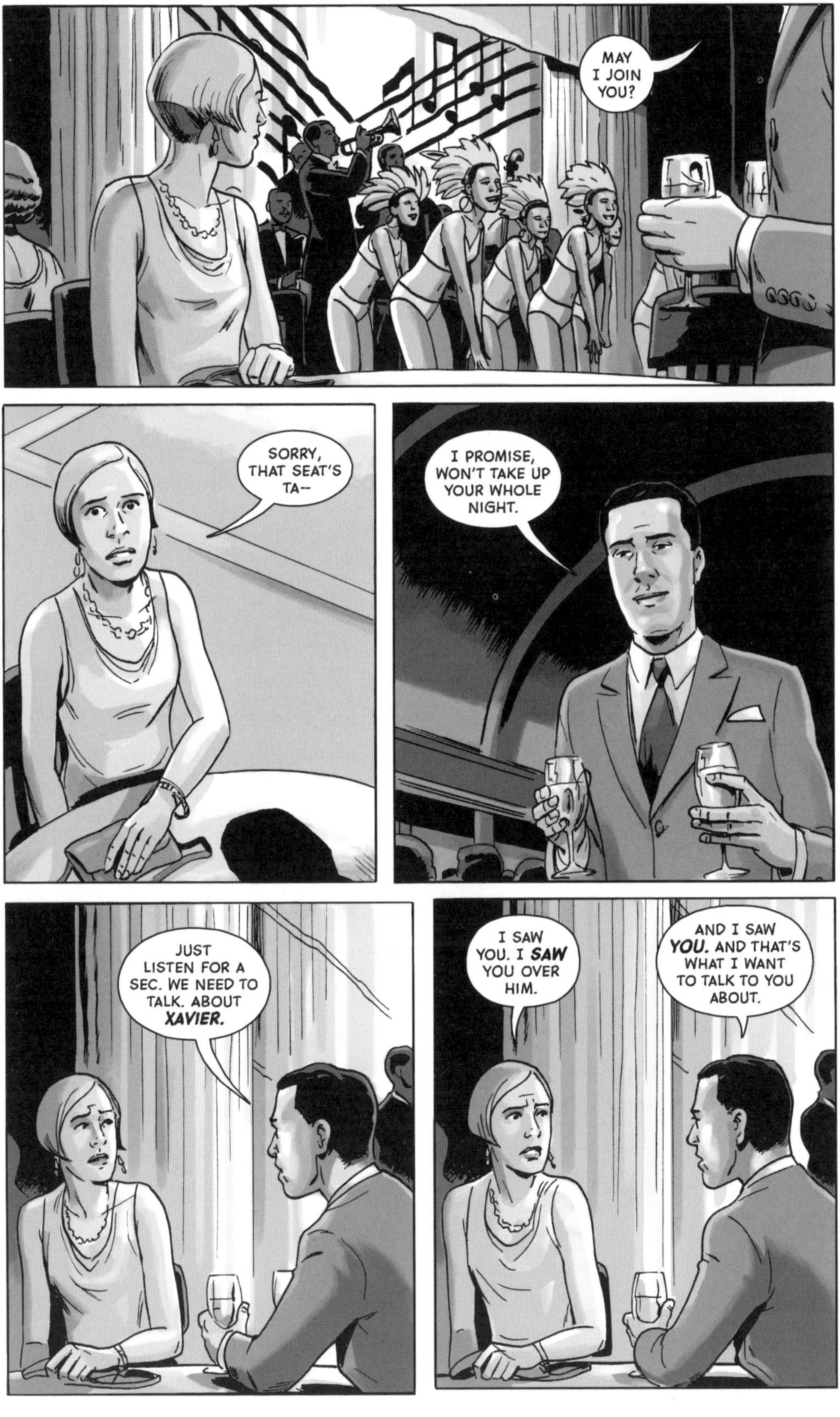
MAY I JOIN YOU?
SORRY, THAT SEAT'S TA--
I PROMISE, WON'T TAKE UP YOUR WHOLE NIGHT.
JUST LISTEN FOR A SEC. WE NEED TO TALK. ABOUT XAVIER.
I SAW YOU. I SAW YOU OVER HIM.
AND I SAW YOU. AND THAT'S WHAT I WANT TO TALK TO YOU ABOUT.

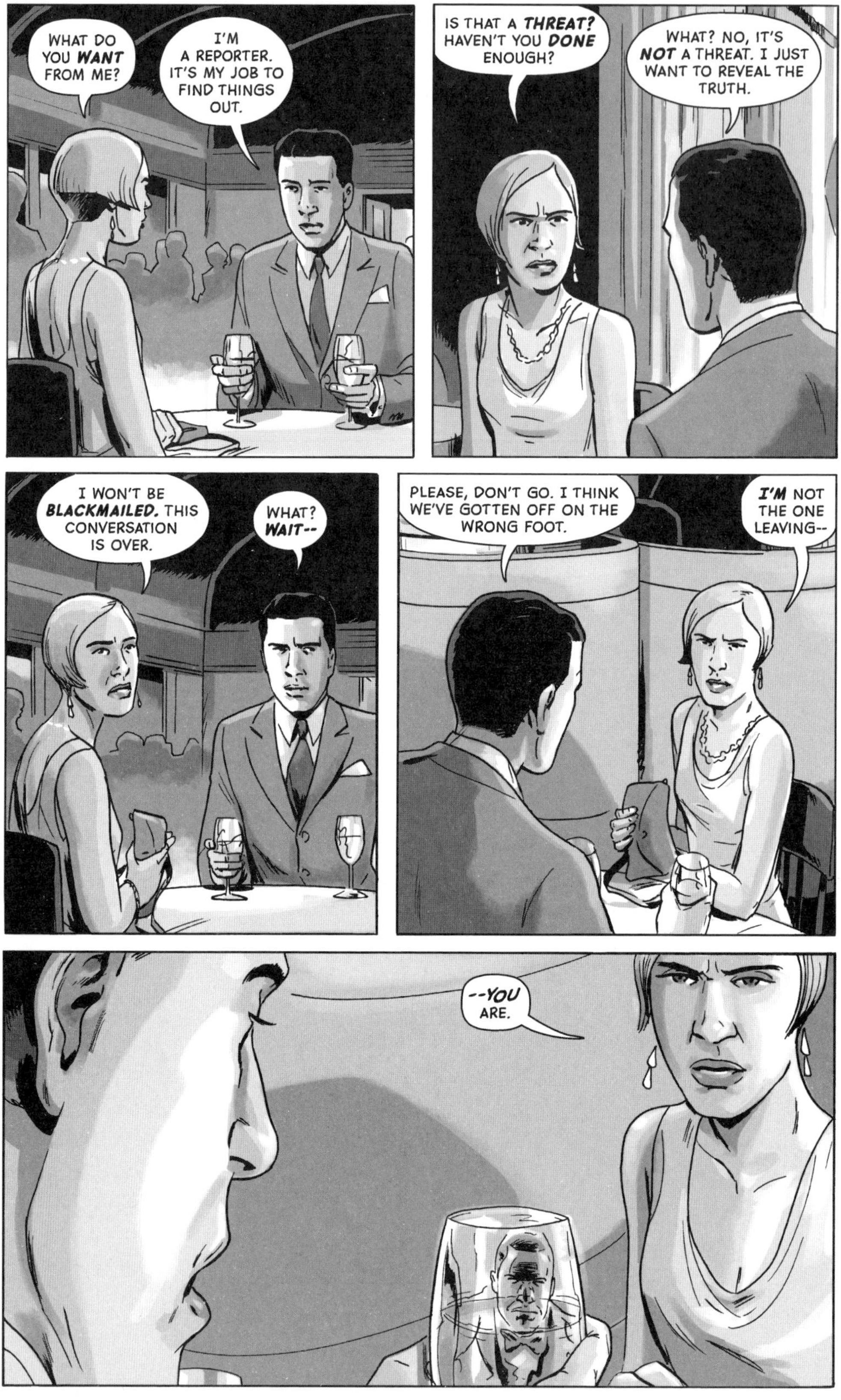
WHAT DO YOU WANT FROM ME?
I'M A REPORTER. IT'S MY JOB TO FIND THINGS OUT.
IS THAT A THREAT? HAVEN'T YOU DONE ENOUGH?
WHAT? NO, IT'S NOT A THREAT. I JUST WANT TO REVEAL THE TRUTH.
I WON'T BE BLACKMAILED. THIS CONVERSATION IS OVER.
WHAT? WAIT--
PLEASE, DON'T GO. I THINK WE'VE GOTTEN OFF ON THE WRONG FOOT.
I'M NOT THE ONE LEAVING--
--YOU ARE.

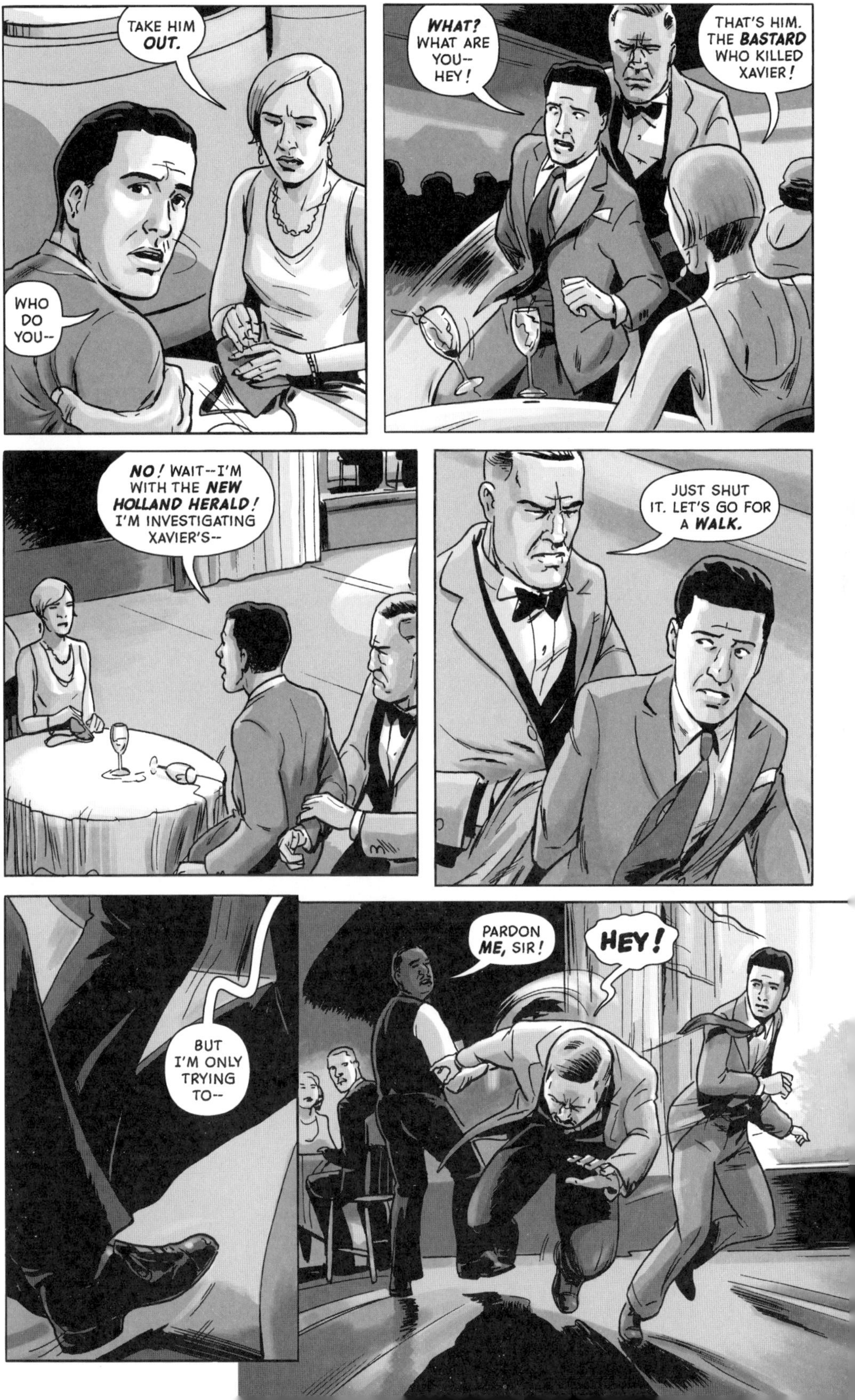
TAKE HIM OUT.
WHO DO YOU--
WHAT? WHAT ARE YOU-- HEY!
THAT'S HIM. THE BASTARD WHO KILLED XAVIER!
NO! WAIT--I'M WITH THE NEW HOLLAND HERALD! I'M INVESTIGATING XAVIER'S--
JUST SHUT IT. LET'S GO FOR A WALK.
BUT I'M ONLY TRYING TO--
PARDON ME, SIR!
HEY!

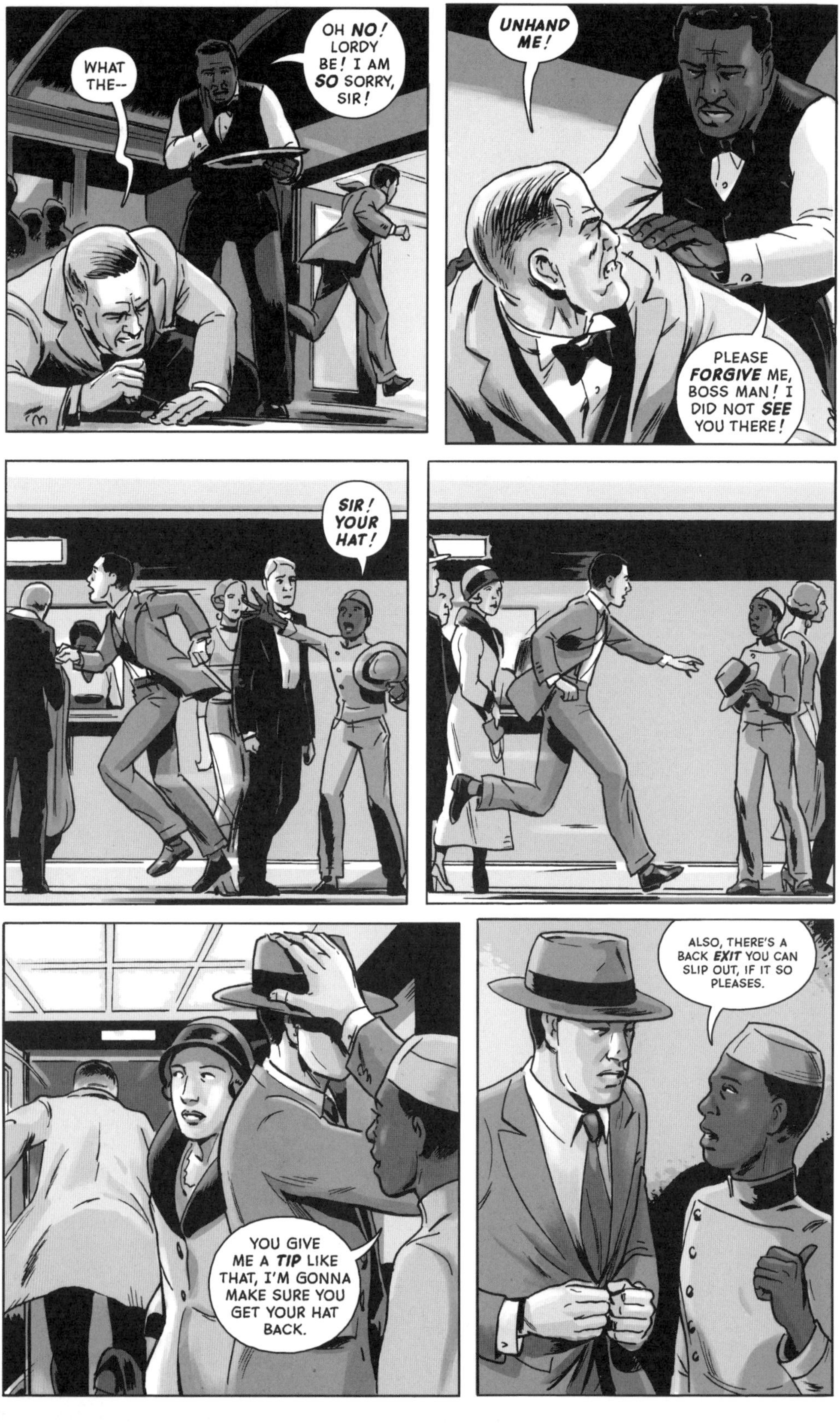
WHAT THE--
OH NO! LORDY BE! I AM SO SORRY, SIR!
UNHAND ME!
PLEASE FORGIVE ME, BOSS MAN! I DID NOT SEE YOU THERE!
SIR! YOUR HAT!
YOU GIVE ME A TIP LIKE THAT, I'M GONNA MAKE SURE YOU GET YOUR HAT BACK.
ALSO, THERE'S A BACK EXIT YOU CAN SLIP OUT, IF IT SO PLEASES.

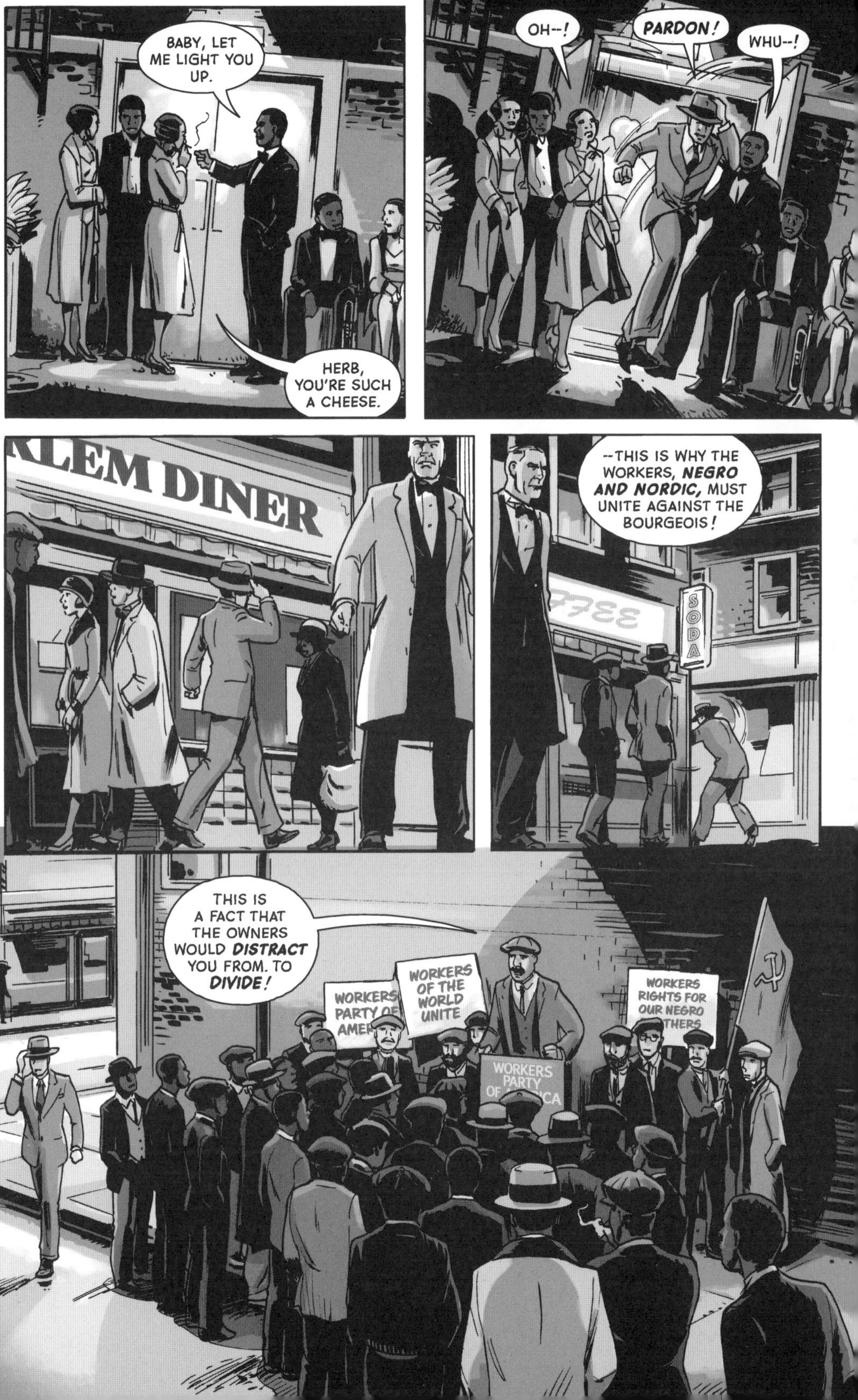
BABY, LET ME LIGHT YOU UP.
HERB, YOU'RE SUCH A CHEESE.
OH--!
PARDON!
WHU--!
LEM DINER
--THIS IS WHY THE WORKERS, NEGRO AND NORDIC, MUST UNITE AGAINST THE BOURGEOIS!
SODA
THIS IS A FACT THAT THE OWNERS WOULD DISTRACT YOU FROM. TO DIVIDE!
WORKERS PARTY OF
WORKERS OF THE WORLD UNITE
WORKERS RIGHTS FOR OUR NEGRO
WORKERS PARTY

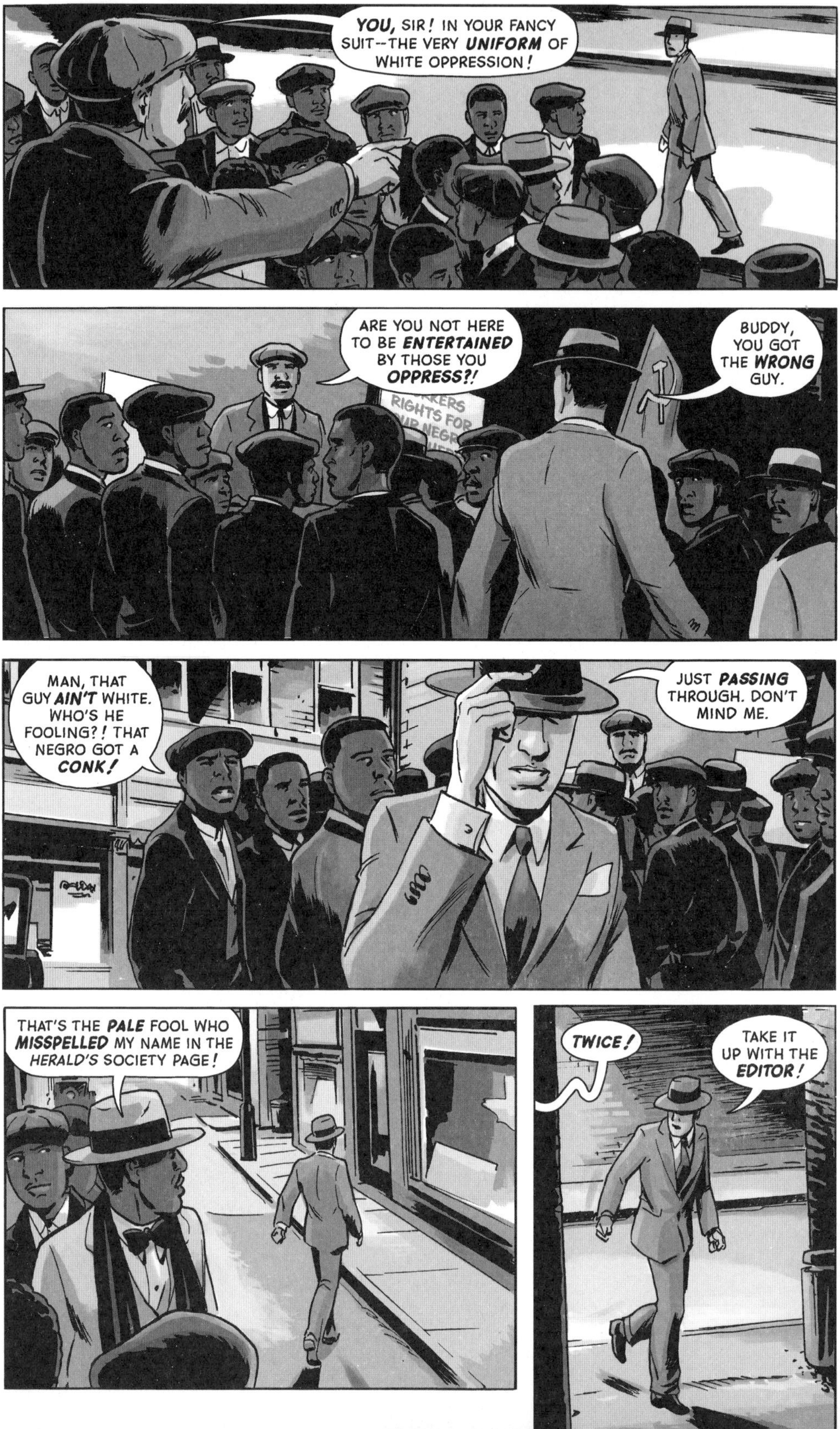

YOU, SIR! IN YOUR FANCY SUIT--THE VERY UNIFORM OF WHITE OPPRESSION!
ARE YOU NOT HERE TO BE ENTERTAINED BY THOSE YOU OPPRESS?!
RIGHTS FOR
BUDDY, YOU GOT THE WRONG GUY.
MAN, THAT GUY AIN'T WHITE. WHO'S HE FOOLING?! THAT NEGRO GOT A CONK!
JUST PASSING THROUGH. DON'T MIND ME.
THAT'S THE PALE FOOL WHO MISSPELLED MY NAME IN THE HERALD'S SOCIETY PAGE!
TWICE!
TAKE IT UP WITH THE EDITOR!

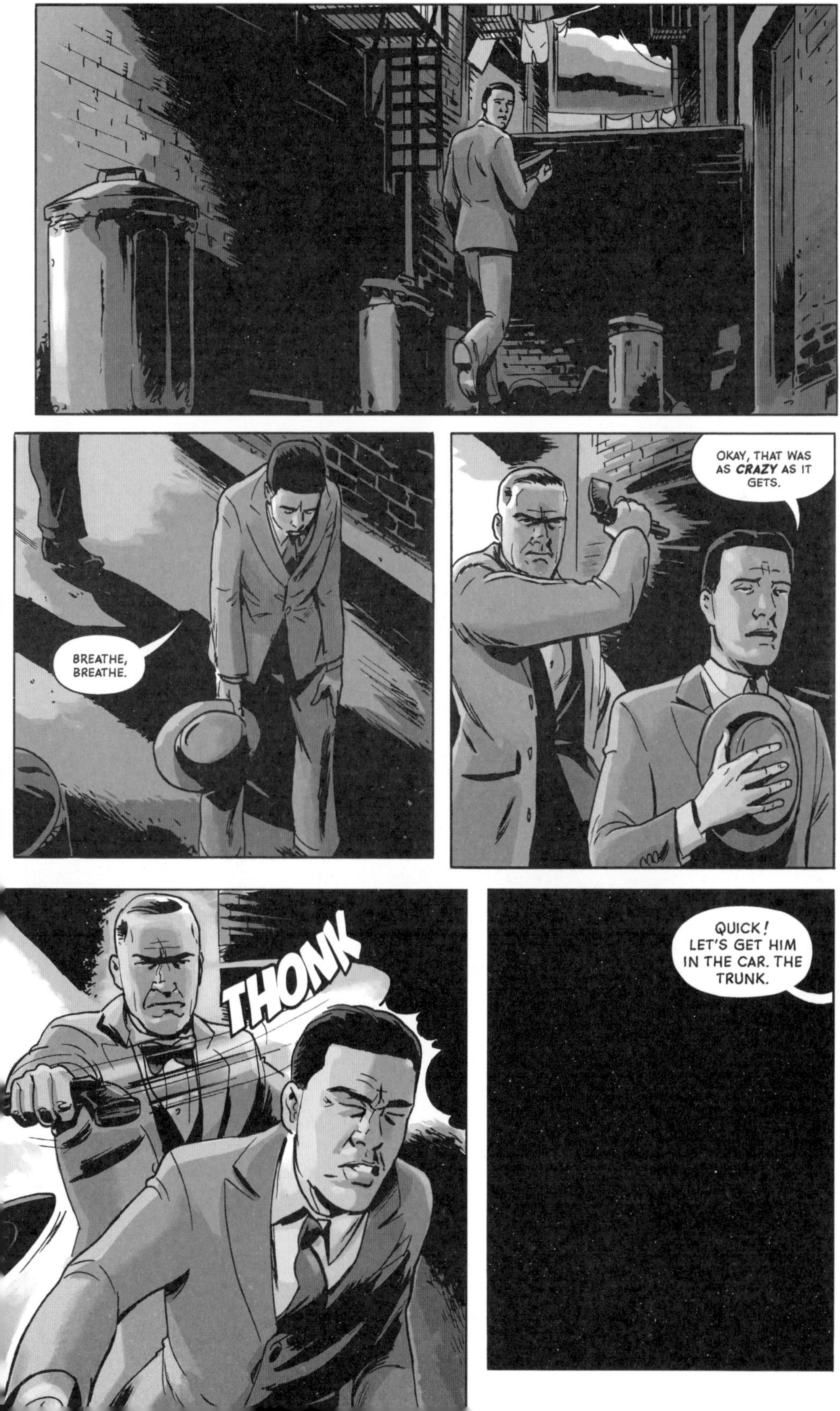
BREATHE, BREATHE.
OKAY, THAT WAS AS CRAZY AS IT GETS.
THONK
QUICK! LET'S GET HIM IN THE CAR. THE TRUNK.

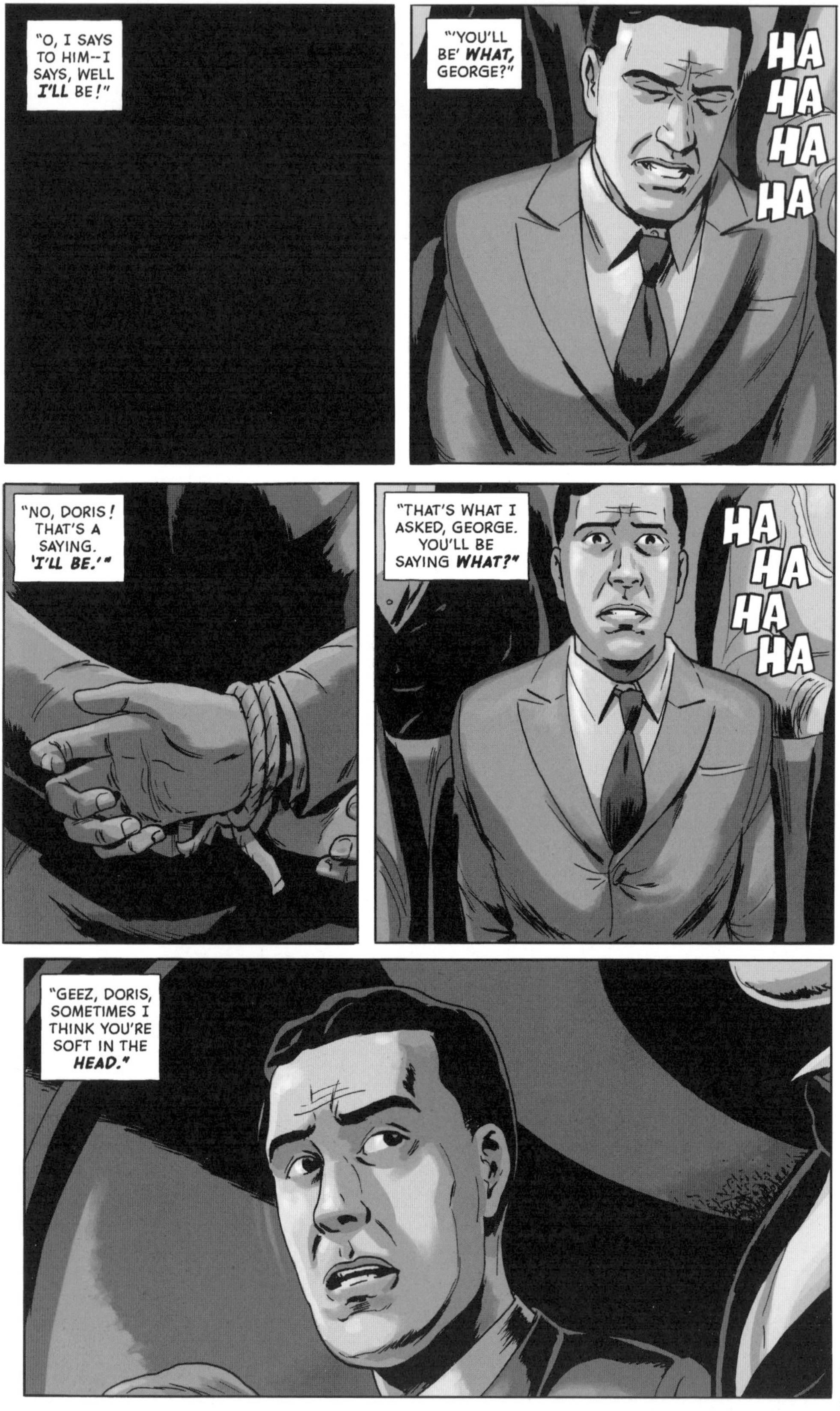
"O, I SAYS TO HIM--I SAYS, WELL I'LL BE!"
"'YOU'LL BE' WHAT, GEORGE?"
HA HA HA HA
"NO, DORIS! THAT'S A SAYING. 'I'LL BE.'"
"THAT'S WHAT I ASKED, GEORGE. YOU'LL BE SAYING WHAT?"
HA HA HA HA
"GEEZ, DORIS, SOMETIMES I THINK YOU'RE SOFT IN THE HEAD."

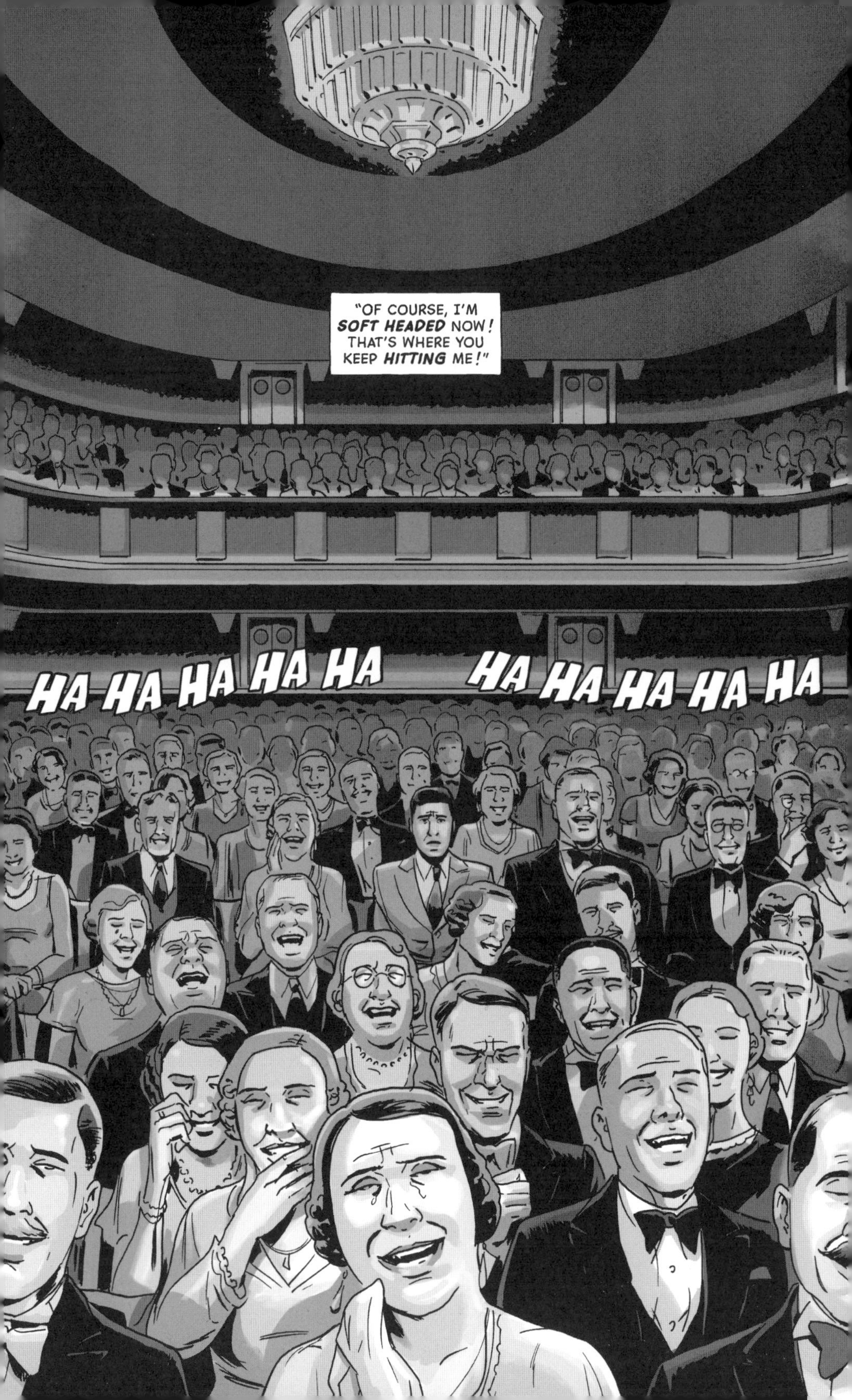
"OF COURSE, I'M SOFT HEADED NOW! THAT'S WHERE YOU KEEP HITTING ME!"
HA HA HA HA HA
HA HA HA HA HA

CHAPTER III

"LIBRETTO"

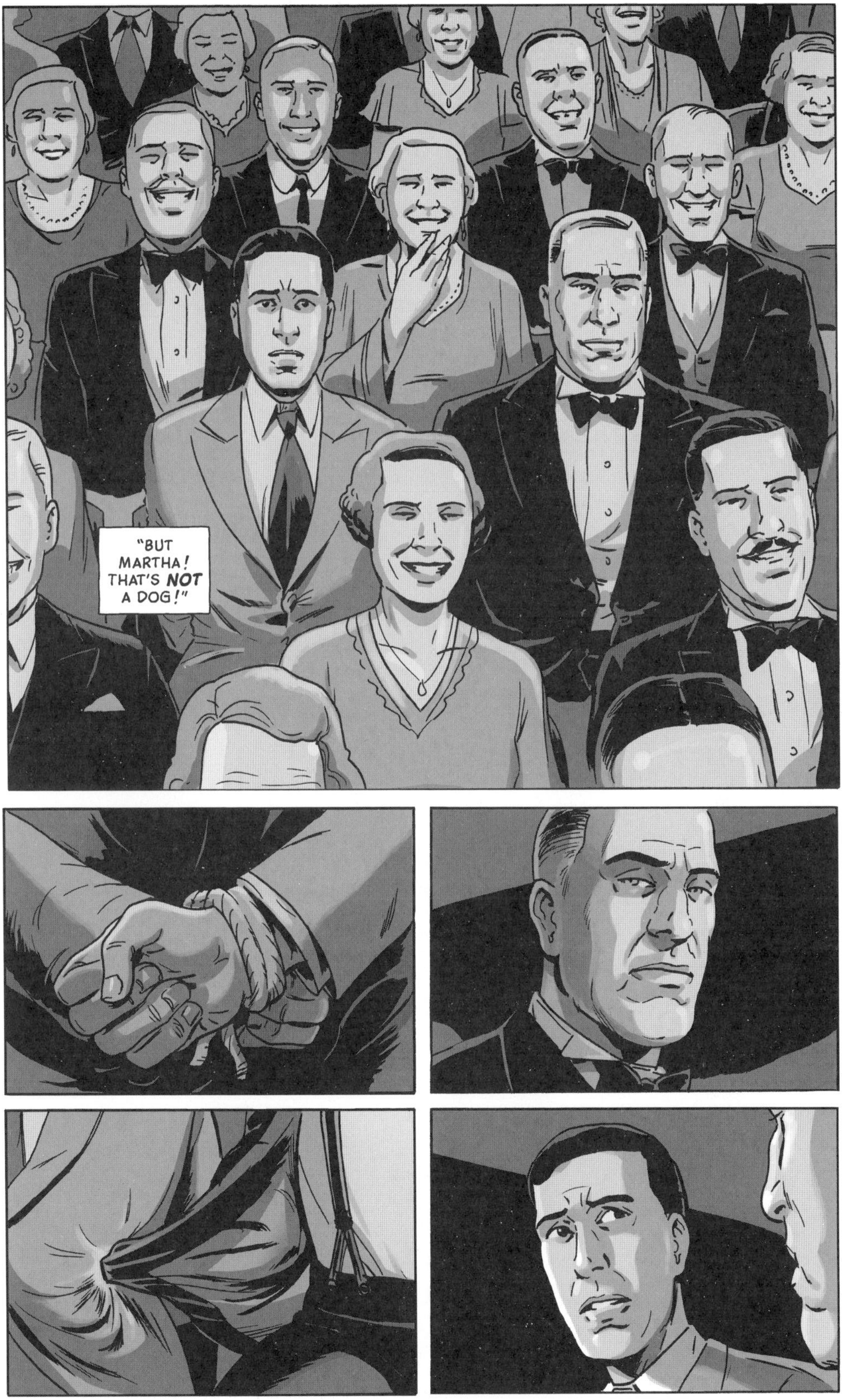
"BUT MARTHA! THAT'S NOT A DOG!"

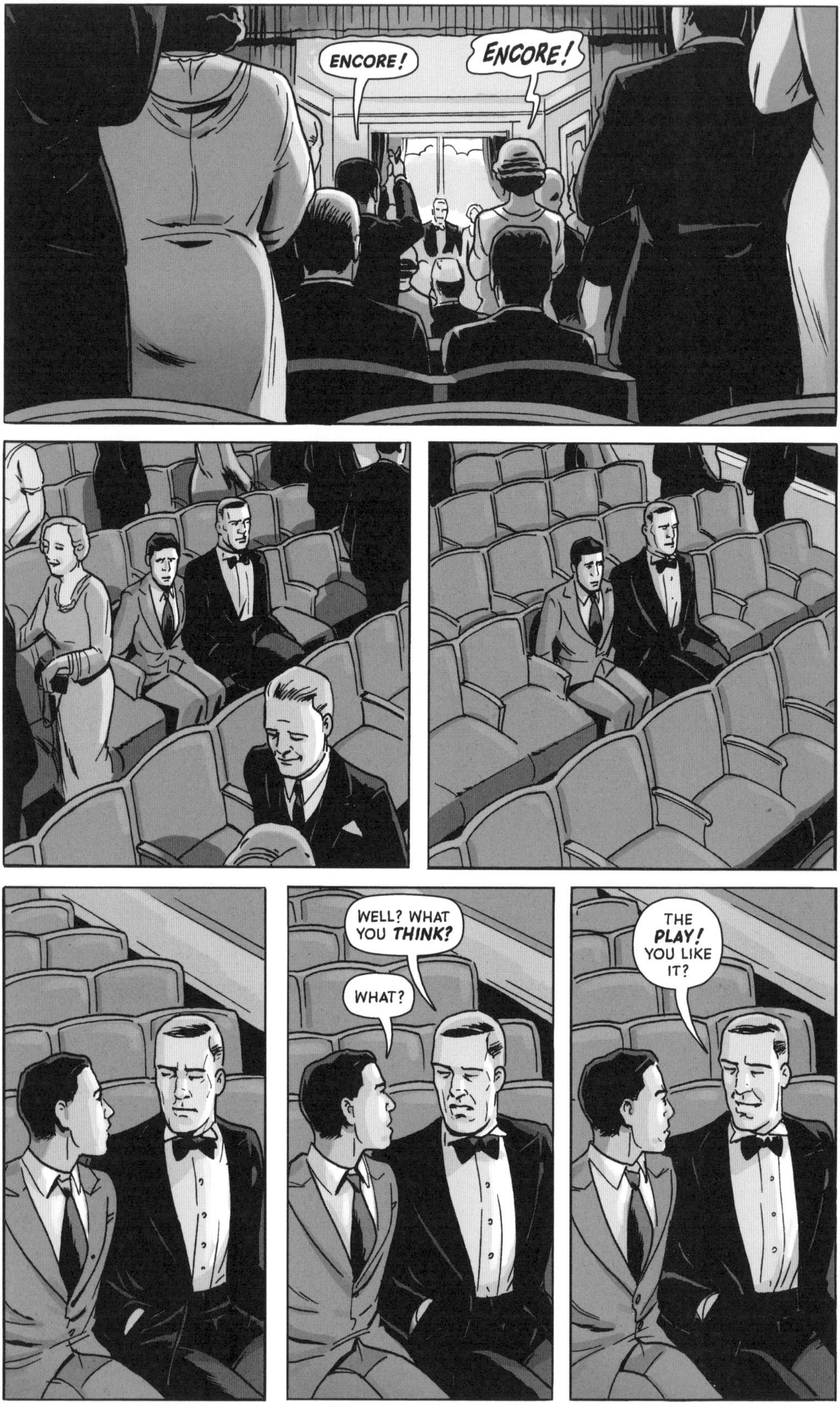
ENCORE!
ENCORE!
WELL? WHAT YOU THINK?
WHAT?
THE PLAY! YOU LIKE IT?

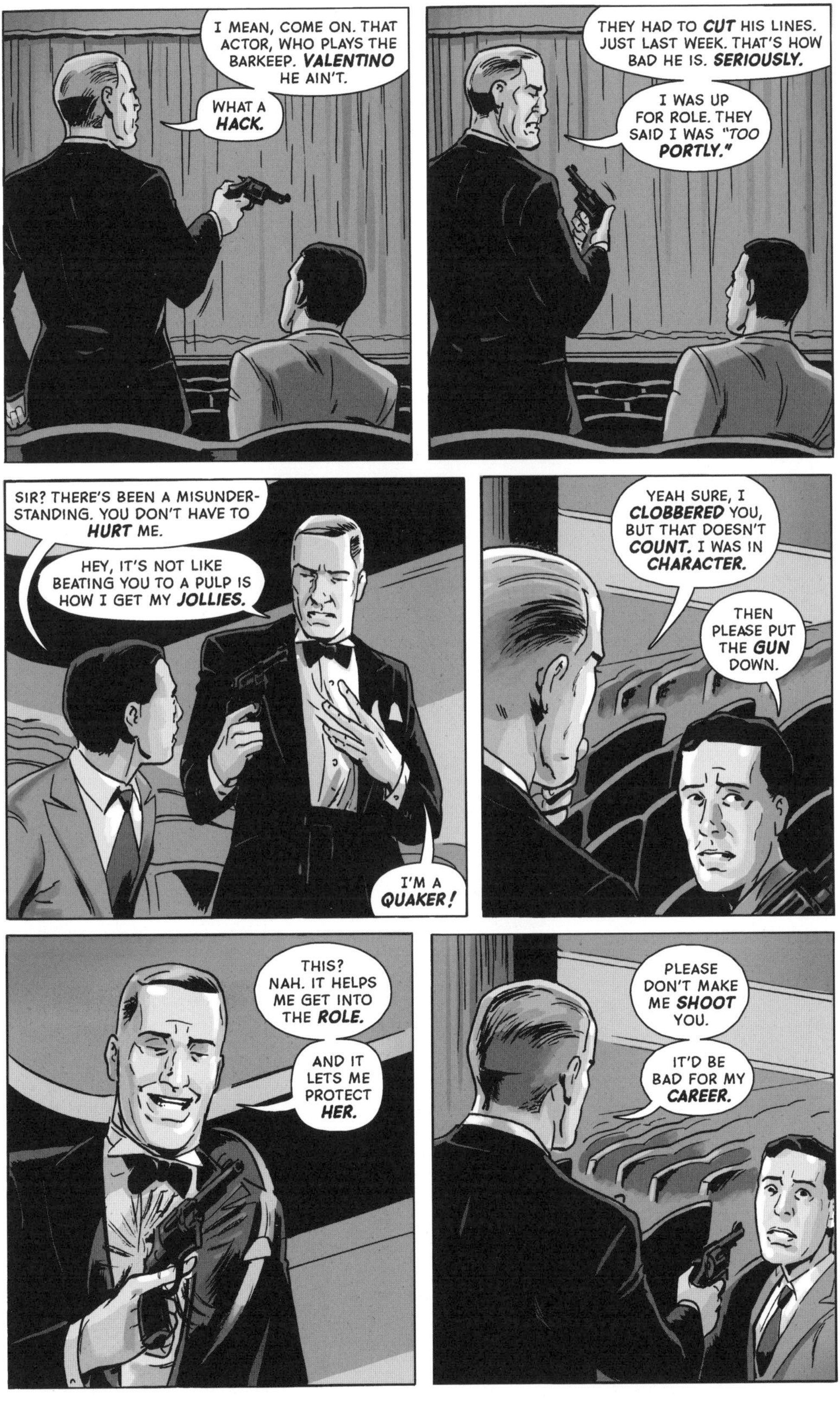
I MEAN, COME ON. THAT ACTOR, WHO PLAYS THE BARKEEP. **VALENTINO** HE AIN'T.
WHAT A **HACK.**
THEY HAD TO **CUT** HIS LINES. JUST LAST WEEK. THAT'S HOW BAD HE IS. **SERIOUSLY.**
I WAS UP FOR ROLE. THEY SAID I WAS *"TOO* **PORTLY."**
SIR? THERE'S BEEN A MISUNDER-STANDING. YOU DON'T HAVE TO **HURT** ME.
HEY, IT'S NOT LIKE BEATING YOU TO A PULP IS HOW I GET MY **JOLLIES.**
I'M A **QUAKER!**
YEAH SURE, I **CLOBBERED** YOU, BUT THAT DOESN'T **COUNT.** I WAS IN **CHARACTER.**
THEN PLEASE PUT THE **GUN** DOWN.
THIS? NAH. IT HELPS ME GET INTO THE **ROLE.**
AND IT LETS ME PROTECT **HER.**
PLEASE DON'T MAKE ME **SHOOT** YOU.
IT'D BE BAD FOR MY **CAREER.**

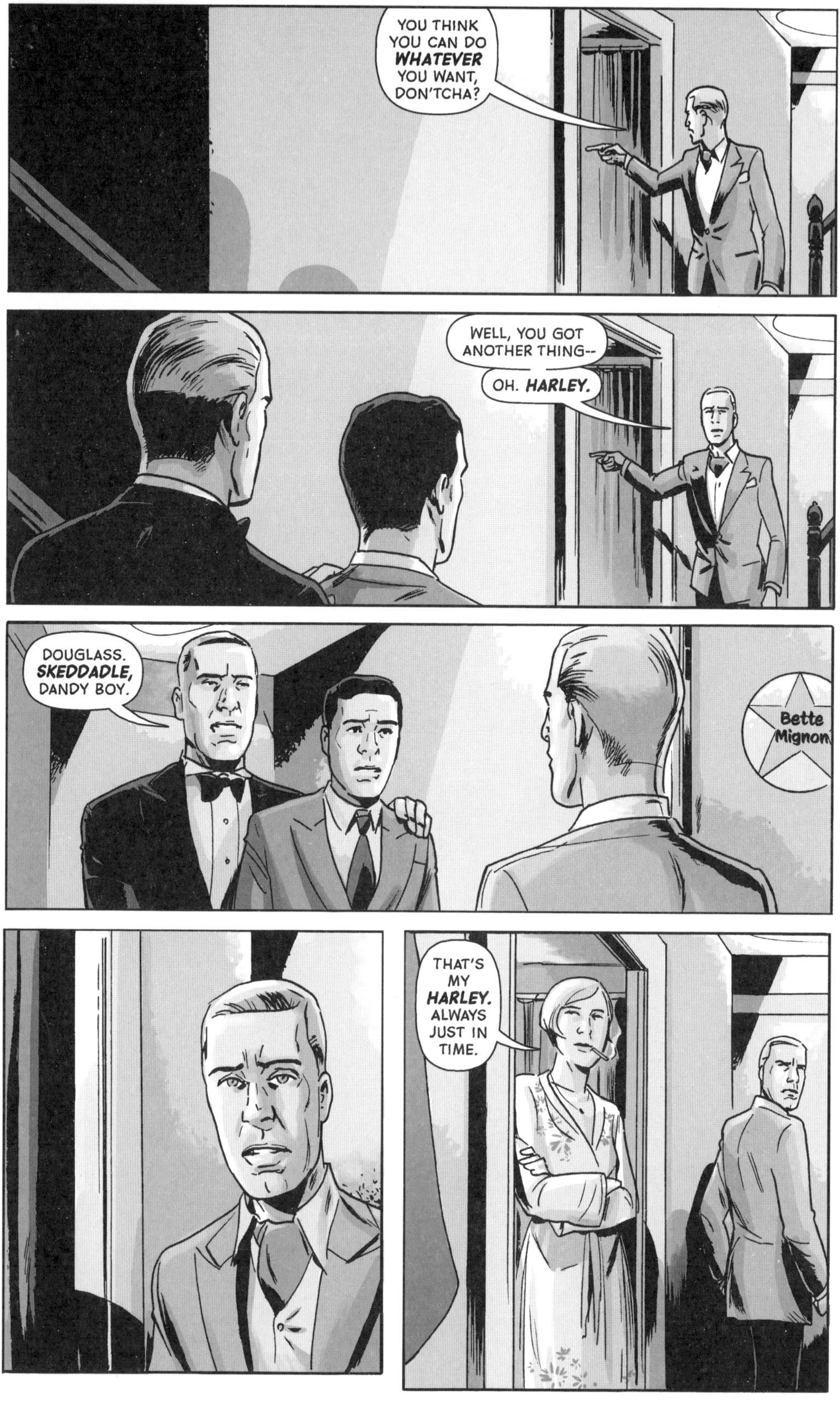
YOU THINK YOU CAN DO **WHATEVER** YOU WANT, DON'TCHA?
WELL, YOU GOT ANOTHER THING--
OH. **HARLEY.**
DOUGLASS. **SKEDDADLE,** DANDY BOY.
Bette Mignon
THAT'S MY **HARLEY.** ALWAYS JUST IN TIME.

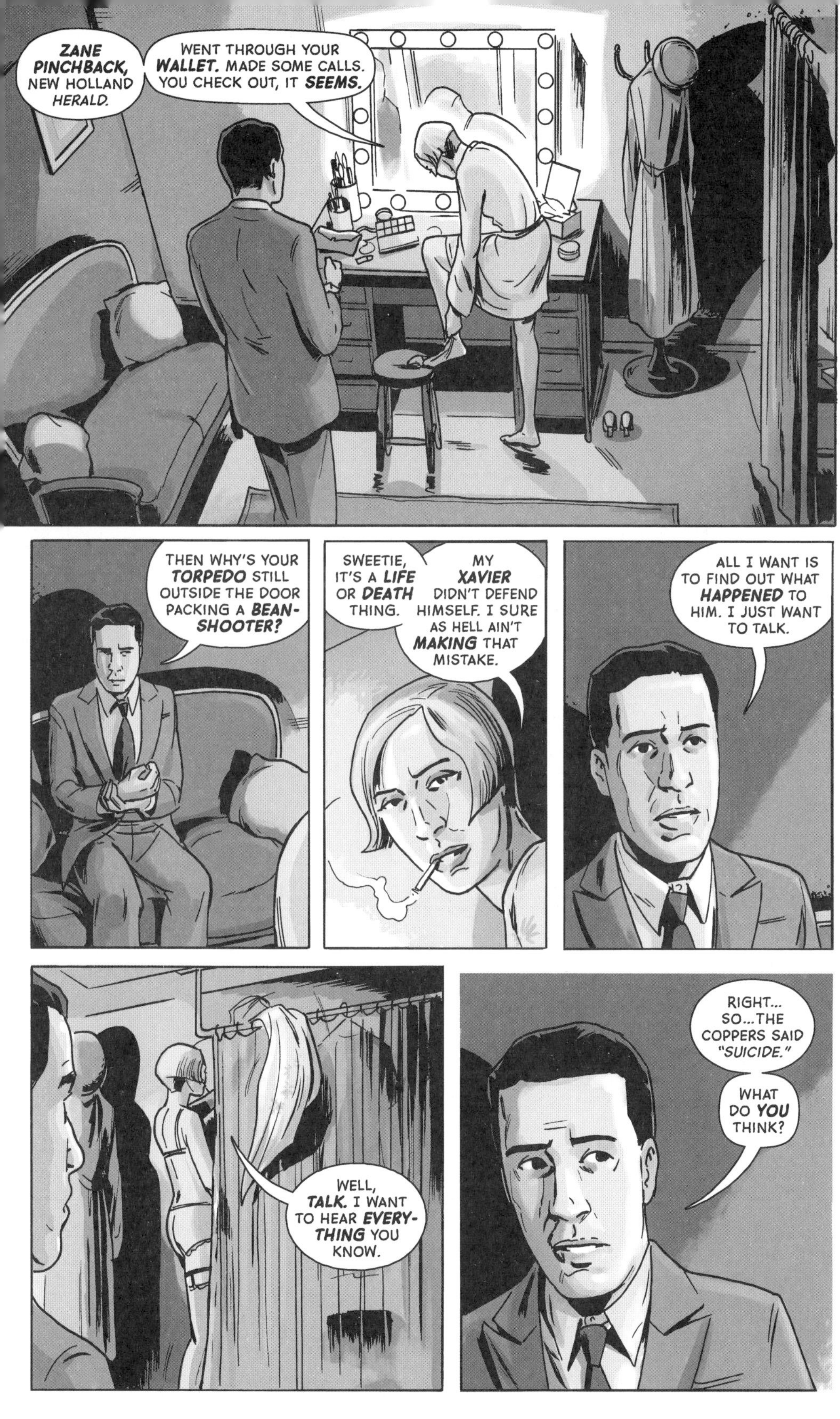

ZANE PINCHBACK, NEW HOLLAND HERALD.
WENT THROUGH YOUR WALLET. MADE SOME CALLS. YOU CHECK OUT, IT SEEMS.
THEN WHY'S YOUR TORPEDO STILL OUTSIDE THE DOOR PACKING A BEAN-SHOOTER?
SWEETIE, IT'S A LIFE OR DEATH THING.
MY XAVIER DIDN'T DEFEND HIMSELF. I SURE AS HELL AIN'T MAKING THAT MISTAKE.
ALL I WANT IS TO FIND OUT WHAT HAPPENED TO HIM. I JUST WANT TO TALK.
WELL, TALK. I WANT TO HEAR EVERY-THING YOU KNOW.
RIGHT... SO...THE COPPERS SAID "SUICIDE."
WHAT DO YOU THINK?

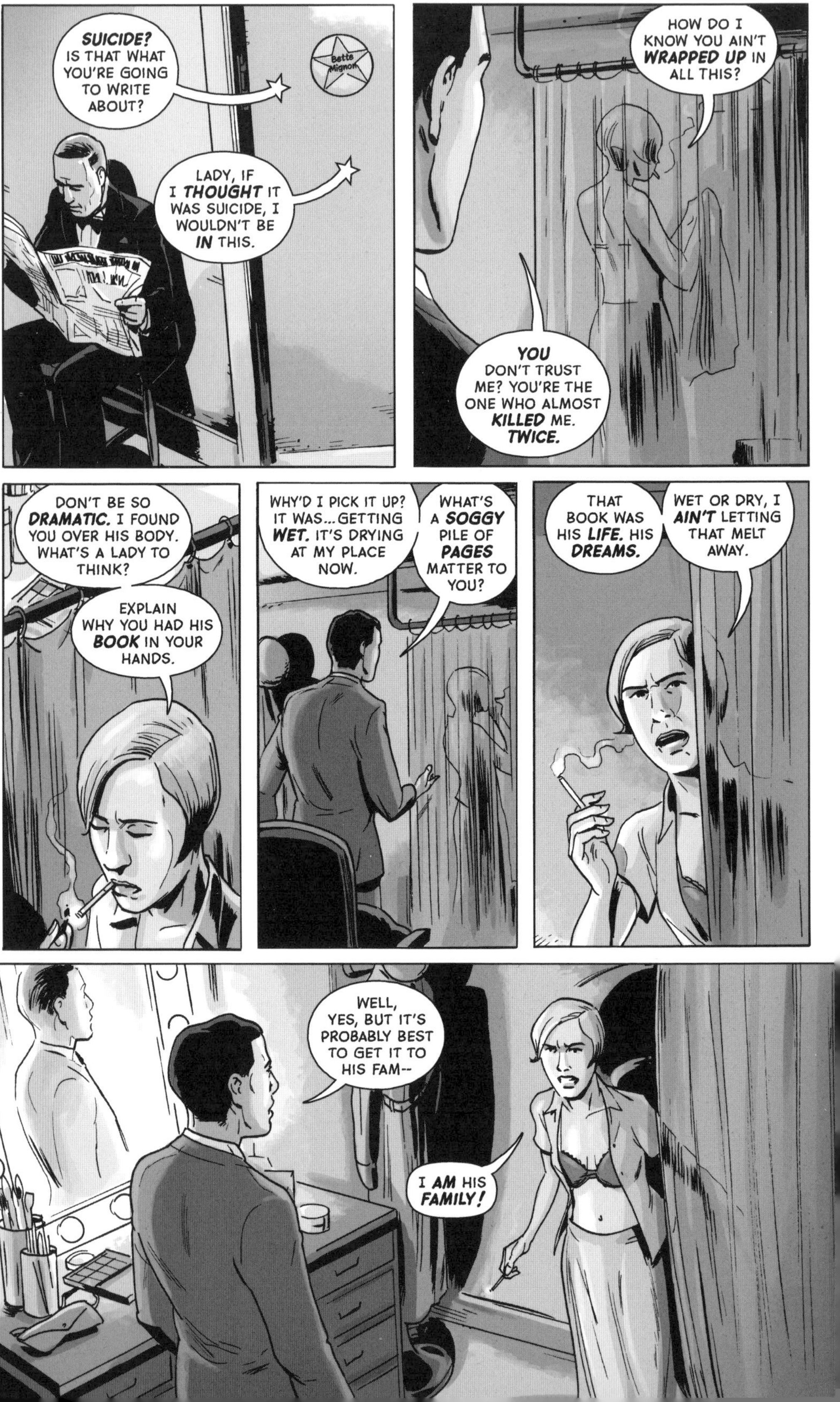

SUICIDE? IS THAT WHAT YOU'RE GOING TO WRITE ABOUT?
Bette Mignon
LADY, IF I THOUGHT IT WAS SUICIDE, I WOULDN'T BE IN THIS.
HOW DO I KNOW YOU AIN'T WRAPPED UP IN ALL THIS?
YOU DON'T TRUST ME? YOU'RE THE ONE WHO ALMOST KILLED ME. TWICE.
DON'T BE SO DRAMATIC. I FOUND YOU OVER HIS BODY. WHAT'S A LADY TO THINK?
EXPLAIN WHY YOU HAD HIS BOOK IN YOUR HANDS.
WHY'D I PICK IT UP? IT WAS...GETTING WET. IT'S DRYING AT MY PLACE NOW.
WHAT'S A SOGGY PILE OF PAGES MATTER TO YOU?
THAT BOOK WAS HIS LIFE. HIS DREAMS.
WET OR DRY, I AIN'T LETTING THAT MELT AWAY.
WELL, YES, BUT IT'S PROBABLY BEST TO GET IT TO HIS FAM--
I AM HIS FAMILY!

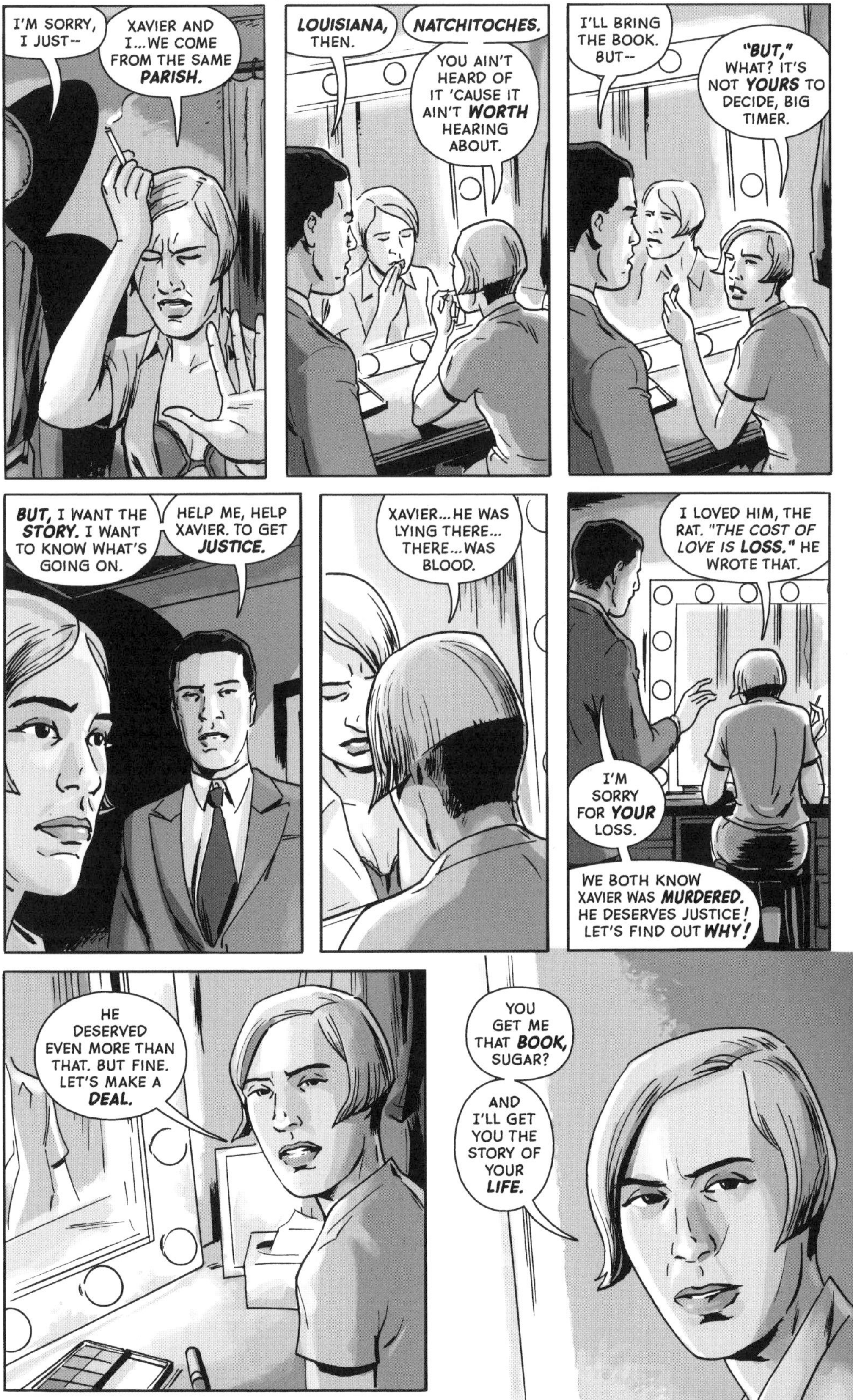
I'M SORRY, I JUST--
XAVIER AND I...WE COME FROM THE SAME PARISH.
LOUISIANA, THEN.
NATCHITOCHES.
YOU AIN'T HEARD OF IT 'CAUSE IT AIN'T WORTH HEARING ABOUT.
I'LL BRING THE BOOK. BUT--
"BUT," WHAT? IT'S NOT YOURS TO DECIDE, BIG TIMER.
BUT, I WANT THE STORY. I WANT TO KNOW WHAT'S GOING ON.
HELP ME, HELP XAVIER. TO GET JUSTICE.
XAVIER...HE WAS LYING THERE... THERE...WAS BLOOD.
I LOVED HIM, THE RAT. "THE COST OF LOVE IS LOSS." HE WROTE THAT.
I'M SORRY FOR YOUR LOSS.
WE BOTH KNOW XAVIER WAS MURDERED. HE DESERVES JUSTICE! LET'S FIND OUT WHY!
HE DESERVED EVEN MORE THAN THAT. BUT FINE. LET'S MAKE A DEAL.
YOU GET ME THAT BOOK, SUGAR?
AND I'LL GET YOU THE STORY OF YOUR LIFE.

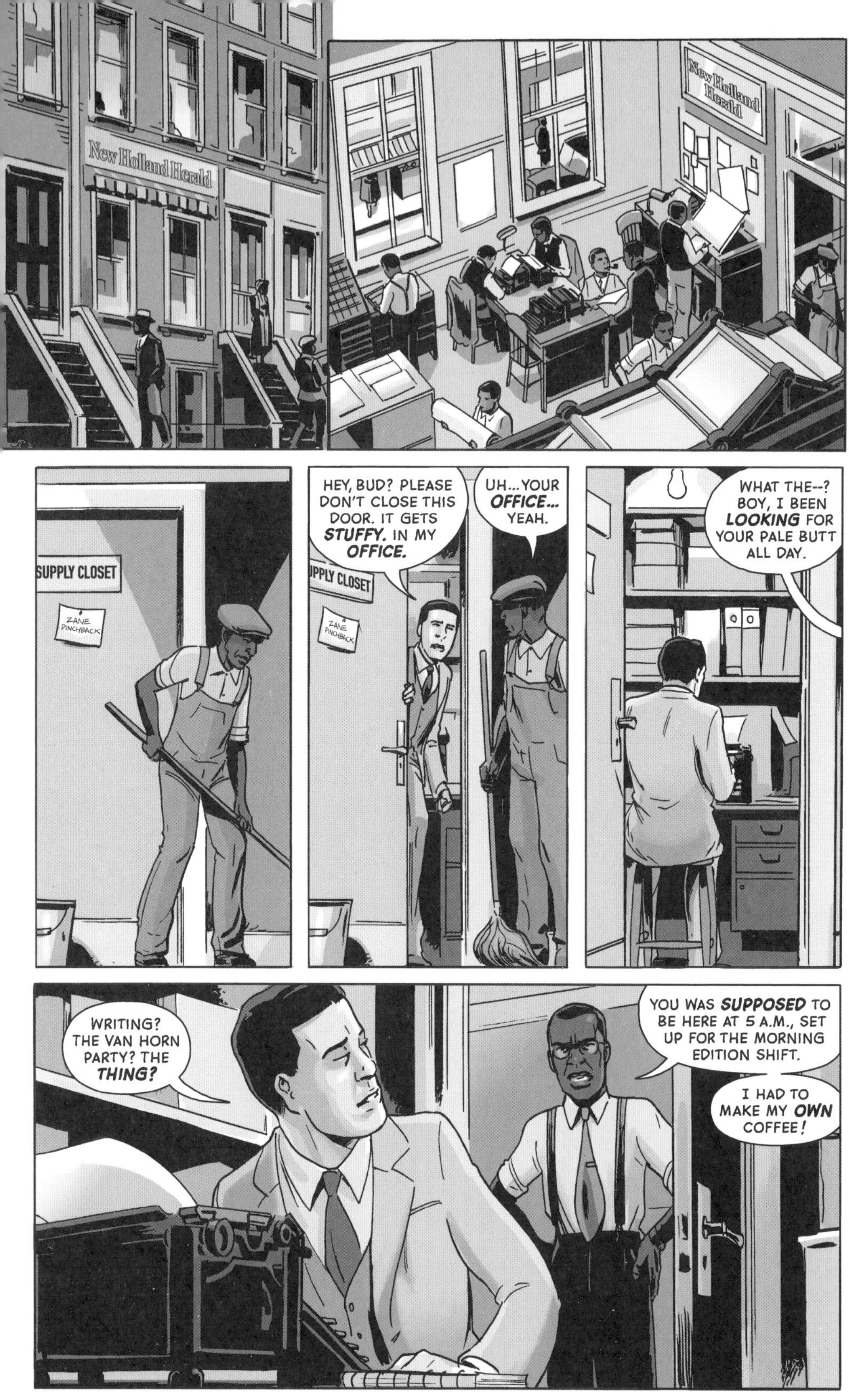

New Holland Herald
New Holland Herald
SUPPLY CLOSET
ZANE PINCHBACK
HEY, BUD? PLEASE DON'T CLOSE THIS DOOR. IT GETS STUFFY. IN MY OFFICE.
UH... YOUR OFFICE... YEAH.
WHAT THE--? BOY, I BEEN LOOKING FOR YOUR PALE BUTT ALL DAY.
YOU WAS SUPPOSED TO BE HERE AT 5 A.M., SET UP FOR THE MORNING EDITION SHIFT.
I HAD TO MAKE MY OWN COFFEE!
WRITING? THE VAN HORN PARTY? THE THING?

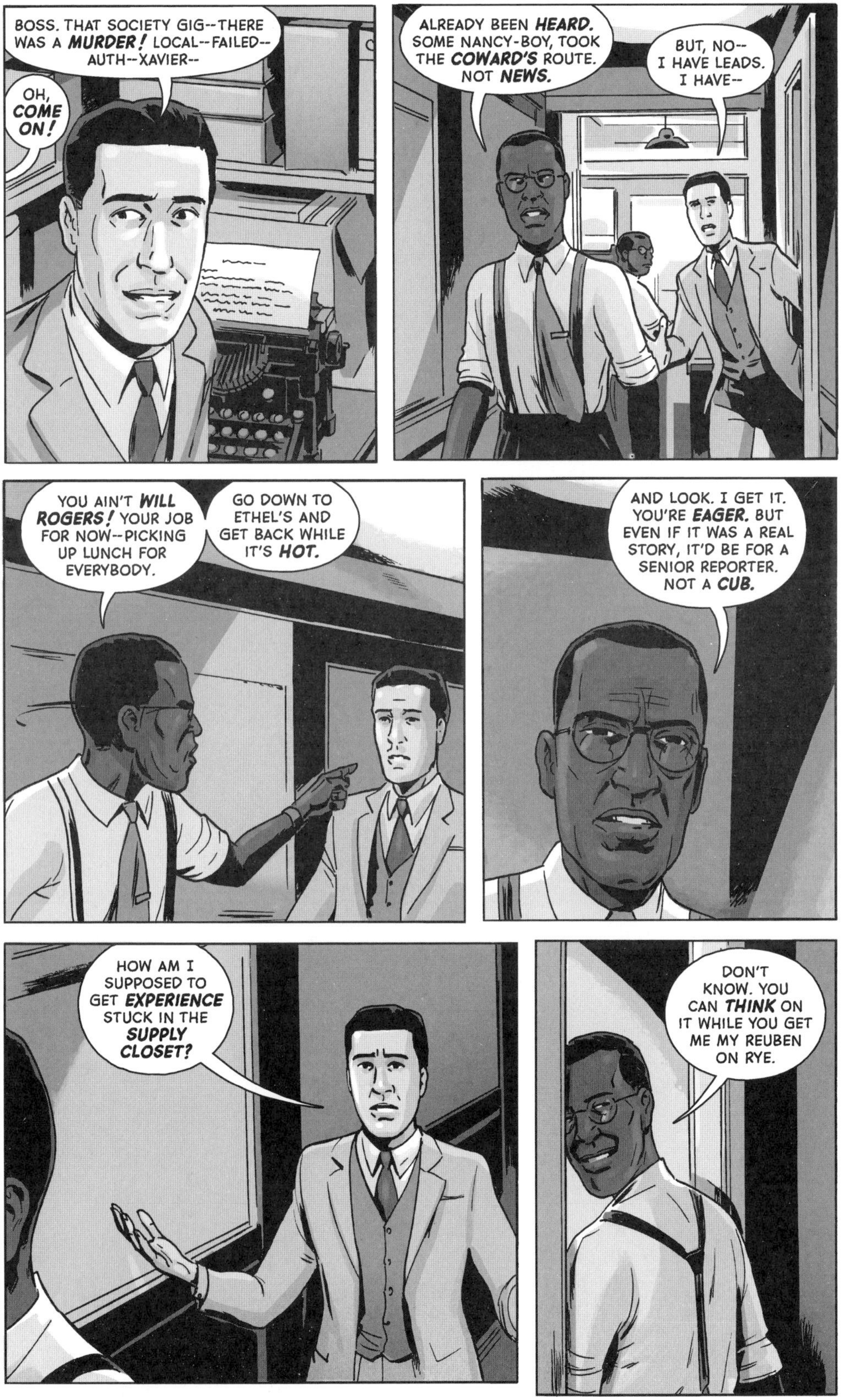
BOSS. THAT SOCIETY GIG--THERE WAS A **MURDER!** LOCAL--FAILED--AUTH--XAVIER--
OH, **COME ON!**
ALREADY BEEN **HEARD.** SOME NANCY-BOY, TOOK THE **COWARD'S** ROUTE. NOT **NEWS.**
BUT, NO--I HAVE LEADS. I HAVE--
YOU AIN'T **WILL ROGERS!** YOUR JOB FOR NOW--PICKING UP LUNCH FOR EVERYBODY.
GO DOWN TO ETHEL'S AND GET BACK WHILE IT'S **HOT.**
AND LOOK. I GET IT. YOU'RE **EAGER.** BUT EVEN IF IT WAS A REAL STORY, IT'D BE FOR A SENIOR REPORTER. NOT A **CUB.**
HOW AM I SUPPOSED TO GET **EXPERIENCE** STUCK IN THE **SUPPLY CLOSET?**
DON'T KNOW. YOU CAN **THINK** ON IT WHILE YOU GET ME MY REUBEN ON RYE.

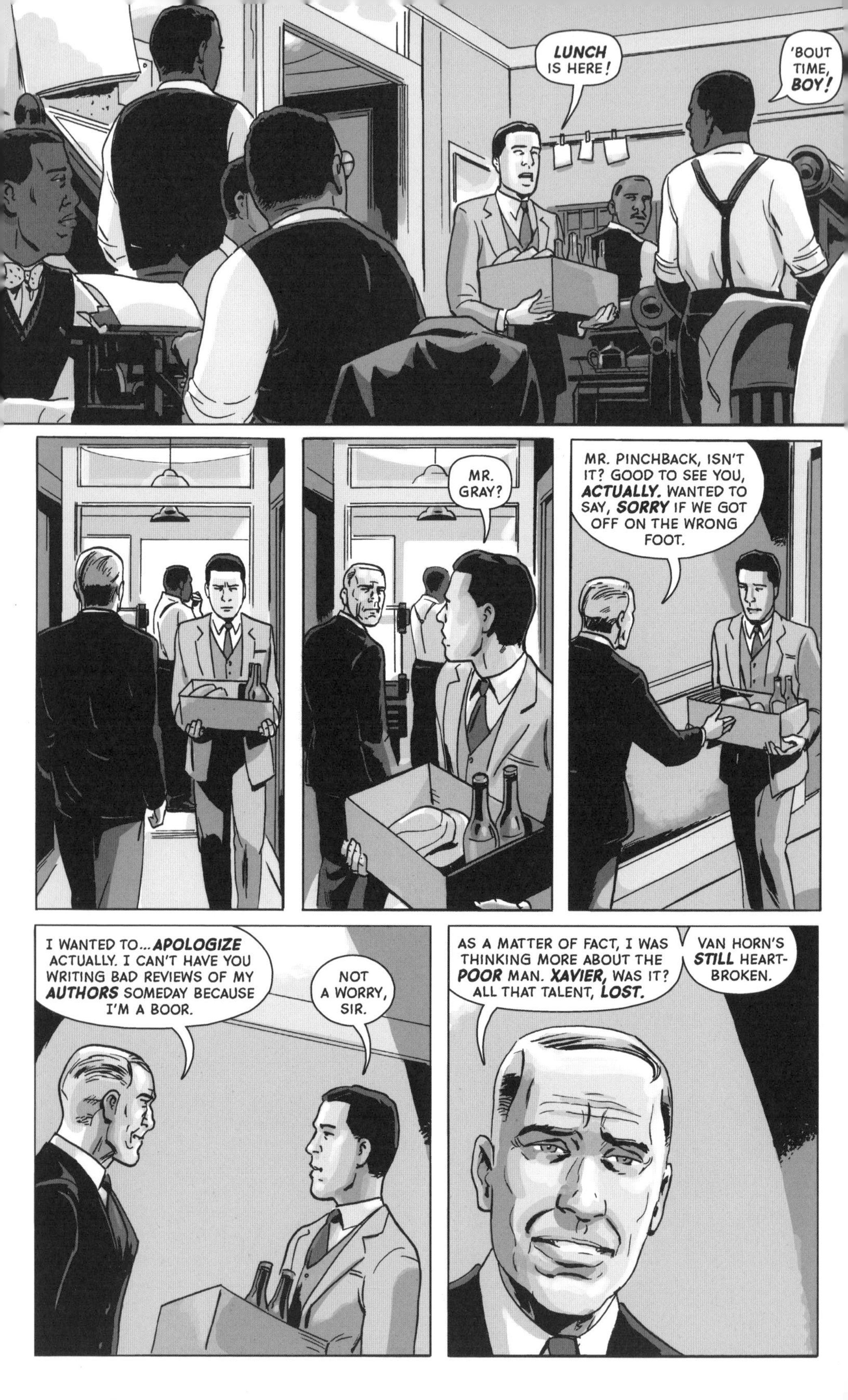
LUNCH IS HERE!
'BOUT TIME, BOY!
MR. GRAY?
MR. PINCHBACK, ISN'T IT? GOOD TO SEE YOU, ACTUALLY. WANTED TO SAY, SORRY IF WE GOT OFF ON THE WRONG FOOT.
I WANTED TO... APOLOGIZE ACTUALLY. I CAN'T HAVE YOU WRITING BAD REVIEWS OF MY AUTHORS SOMEDAY BECAUSE I'M A BOOR.
NOT A WORRY, SIR.
AS A MATTER OF FACT, I WAS THINKING MORE ABOUT THE POOR MAN. XAVIER, WAS IT? ALL THAT TALENT, LOST.
VAN HORN'S STILL HEART-BROKEN.

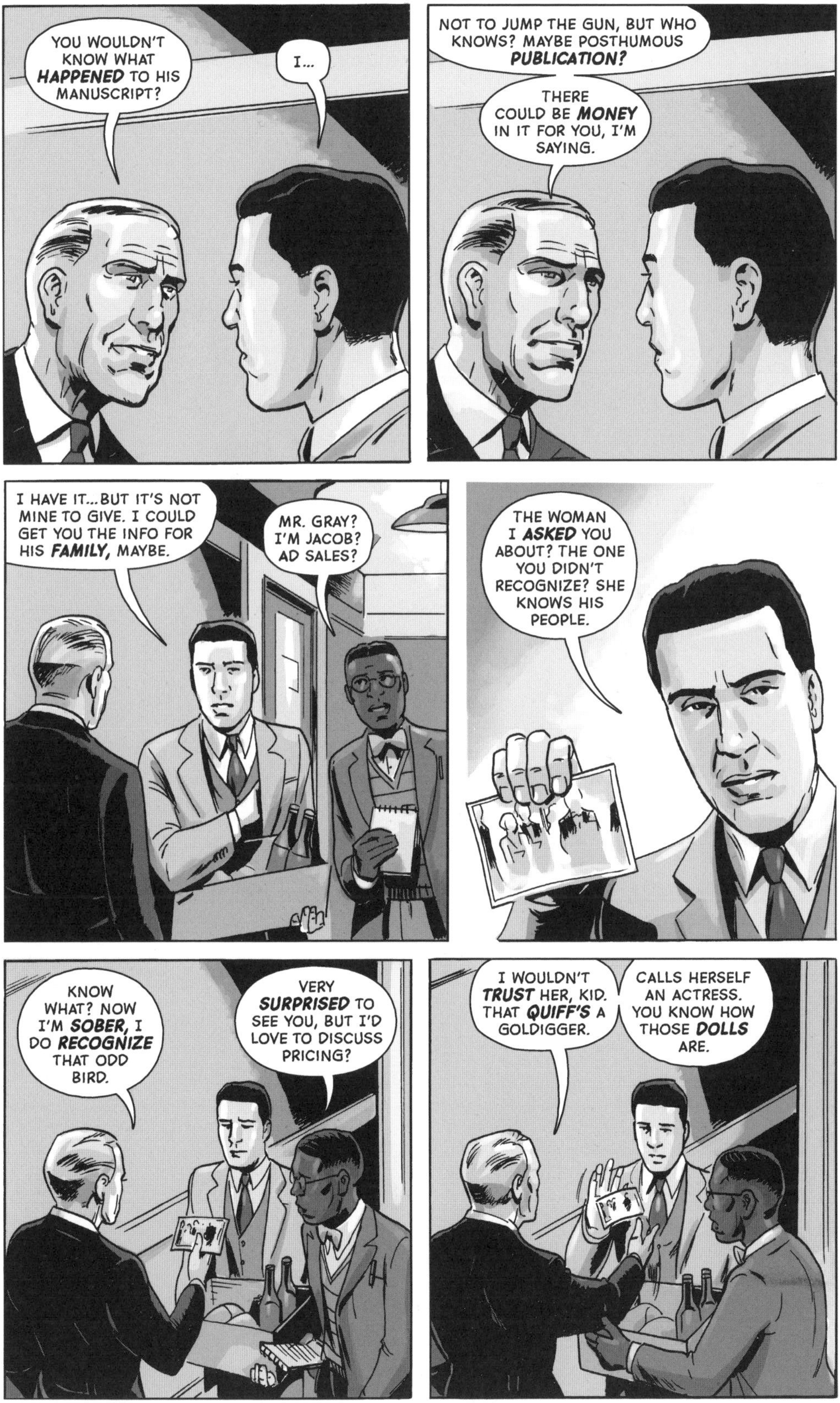
YOU WOULDN'T KNOW WHAT HAPPENED TO HIS MANUSCRIPT?
I...
NOT TO JUMP THE GUN, BUT WHO KNOWS? MAYBE POSTHUMOUS PUBLICATION?
THERE COULD BE MONEY IN IT FOR YOU, I'M SAYING.
I HAVE IT...BUT IT'S NOT MINE TO GIVE. I COULD GET YOU THE INFO FOR HIS FAMILY, MAYBE.
MR. GRAY? I'M JACOB? AD SALES?
THE WOMAN I ASKED YOU ABOUT? THE ONE YOU DIDN'T RECOGNIZE? SHE KNOWS HIS PEOPLE.
KNOW WHAT? NOW I'M SOBER, I DO RECOGNIZE THAT ODD BIRD.
VERY SURPRISED TO SEE YOU, BUT I'D LOVE TO DISCUSS PRICING?
I WOULDN'T TRUST HER, KID. THAT QUIFF'S A GOLDIGGER.
CALLS HERSELF AN ACTRESS. YOU KNOW HOW THOSE DOLLS ARE.

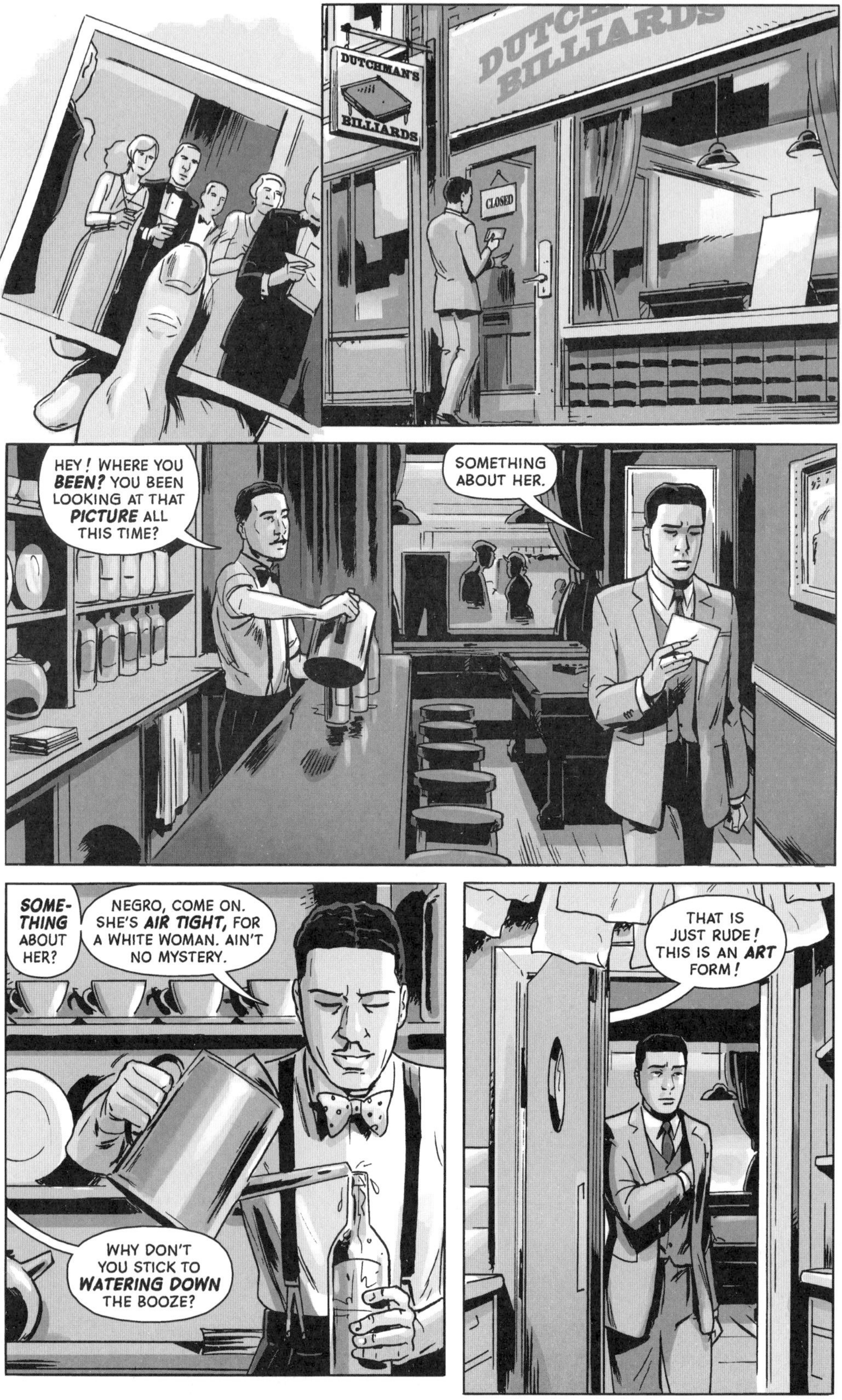
DUTCHMAN'S BILLIARDS
CLOSED
DUTCH BILLIARDS
HEY! WHERE YOU BEEN? YOU BEEN LOOKING AT THAT PICTURE ALL THIS TIME?
SOMETHING ABOUT HER.
SOMETHING ABOUT HER?
NEGRO, COME ON. SHE'S AIR TIGHT, FOR A WHITE WOMAN. AIN'T NO MYSTERY.
WHY DON'T YOU STICK TO WATERING DOWN THE BOOZE?
THAT IS JUST RUDE! THIS IS AN ART FORM!

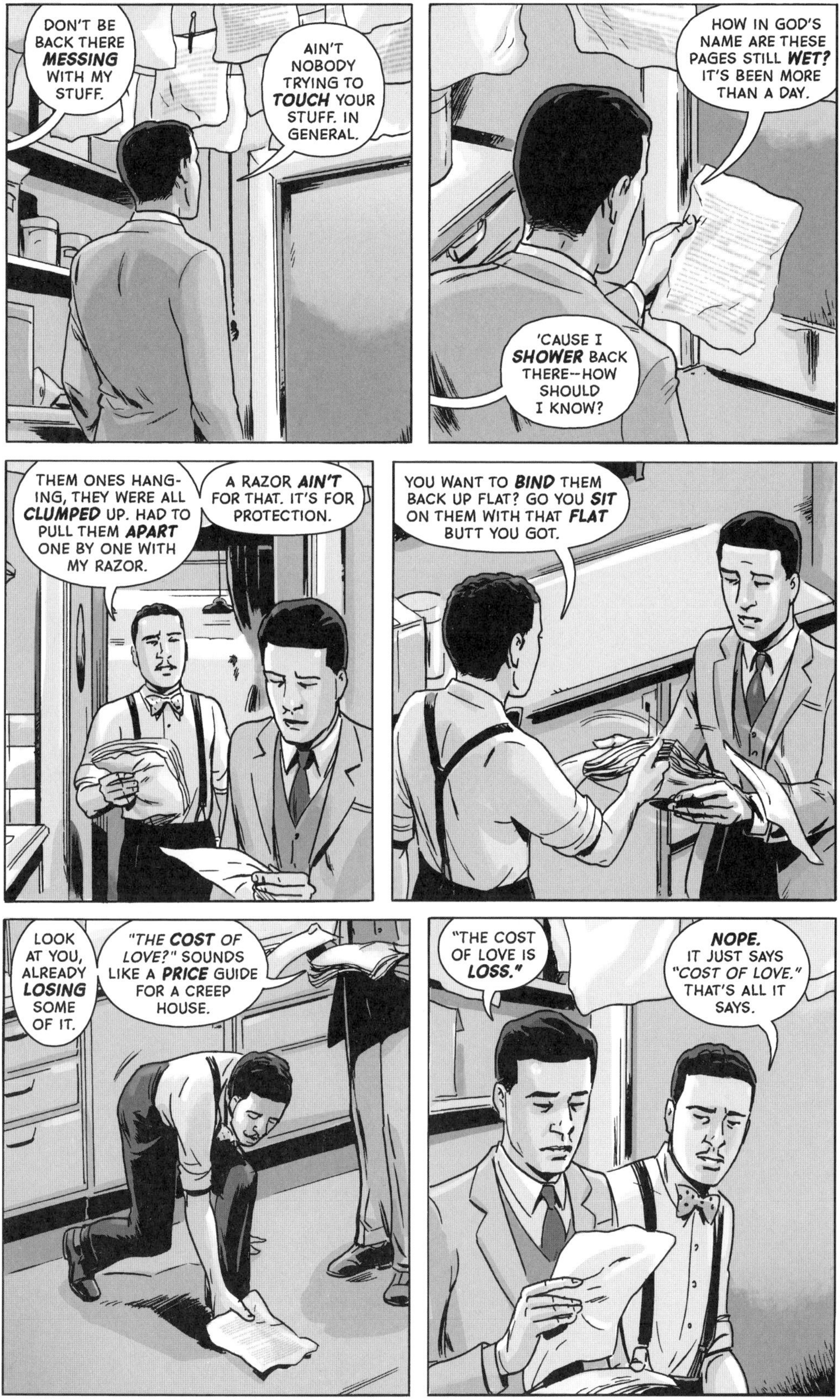
DON'T BE BACK THERE **MESSING** WITH MY STUFF.
AIN'T NOBODY TRYING TO **TOUCH** YOUR STUFF. IN GENERAL.
HOW IN GOD'S NAME ARE THESE PAGES STILL **WET?** IT'S BEEN MORE THAN A DAY.
'CAUSE I **SHOWER** BACK THERE--HOW SHOULD I KNOW?
THEM ONES HANG-ING, THEY WERE ALL **CLUMPED** UP. HAD TO PULL THEM **APART** ONE BY ONE WITH MY RAZOR.
A RAZOR **AIN'T** FOR THAT. IT'S FOR PROTECTION.
YOU WANT TO **BIND** THEM BACK UP FLAT? GO YOU **SIT** ON THEM WITH THAT **FLAT** BUTT YOU GOT.
LOOK AT YOU, ALREADY **LOSING** SOME OF IT.
*"THE **COST** OF LOVE?"* SOUNDS LIKE A **PRICE** GUIDE FOR A CREEP HOUSE.
"THE COST OF LOVE IS **LOSS."**
NOPE. IT JUST SAYS *"COST OF LOVE."* THAT'S ALL IT SAYS.

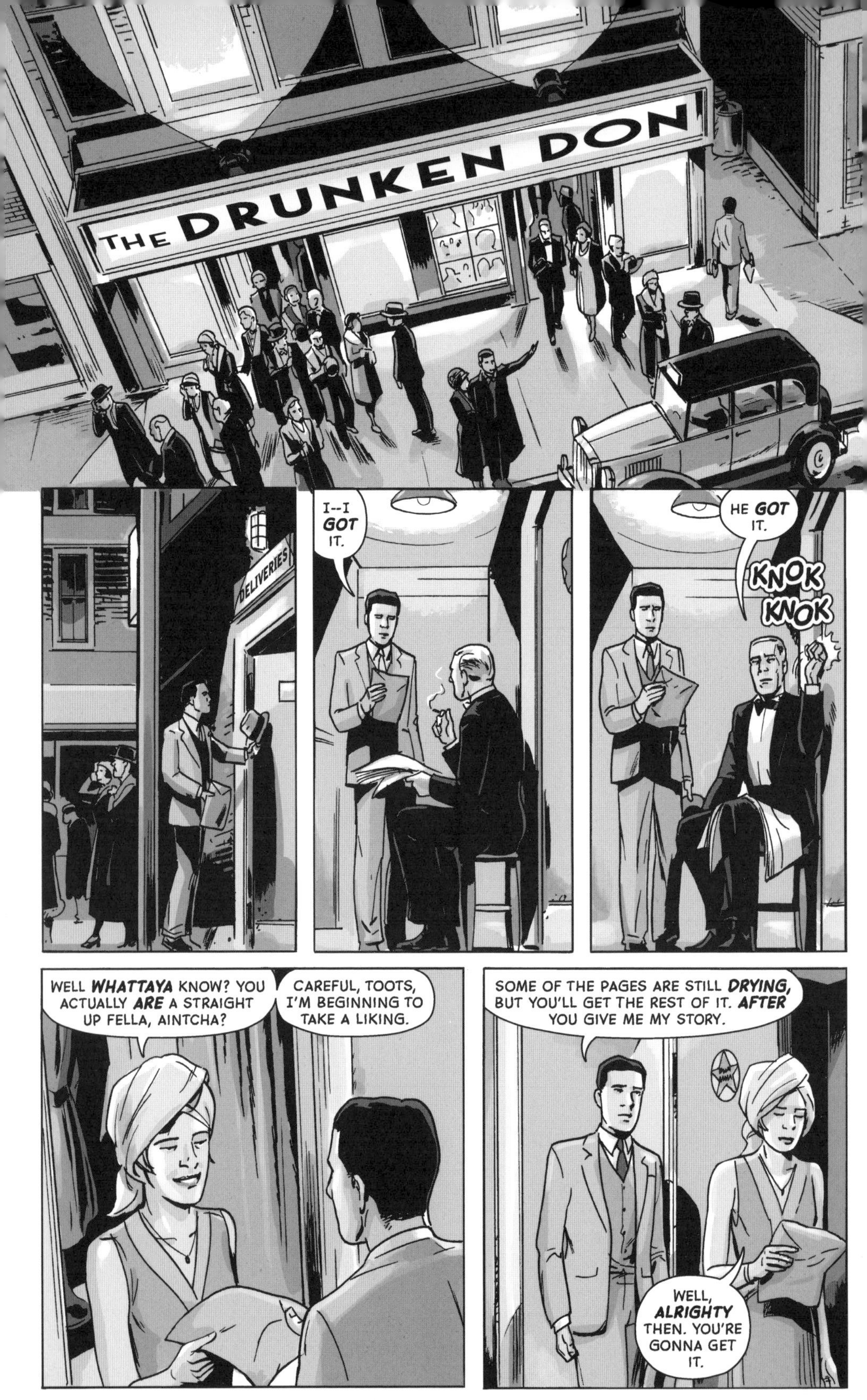
THE DRUNKEN DON
DELIVERIES
I--I GOT IT.
HE GOT IT.
KNOK KNOK
WELL WHATTAYA KNOW? YOU ACTUALLY ARE A STRAIGHT UP FELLA, AINTCHA?
CAREFUL, TOOTS, I'M BEGINNING TO TAKE A LIKING.
SOME OF THE PAGES ARE STILL DRYING, BUT YOU'LL GET THE REST OF IT. AFTER YOU GIVE ME MY STORY.
WELL, ALRIGHTY THEN. YOU'RE GONNA GET IT.

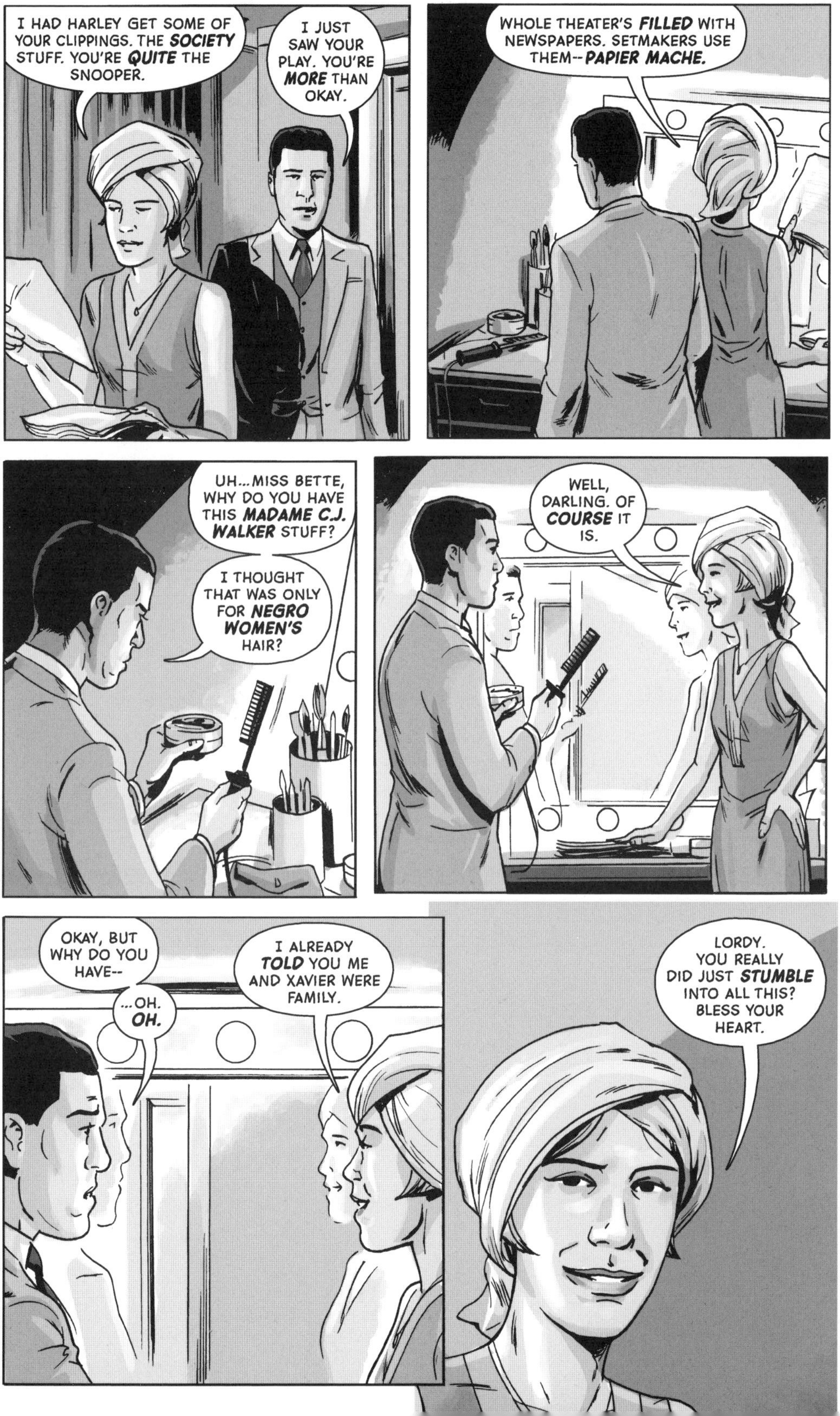
I HAD HARLEY GET SOME OF YOUR CLIPPINGS. THE SOCIETY STUFF. YOU'RE QUITE THE SNOOPER.
I JUST SAW YOUR PLAY. YOU'RE MORE THAN OKAY.
WHOLE THEATER'S FILLED WITH NEWSPAPERS. SETMAKERS USE THEM--PAPIER MACHE.
UH...MISS BETTE, WHY DO YOU HAVE THIS MADAME C.J. WALKER STUFF?
I THOUGHT THAT WAS ONLY FOR NEGRO WOMEN'S HAIR?
WELL, DARLING. OF COURSE IT IS.
OKAY, BUT WHY DO YOU HAVE--
...OH. OH.
I ALREADY TOLD YOU ME AND XAVIER WERE FAMILY.
LORDY. YOU REALLY DID JUST STUMBLE INTO ALL THIS? BLESS YOUR HEART.

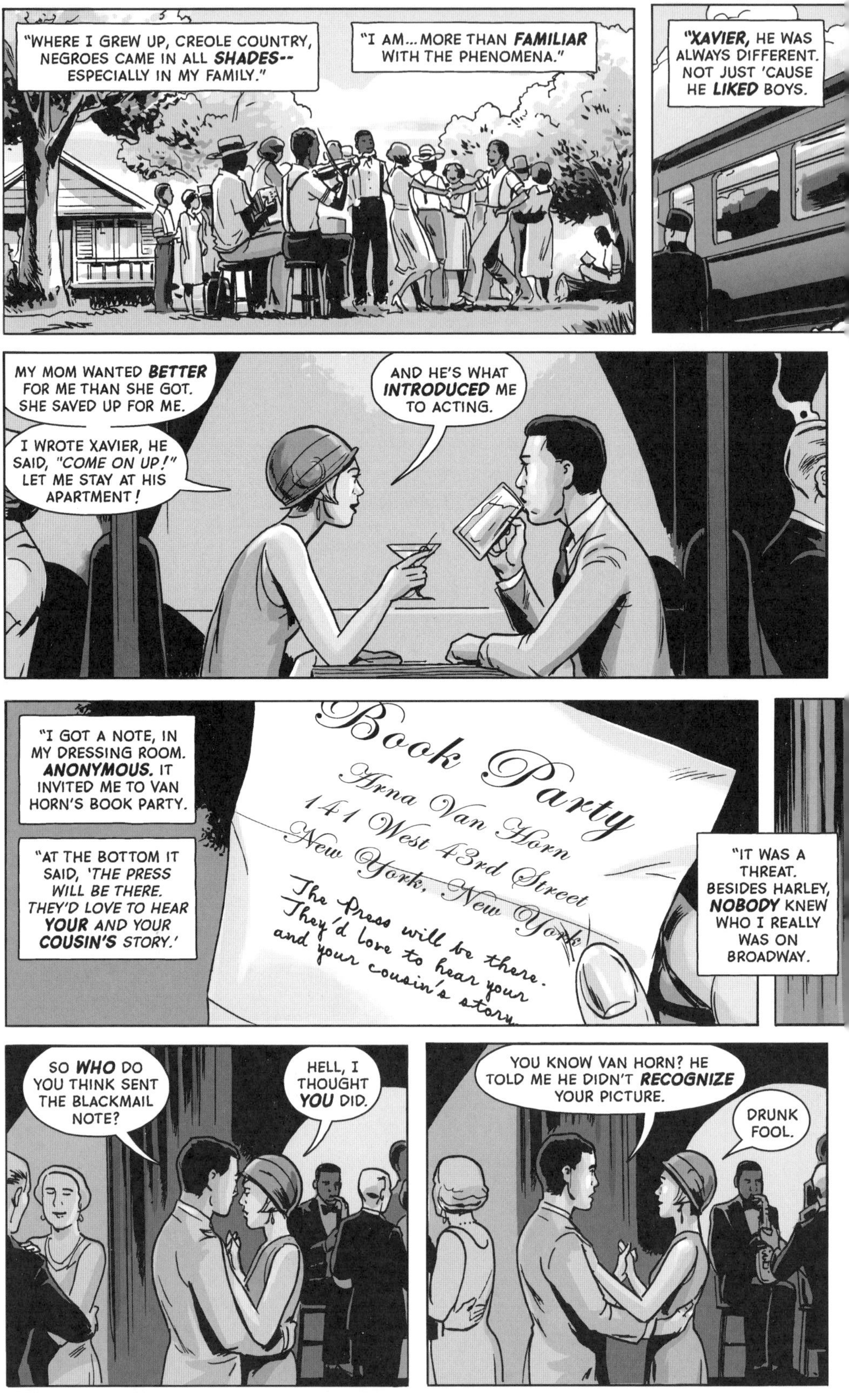
"WHERE I GREW UP, CREOLE COUNTRY, NEGROES CAME IN ALL SHADES-- ESPECIALLY IN MY FAMILY."
"I AM... MORE THAN FAMILIAR WITH THE PHENOMENA."
"XAVIER, HE WAS ALWAYS DIFFERENT. NOT JUST 'CAUSE HE LIKED BOYS.
MY MOM WANTED BETTER FOR ME THAN SHE GOT. SHE SAVED UP FOR ME.
I WROTE XAVIER, HE SAID, "COME ON UP!" LET ME STAY AT HIS APARTMENT!
AND HE'S WHAT INTRODUCED ME TO ACTING.
"I GOT A NOTE, IN MY DRESSING ROOM. ANONYMOUS. IT INVITED ME TO VAN HORN'S BOOK PARTY.
"AT THE BOTTOM IT SAID, 'THE PRESS WILL BE THERE. THEY'D LOVE TO HEAR YOUR AND YOUR COUSIN'S STORY.'
Book Party
Arna Van Horn
141 West 43rd Street
New York, New York
The Press will be there.
They'd love to hear your
and your cousin's story.
"IT WAS A THREAT. BESIDES HARLEY, NOBODY KNEW WHO I REALLY WAS ON BROADWAY.
SO WHO DO YOU THINK SENT THE BLACKMAIL NOTE?
HELL, I THOUGHT YOU DID.
YOU KNOW VAN HORN? HE TOLD ME HE DIDN'T RECOGNIZE YOUR PICTURE.
DRUNK FOOL.

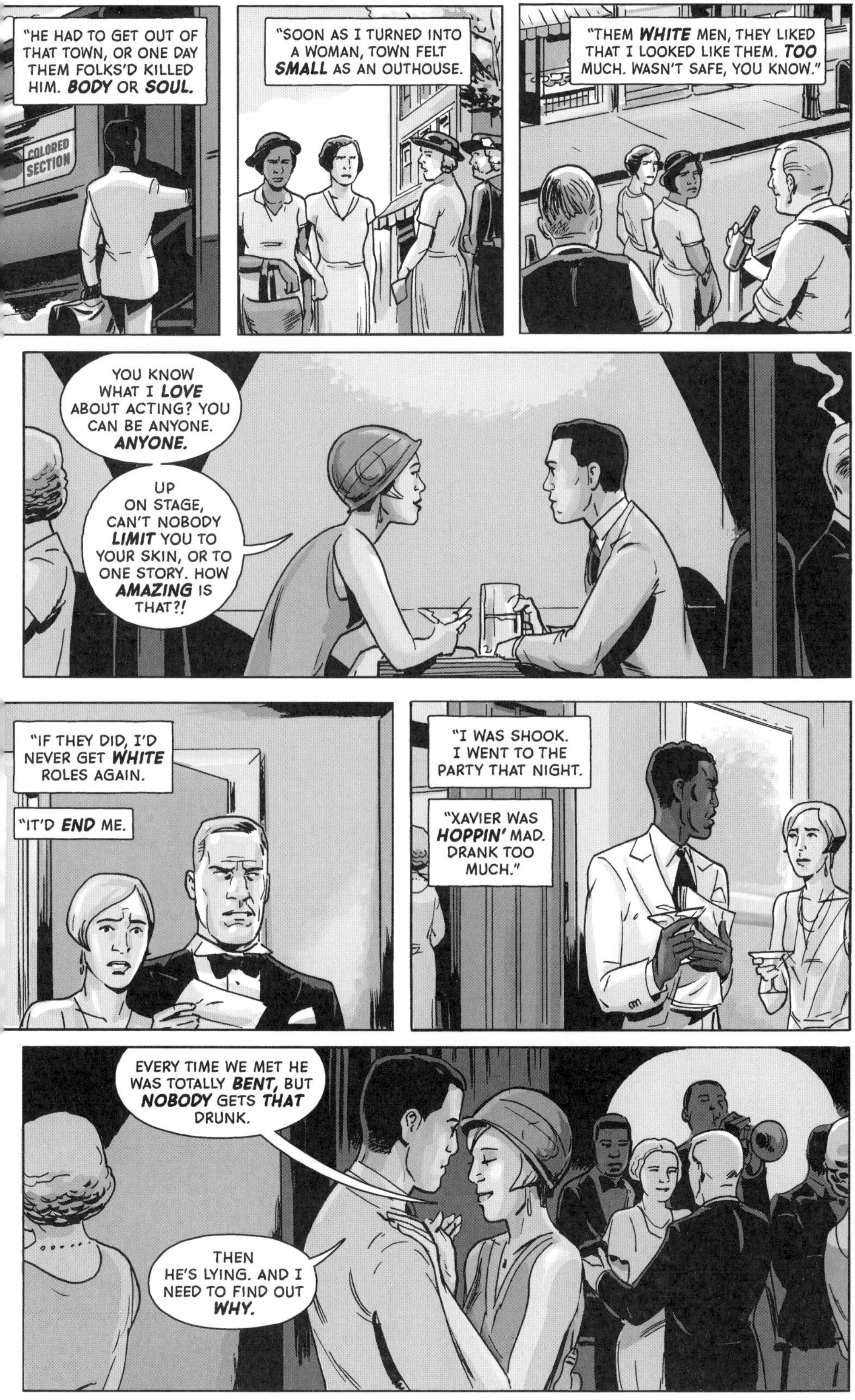
"HE HAD TO GET OUT OF THAT TOWN, OR ONE DAY THEM FOLKS'D KILLED HIM. BODY OR SOUL.
COLORED SECTION
"SOON AS I TURNED INTO A WOMAN, TOWN FELT SMALL AS AN OUTHOUSE.
"THEM WHITE MEN, THEY LIKED THAT I LOOKED LIKE THEM. TOO MUCH. WASN'T SAFE, YOU KNOW."
YOU KNOW WHAT I LOVE ABOUT ACTING? YOU CAN BE ANYONE. ANYONE.
UP ON STAGE, CAN'T NOBODY LIMIT YOU TO YOUR SKIN, OR TO ONE STORY. HOW AMAZING IS THAT?!
"IF THEY DID, I'D NEVER GET WHITE ROLES AGAIN.
"IT'D END ME.
"I WAS SHOOK. I WENT TO THE PARTY THAT NIGHT.
"XAVIER WAS HOPPIN' MAD. DRANK TOO MUCH."
EVERY TIME WE MET HE WAS TOTALLY BENT, BUT NOBODY GETS THAT DRUNK.
THEN HE'S LYING. AND I NEED TO FIND OUT WHY.

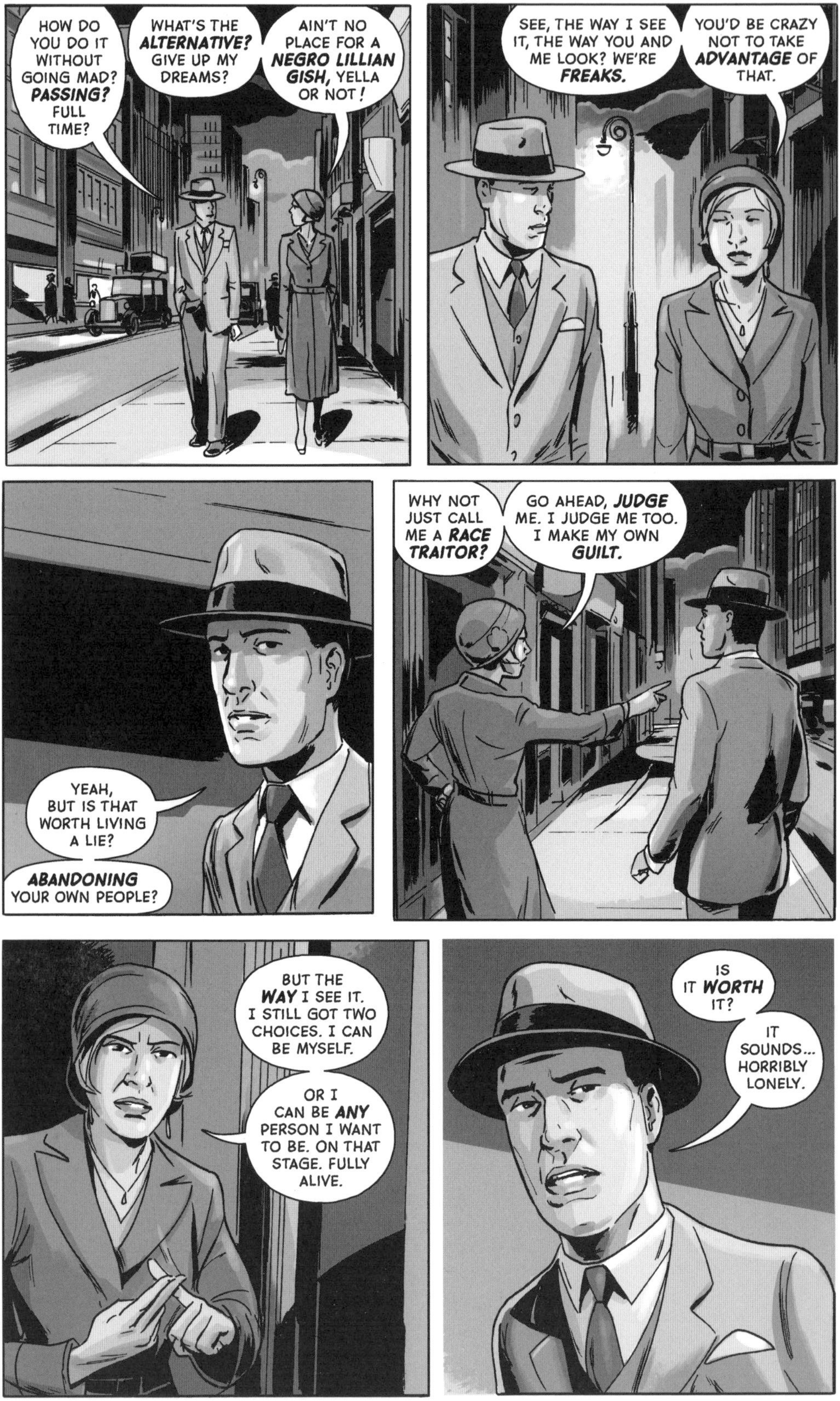
HOW DO YOU DO IT WITHOUT GOING MAD? PASSING? FULL TIME?
WHAT'S THE ALTERNATIVE? GIVE UP MY DREAMS?
AIN'T NO PLACE FOR A NEGRO LILLIAN GISH, YELLA OR NOT!
SEE, THE WAY I SEE IT, THE WAY YOU AND ME LOOK? WE'RE FREAKS.
YOU'D BE CRAZY NOT TO TAKE ADVANTAGE OF THAT.
YEAH, BUT IS THAT WORTH LIVING A LIE?
ABANDONING YOUR OWN PEOPLE?
WHY NOT JUST CALL ME A RACE TRAITOR?
GO AHEAD, JUDGE ME. I JUDGE ME TOO. I MAKE MY OWN GUILT.
BUT THE WAY I SEE IT. I STILL GOT TWO CHOICES. I CAN BE MYSELF.
OR I CAN BE ANY PERSON I WANT TO BE. ON THAT STAGE. FULLY ALIVE.
IS IT WORTH IT?
IT SOUNDS... HORRIBLY LONELY.

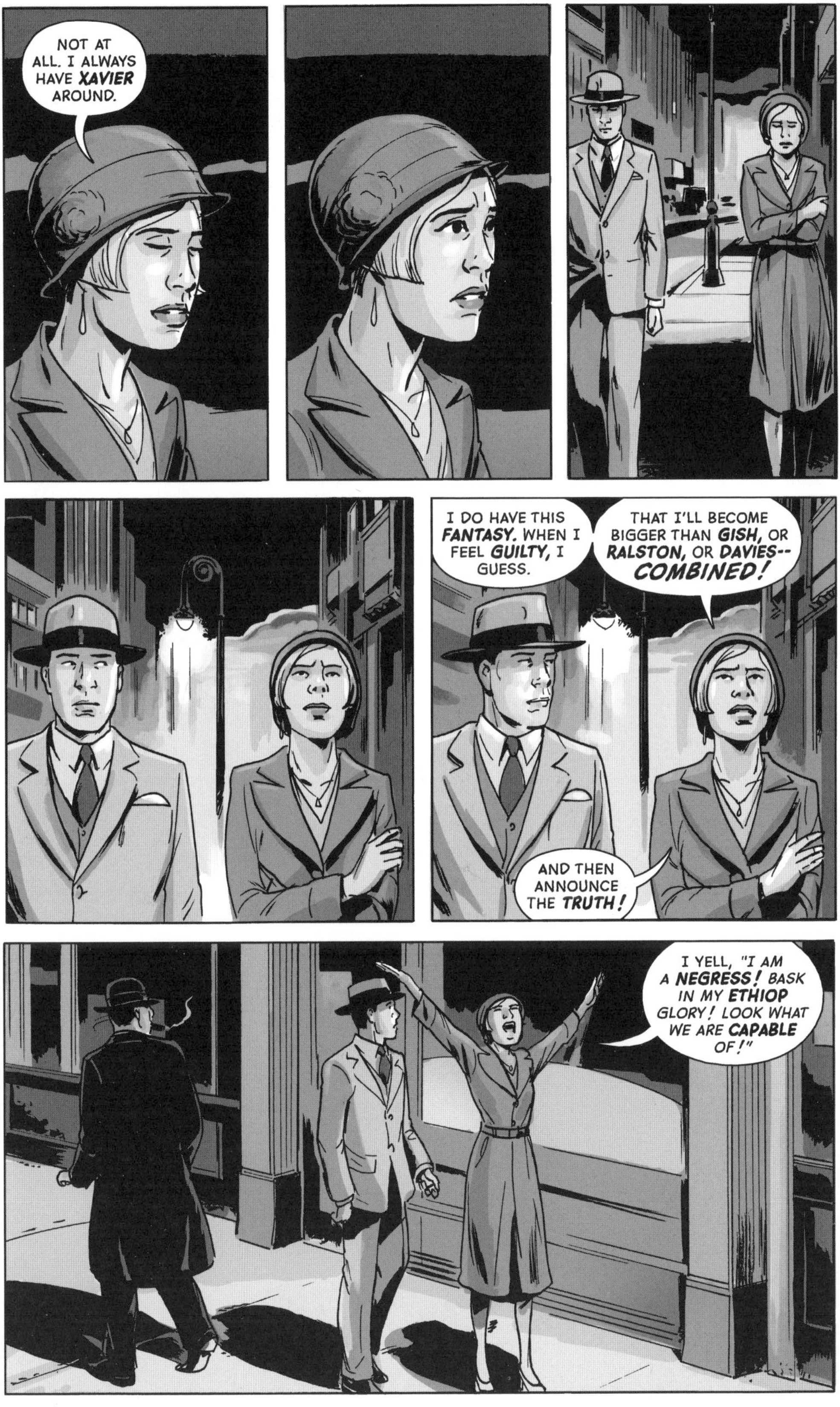
NOT AT ALL. I ALWAYS HAVE XAVIER AROUND.
I DO HAVE THIS FANTASY. WHEN I FEEL GUILTY, I GUESS.
THAT I'LL BECOME BIGGER THAN GISH, OR RALSTON, OR DAVIES-- COMBINED!
AND THEN ANNOUNCE THE TRUTH!
I YELL, "I AM A NEGRESS! BASK IN MY ETHIOP GLORY! LOOK WHAT WE ARE CAPABLE OF!"

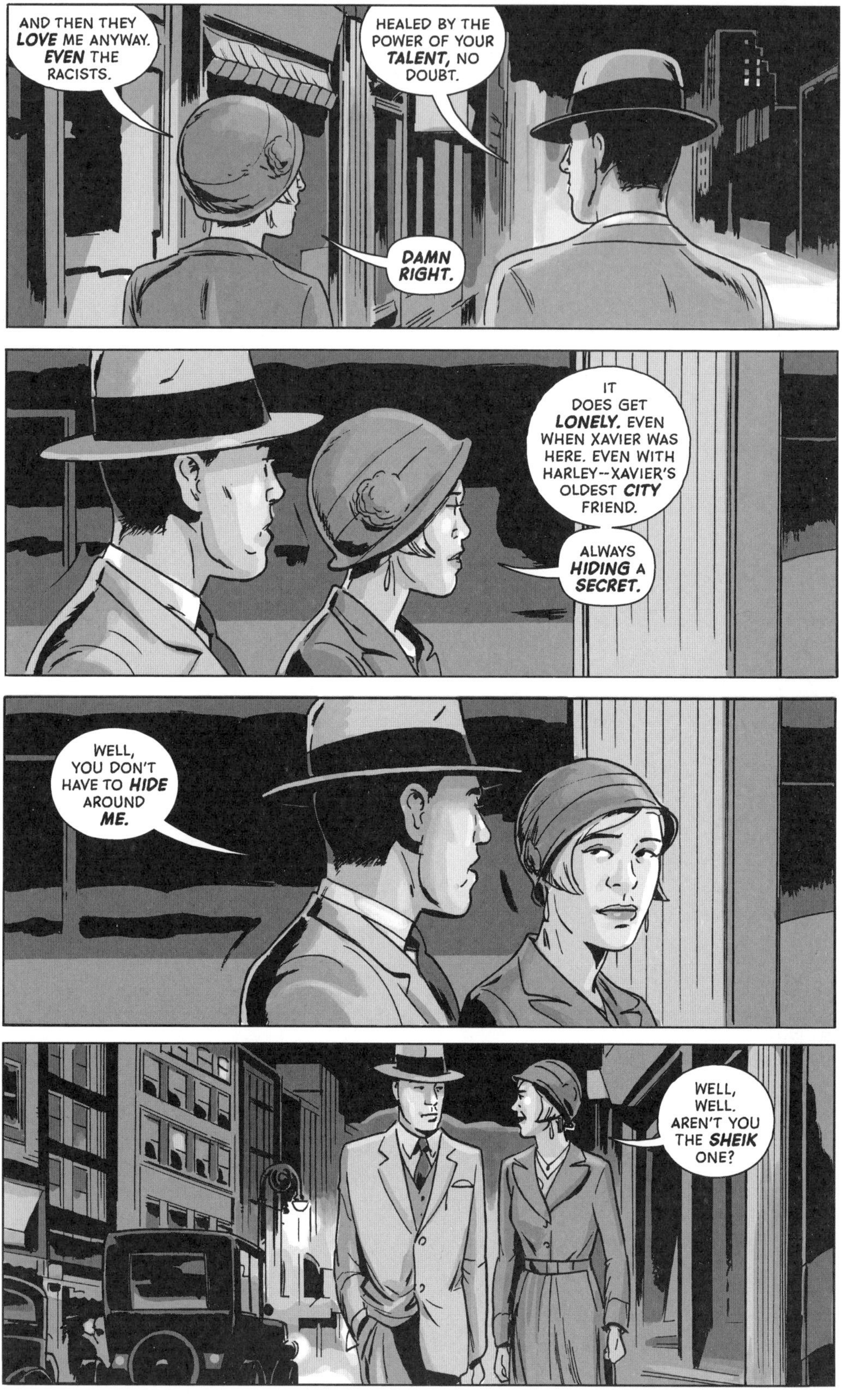
AND THEN THEY **LOVE** ME ANYWAY. **EVEN** THE RACISTS.
HEALED BY THE POWER OF YOUR **TALENT,** NO DOUBT.
DAMN RIGHT.
IT DOES GET **LONELY.** EVEN WHEN XAVIER WAS HERE. EVEN WITH HARLEY--XAVIER'S OLDEST **CITY** FRIEND.
ALWAYS **HIDING** A **SECRET.**
WELL, YOU DON'T HAVE TO **HIDE** AROUND **ME.**
WELL, WELL. AREN'T YOU THE **SHEIK** ONE?

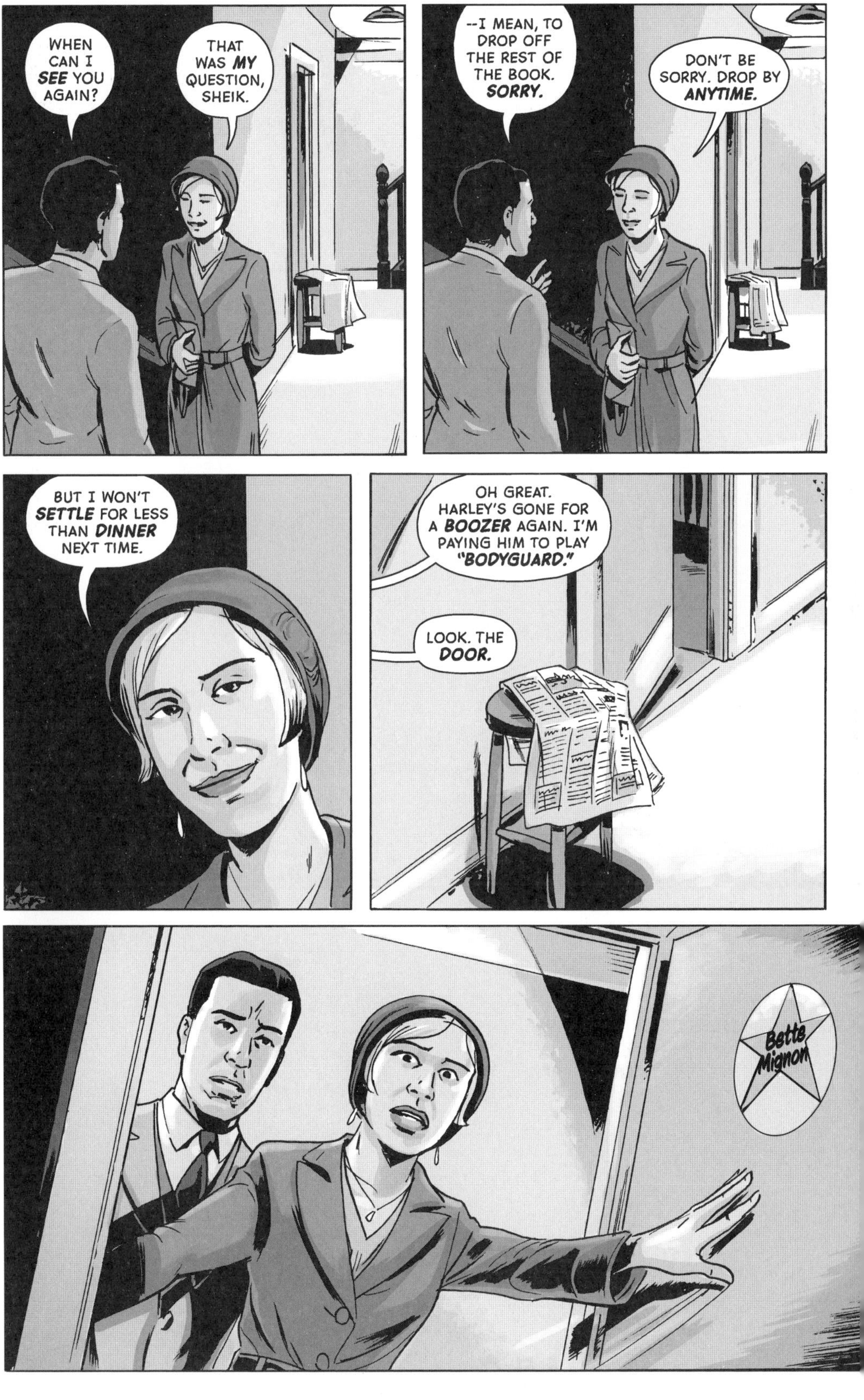
WHEN CAN I SEE YOU AGAIN?
THAT WAS MY QUESTION, SHEIK.
--I MEAN, TO DROP OFF THE REST OF THE BOOK. SORRY.
DON'T BE SORRY. DROP BY ANYTIME.
BUT I WON'T SETTLE FOR LESS THAN DINNER NEXT TIME.
OH GREAT. HARLEY'S GONE FOR A BOOZER AGAIN. I'M PAYING HIM TO PLAY "BODYGUARD."
LOOK. THE DOOR.
Bette Mignon

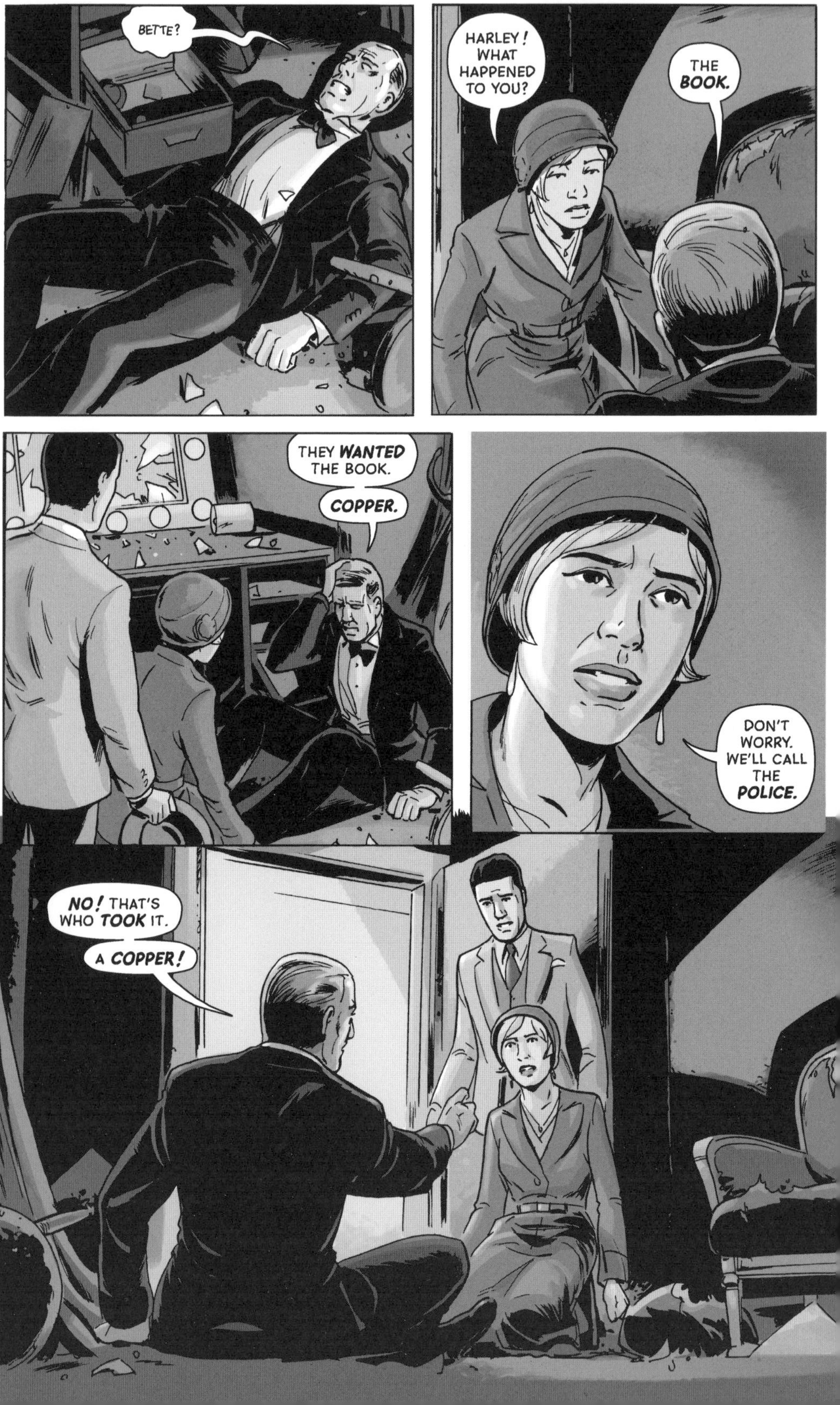
BETTE?
HARLEY! WHAT HAPPENED TO YOU?
THE BOOK.
THEY WANTED THE BOOK.
COPPER.
DON'T WORRY. WE'LL CALL THE POLICE.
NO! THAT'S WHO TOOK IT.
A COPPER!

CHAPTER IV

"PIGEONS"

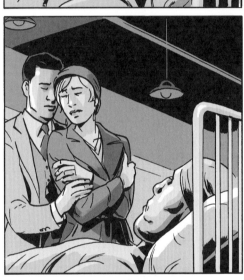
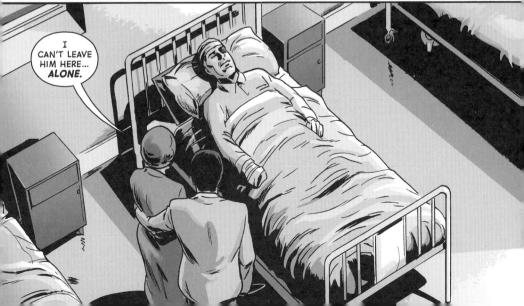

I CAN'T LEAVE HIM HERE... **ALONE.**

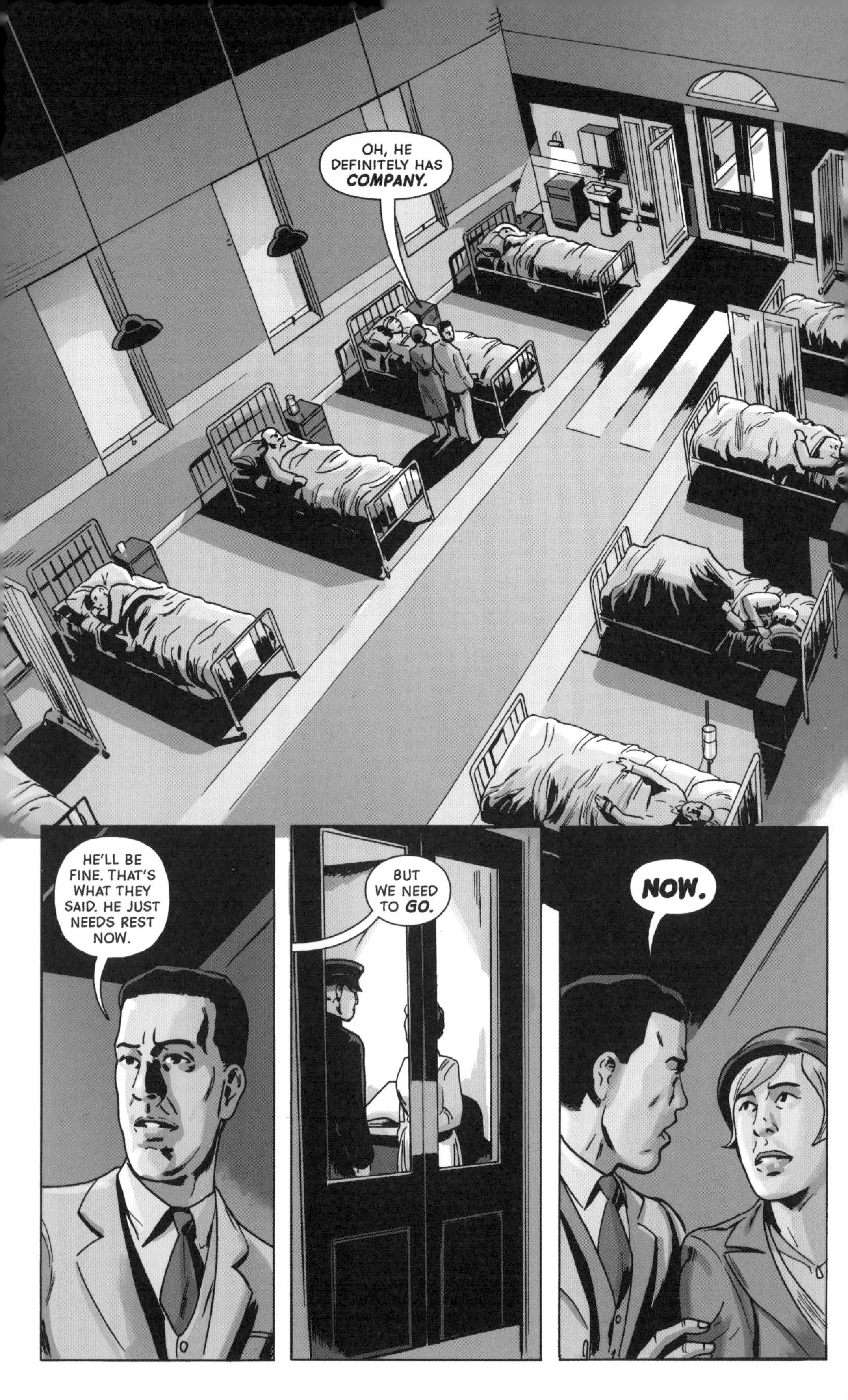
OH, HE DEFINITELY HAS COMPANY.
HE'LL BE FINE. THAT'S WHAT THEY SAID. HE JUST NEEDS REST NOW.
BUT WE NEED TO GO.
NOW.

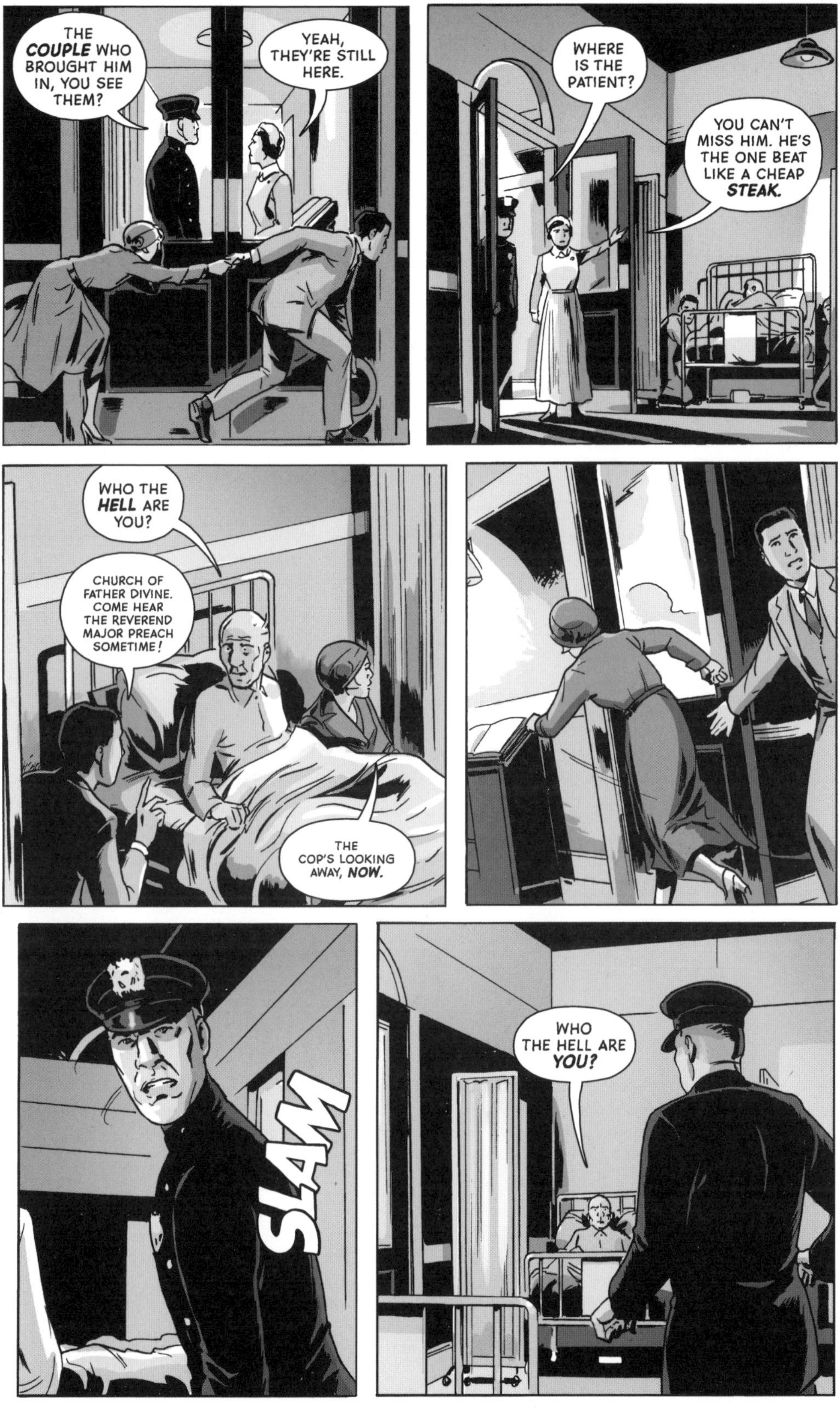
THE COUPLE WHO BROUGHT HIM IN, YOU SEE THEM?
YEAH, THEY'RE STILL HERE.
WHERE IS THE PATIENT?
YOU CAN'T MISS HIM. HE'S THE ONE BEAT LIKE A CHEAP STEAK.
WHO THE HELL ARE YOU?
CHURCH OF FATHER DIVINE. COME HEAR THE REVEREND MAJOR PREACH SOMETIME!
THE COP'S LOOKING AWAY, NOW.
SLAM
WHO THE HELL ARE YOU?

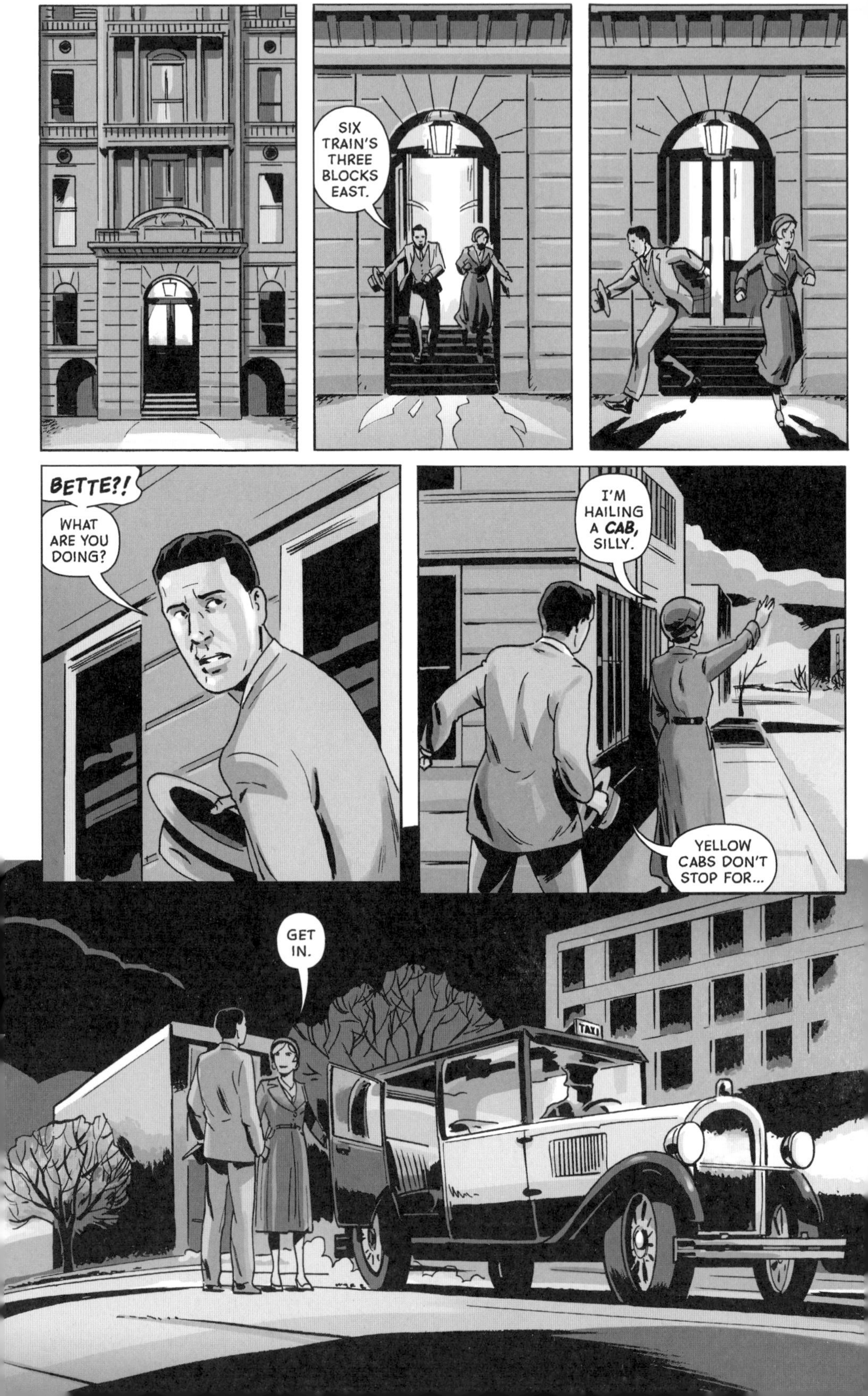
SIX TRAIN'S THREE BLOCKS EAST.
BETTE?!
WHAT ARE YOU DOING?
I'M HAILING A CAB, SILLY.
YELLOW CABS DON'T STOP FOR...
GET IN.
TAXI

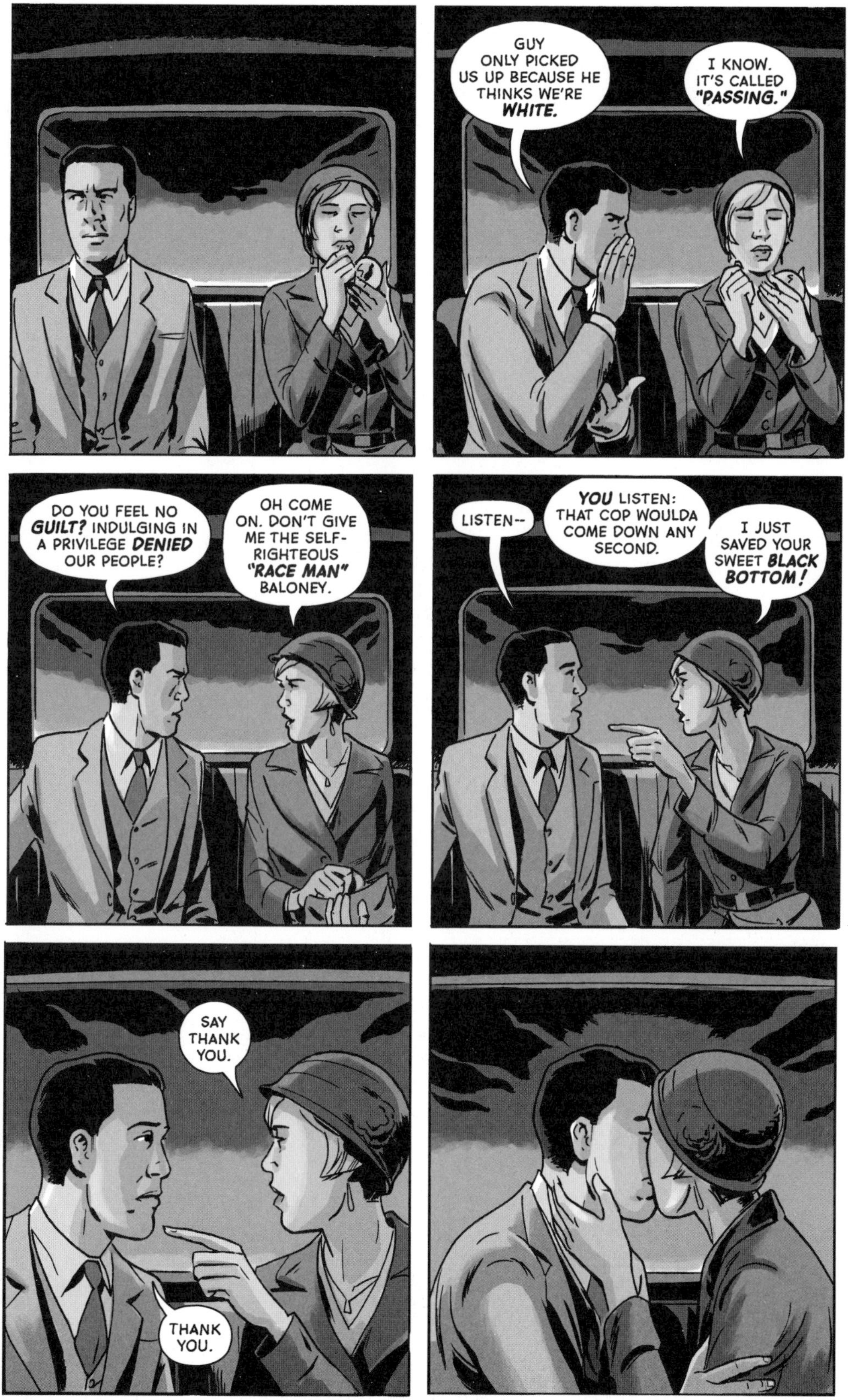
GUY ONLY PICKED US UP BECAUSE HE THINKS WE'RE WHITE.
I KNOW. IT'S CALLED "PASSING."
DO YOU FEEL NO GUILT? INDULGING IN A PRIVILEGE DENIED OUR PEOPLE?
OH COME ON. DON'T GIVE ME THE SELF-RIGHTEOUS "RACE MAN" BALONEY.
LISTEN--
YOU LISTEN: THAT COP WOULDA COME DOWN ANY SECOND.
I JUST SAVED YOUR SWEET BLACK BOTTOM!
SAY THANK YOU.
THANK YOU.

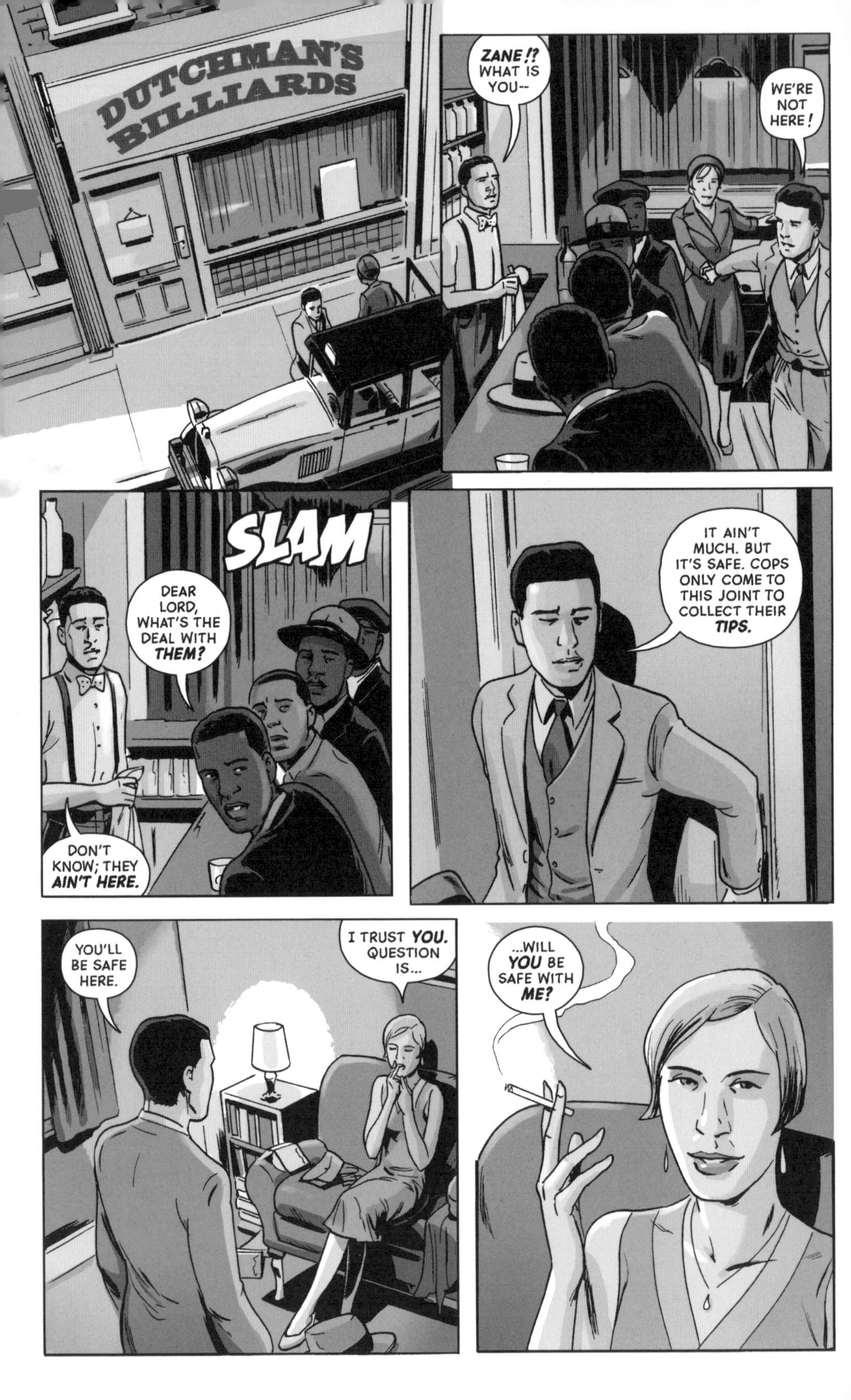
DUTCHMAN'S BILLIARDS
ZANE!? WHAT IS YOU--
WE'RE NOT HERE!
SLAM
DEAR LORD, WHAT'S THE DEAL WITH THEM?
DON'T KNOW; THEY AIN'T HERE.
IT AIN'T MUCH. BUT IT'S SAFE. COPS ONLY COME TO THIS JOINT TO COLLECT THEIR TIPS.
YOU'LL BE SAFE HERE.
I TRUST YOU. QUESTION IS...
...WILL YOU BE SAFE WITH ME?

"UNDER THE BAMBOO TREE."

WHAT?

WHATCHU HUMMING? THE SONG?

I DIDN'T EVEN REALIZE I WAS. *XAVIER* LOVED THAT SONG.

HE HAD AN EYE FOR *BEAUTY*--BUT LORDY, HE WAS AN *UGLY* WRITER.

I PIECED TOGETHER A CHAPTER, BUT I CAN BARELY READ IT. THE WHOLE THING'S OUT THE MOUTH OF A *PIGEON!*

A DAMN *PIGEON!* WHAT A MESS. BREAKS MY HEART TO READ IT.

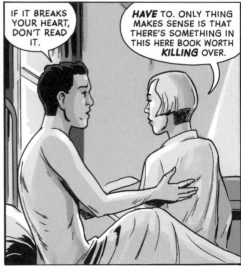

IF IT BREAKS YOUR HEART, DON'T READ IT.

HAVE TO. ONLY THING MAKES SENSE IS THAT THERE'S SOMETHING IN THIS HERE BOOK WORTH *KILLING* OVER.

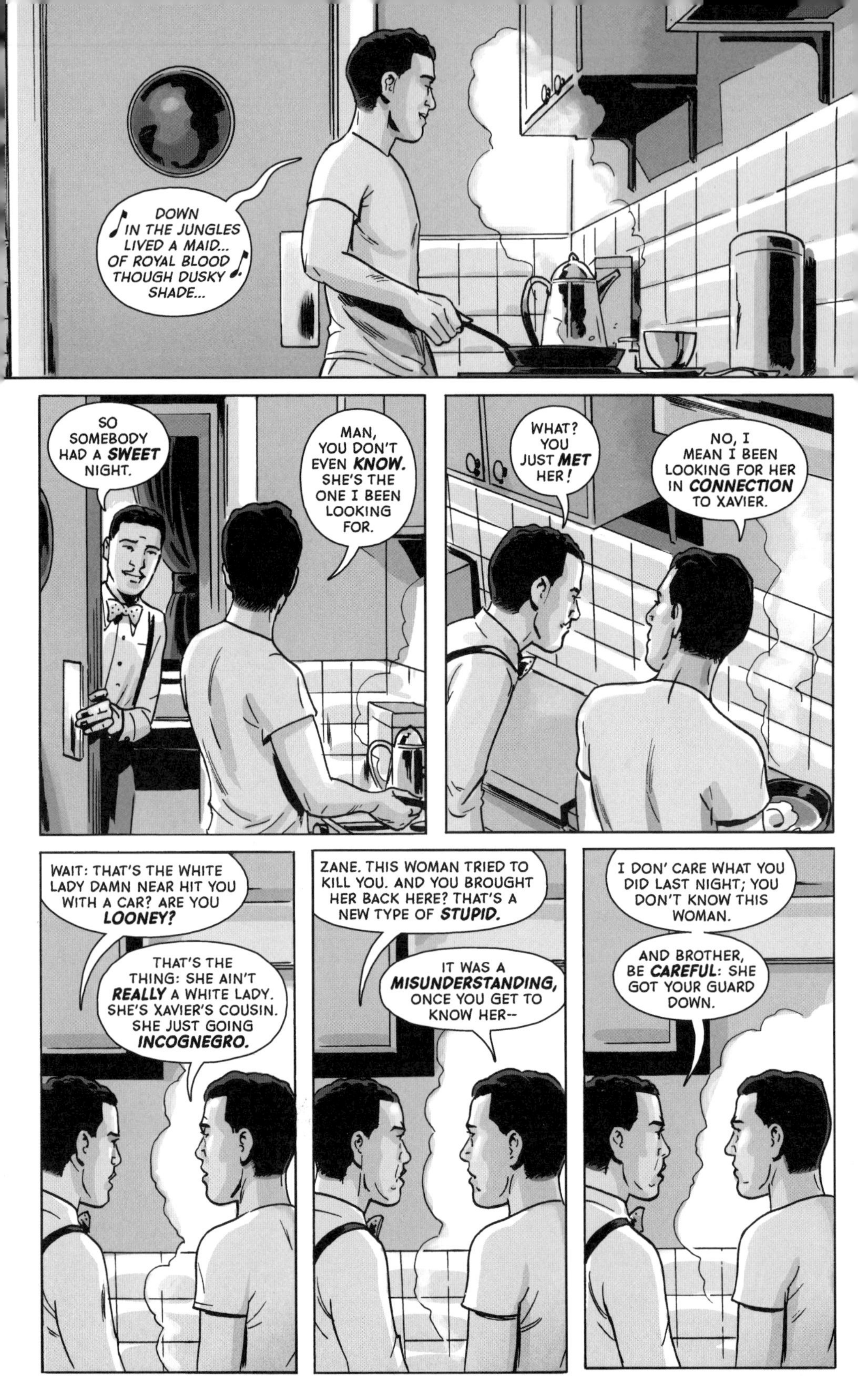
DOWN IN THE JUNGLES LIVED A MAID... OF ROYAL BLOOD THOUGH DUSKY SHADE...
SO SOMEBODY HAD A **SWEET** NIGHT.
MAN, YOU DON'T EVEN **KNOW.** SHE'S THE ONE I BEEN LOOKING FOR.
WHAT? YOU JUST **MET** HER!
NO, I MEAN I BEEN LOOKING FOR HER IN **CONNECTION** TO XAVIER.
WAIT: THAT'S THE WHITE LADY DAMN NEAR HIT YOU WITH A CAR? ARE YOU **LOONEY?**
THAT'S THE THING: SHE AIN'T **REALLY** A WHITE LADY. SHE'S XAVIER'S COUSIN. SHE JUST GOING **INCOGNEGRO.**
ZANE. THIS WOMAN TRIED TO KILL YOU. AND YOU BROUGHT HER BACK HERE? THAT'S A NEW TYPE OF **STUPID.**
IT WAS A **MISUNDERSTANDING,** ONCE YOU GET TO KNOW HER--
I DON' CARE WHAT YOU DID LAST NIGHT; YOU DON'T KNOW THIS WOMAN.
AND BROTHER, BE **CAREFUL**: SHE GOT YOUR GUARD DOWN.

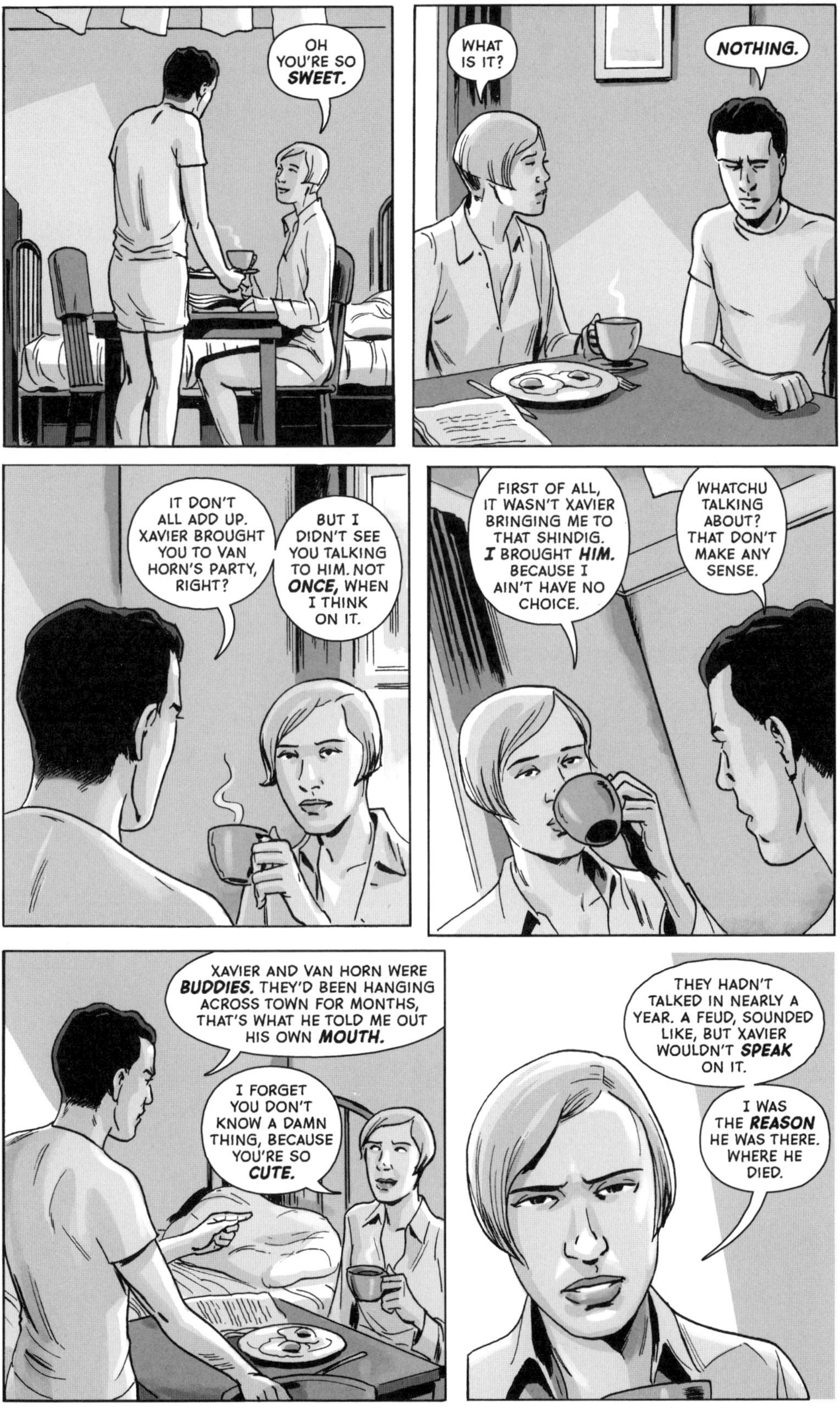
OH YOU'RE SO **SWEET.**
WHAT IS IT?
NOTHING.
IT DON'T ALL ADD UP. XAVIER BROUGHT YOU TO VAN HORN'S PARTY, RIGHT?
BUT I DIDN'T SEE YOU TALKING TO HIM. NOT **ONCE,** WHEN I THINK ON IT.
FIRST OF ALL, IT WASN'T XAVIER BRINGING ME TO THAT SHINDIG. **I** BROUGHT **HIM.** BECAUSE I AIN'T HAVE NO CHOICE.
WHATCHU TALKING ABOUT? THAT DON'T MAKE ANY SENSE.
XAVIER AND VAN HORN WERE **BUDDIES.** THEY'D BEEN HANGING ACROSS TOWN FOR MONTHS, THAT'S WHAT HE TOLD ME OUT HIS OWN **MOUTH.**
I FORGET YOU DON'T KNOW A DAMN THING, BECAUSE YOU'RE SO **CUTE.**
THEY HADN'T TALKED IN NEARLY A YEAR. A FEUD, SOUNDED LIKE, BUT XAVIER WOULDN'T **SPEAK** ON IT.
I WAS THE **REASON** HE WAS THERE. WHERE HE DIED.

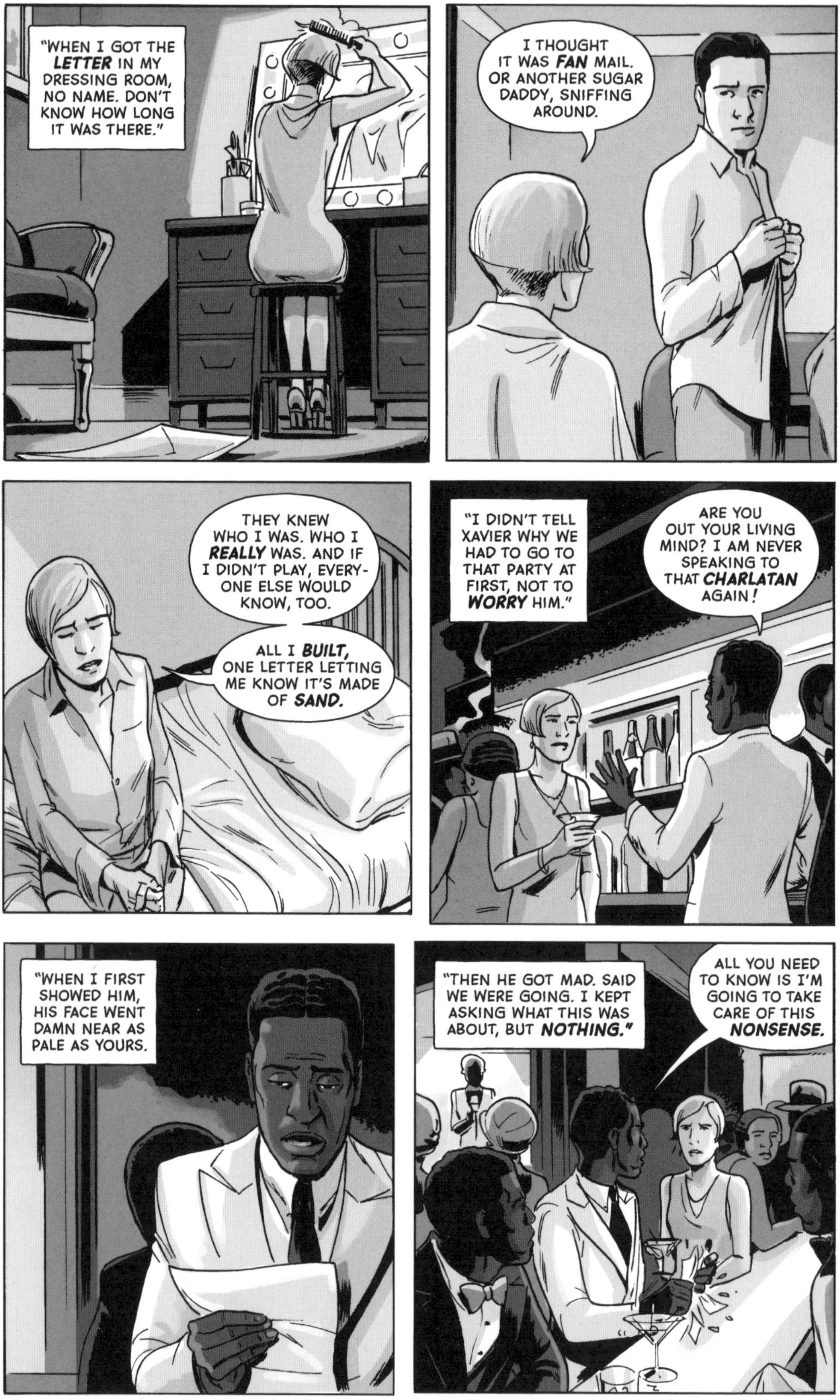
"WHEN I GOT THE LETTER IN MY DRESSING ROOM, NO NAME. DON'T KNOW HOW LONG IT WAS THERE."
I THOUGHT IT WAS FAN MAIL. OR ANOTHER SUGAR DADDY, SNIFFING AROUND.
THEY KNEW WHO I WAS. WHO I REALLY WAS. AND IF I DIDN'T PLAY, EVERY-ONE ELSE WOULD KNOW, TOO.
ALL I BUILT, ONE LETTER LETTING ME KNOW IT'S MADE OF SAND.
"I DIDN'T TELL XAVIER WHY WE HAD TO GO TO THAT PARTY AT FIRST, NOT TO WORRY HIM."
ARE YOU OUT YOUR LIVING MIND? I AM NEVER SPEAKING TO THAT CHARLATAN AGAIN!
"WHEN I FIRST SHOWED HIM, HIS FACE WENT DAMN NEAR AS PALE AS YOURS.
"THEN HE GOT MAD. SAID WE WERE GOING. I KEPT ASKING WHAT THIS WAS ABOUT, BUT NOTHING."
ALL YOU NEED TO KNOW IS I'M GOING TO TAKE CARE OF THIS NONSENSE.

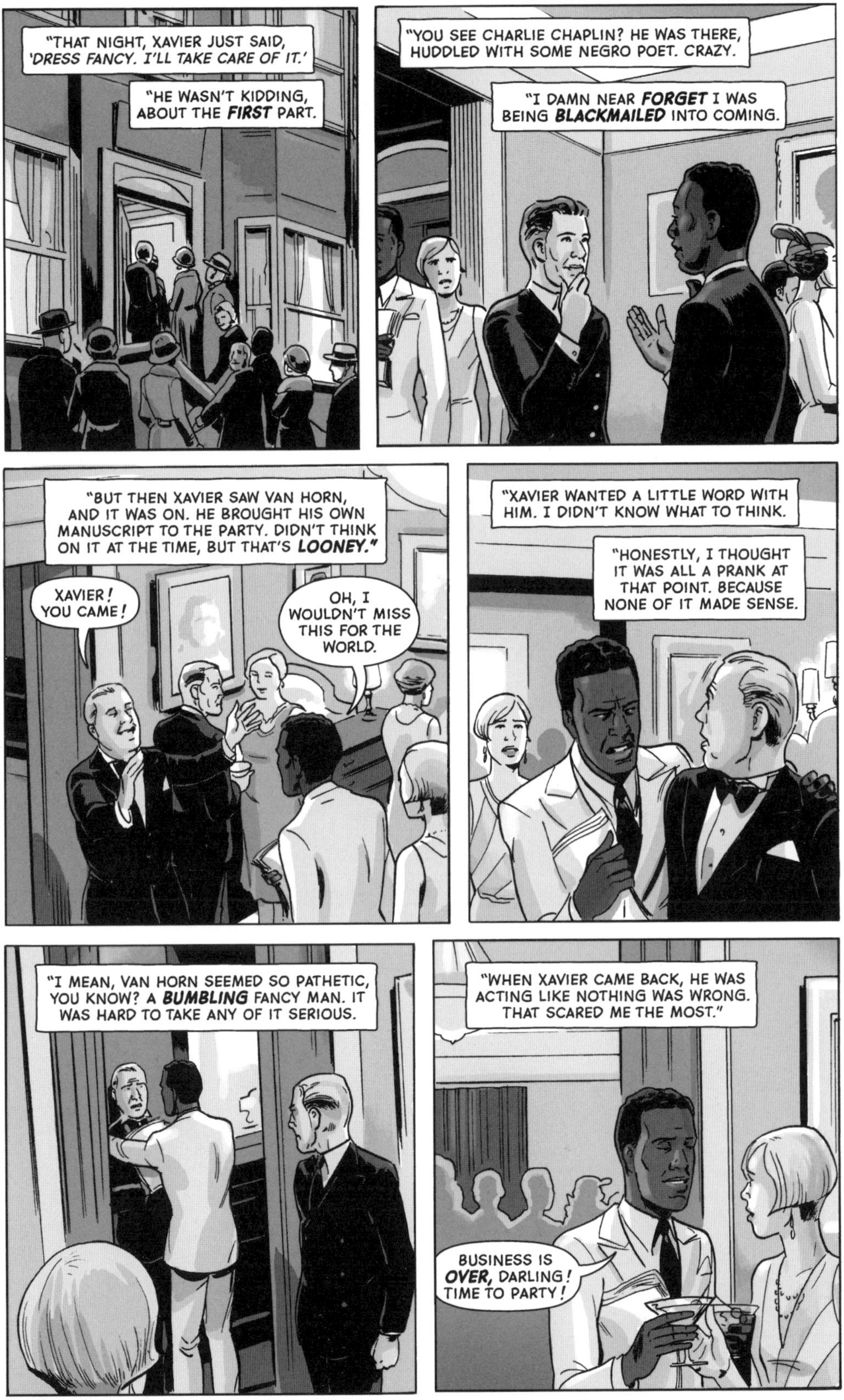
"THAT NIGHT, XAVIER JUST SAID, *'DRESS FANCY. I'LL TAKE CARE OF IT.'*
"HE WASN'T KIDDING, ABOUT THE ***FIRST*** PART.
"YOU SEE CHARLIE CHAPLIN? HE WAS THERE, HUDDLED WITH SOME NEGRO POET. CRAZY.
"I DAMN NEAR ***FORGET*** I WAS BEING ***BLACKMAILED*** INTO COMING.
"BUT THEN XAVIER SAW VAN HORN, AND IT WAS ON. HE BROUGHT HIS OWN MANUSCRIPT TO THE PARTY. DIDN'T THINK ON IT AT THE TIME, BUT THAT'S ***LOONEY."***
XAVIER! YOU CAME!
OH, I WOULDN'T MISS THIS FOR THE WORLD.
"XAVIER WANTED A LITTLE WORD WITH HIM. I DIDN'T KNOW WHAT TO THINK.
"HONESTLY, I THOUGHT IT WAS ALL A PRANK AT THAT POINT. BECAUSE NONE OF IT MADE SENSE.
"I MEAN, VAN HORN SEEMED SO PATHETIC, YOU KNOW? A ***BUMBLING*** FANCY MAN. IT WAS HARD TO TAKE ANY OF IT SERIOUS.
"WHEN XAVIER CAME BACK, HE WAS ACTING LIKE NOTHING WAS WRONG. THAT SCARED ME THE MOST."
BUSINESS IS ***OVER,*** DARLING! TIME TO PARTY!

"I SAID TO HIM, 'WHAT ABOUT **ME?** THE **BLACKMAIL?**'"

AIN'T NOTHING TO **WORRY** ABOUT. JUST SOME CATTY BULL. I STOPPED THAT NONSENSE.

THAT LETTER, THAT WAS JUST SOMEONE PLAYING GAMES. BUT THEY **OVERPLAYED** THEIR HAND, BABY. WE'RE GOOD.

"AND HE MUST HAVE THOUGHT WE WERE GOOD. BECAUSE HIS GUARD FELL TO THE DANCE FLOOR. HE WAS OUT OF **CONTROL.**"

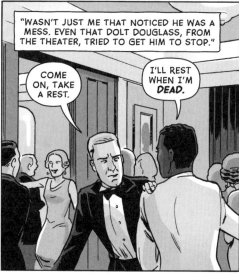

"WASN'T JUST ME THAT NOTICED HE WAS A MESS. EVEN THAT DOLT DOUGLASS, FROM THE THEATER, TRIED TO GET HIM TO STOP."

COME ON, TAKE A REST.

I'LL REST WHEN I'M **DEAD.**

WHY WAS THAT ACTOR EVEN THERE? DID HE COME WITH YOU?

DOUGLASS? HE SHOWS UP WHENEVER A SOCIALITE POPS A CORK. HE AND XAVIER USED TO PARTY, BUT THEY FELL OUT. HE'S JUST A BORE.

I TALKED TO HIM THAT NIGHT, HE'S NO FAN OF YOURS EITHER. SO HE'S A BORE WITH **OPPORTUNITY.**

AND MAYBE EVEN **MOTIVE.**

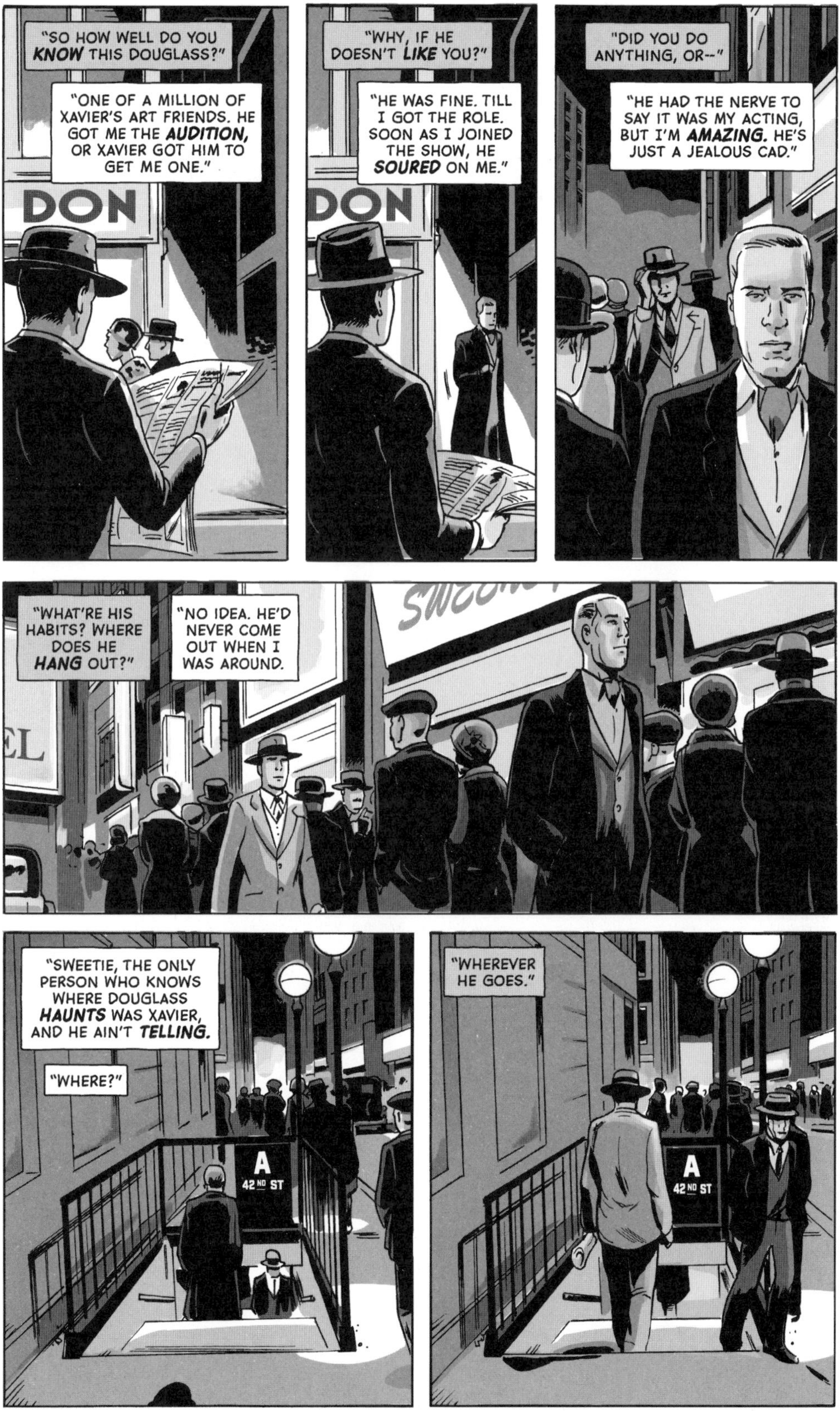
"SO HOW WELL DO YOU KNOW THIS DOUGLASS?"
"ONE OF A MILLION OF XAVIER'S ART FRIENDS. HE GOT ME THE AUDITION, OR XAVIER GOT HIM TO GET ME ONE."
DON
"WHY, IF HE DOESN'T LIKE YOU?"
"HE WAS FINE. TILL I GOT THE ROLE. SOON AS I JOINED THE SHOW, HE SOURED ON ME."
DON
"DID YOU DO ANYTHING, OR--"
"HE HAD THE NERVE TO SAY IT WAS MY ACTING, BUT I'M AMAZING. HE'S JUST A JEALOUS CAD."
"WHAT'RE HIS HABITS? WHERE DOES HE HANG OUT?"
"NO IDEA. HE'D NEVER COME OUT WHEN I WAS AROUND.
"SWEETIE, THE ONLY PERSON WHO KNOWS WHERE DOUGLASS HAUNTS WAS XAVIER, AND HE AIN'T TELLING.
"WHERE?"
A
42ND ST
"WHEREVER HE GOES."
A
42ND ST

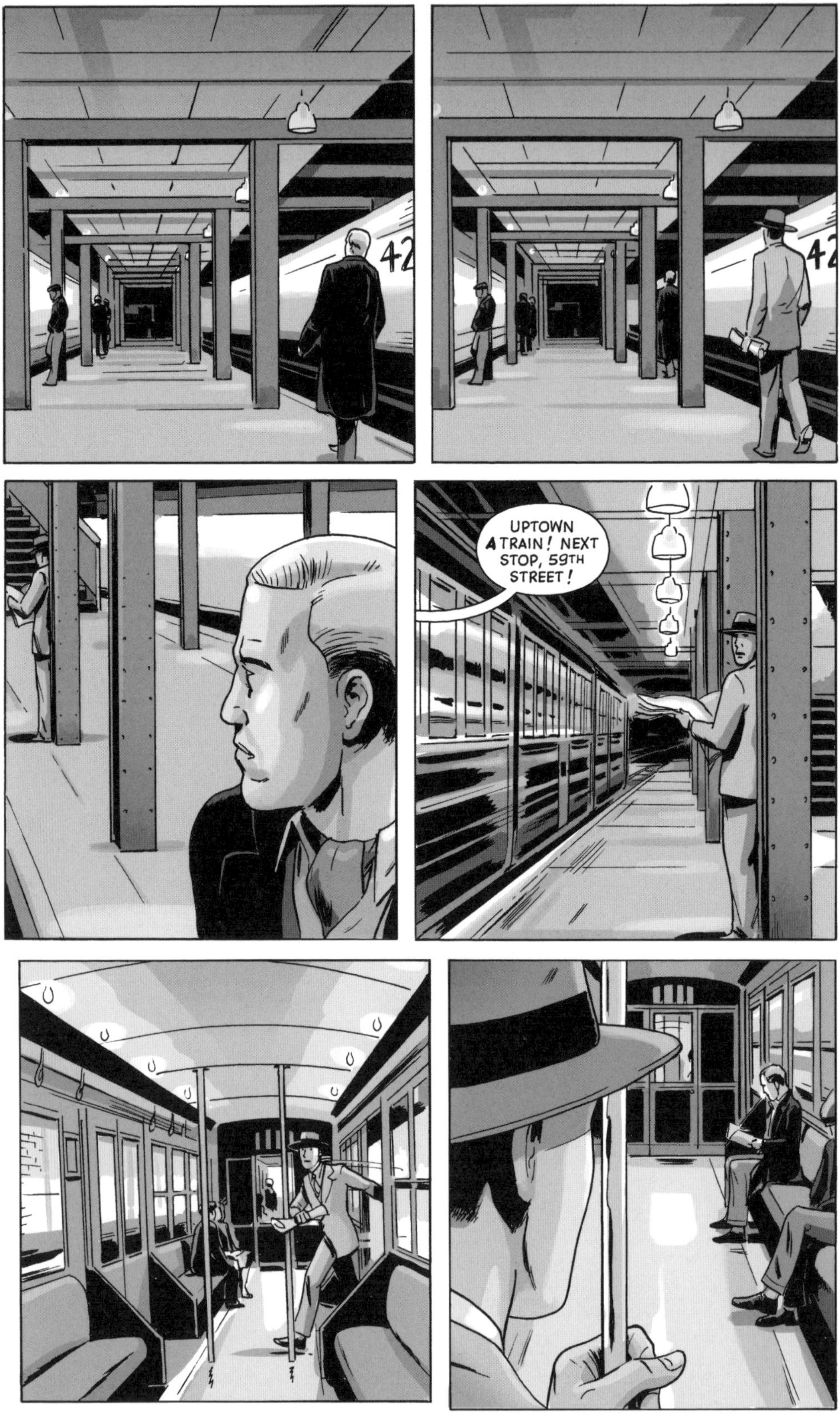
UPTOWN A TRAIN! NEXT STOP, 59TH STREET!

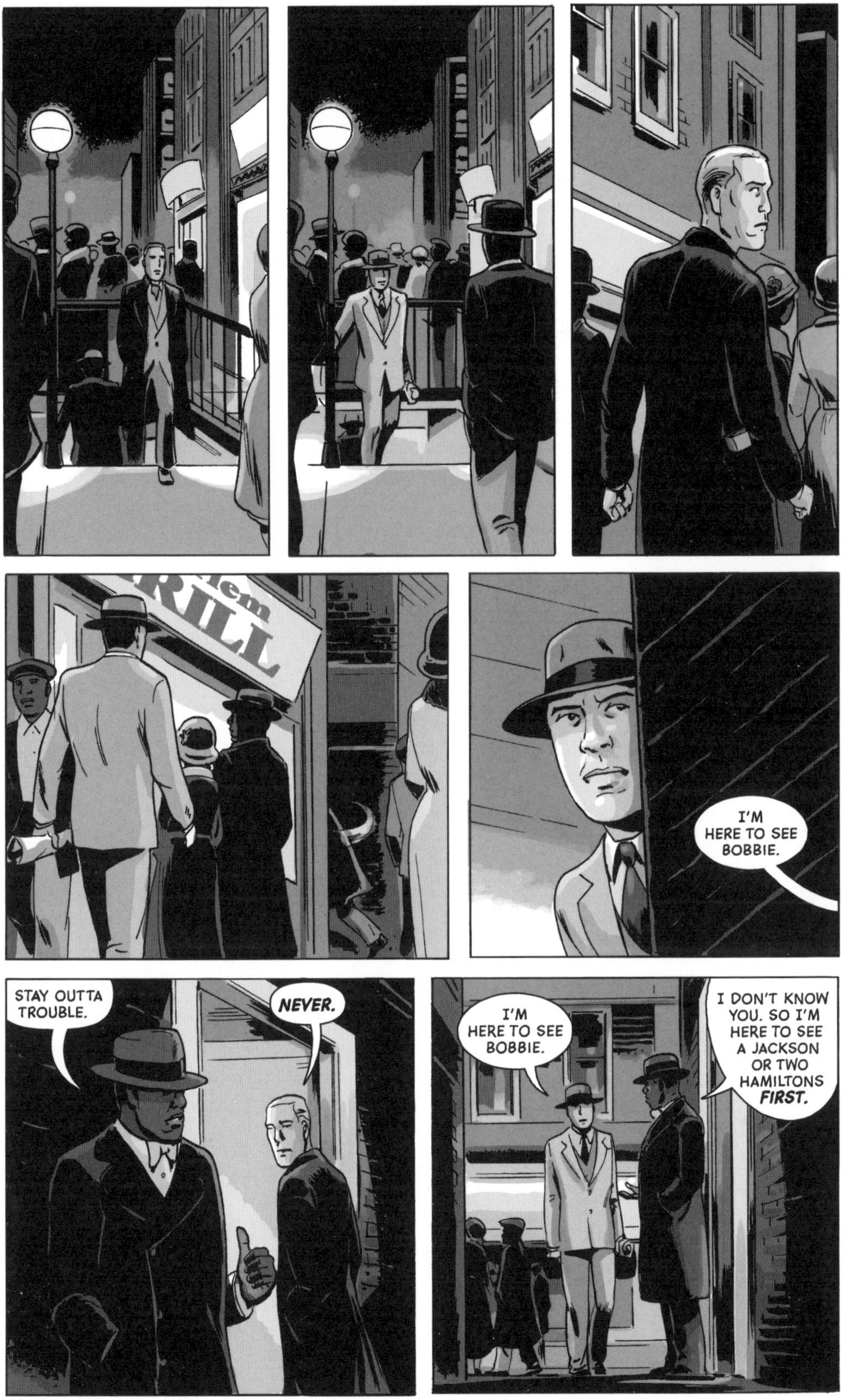
I'M HERE TO SEE BOBBIE.
STAY OUTTA TROUBLE.
NEVER.
I'M HERE TO SEE BOBBIE.
I DON'T KNOW YOU. SO I'M HERE TO SEE A JACKSON OR TWO HAMILTONS FIRST.

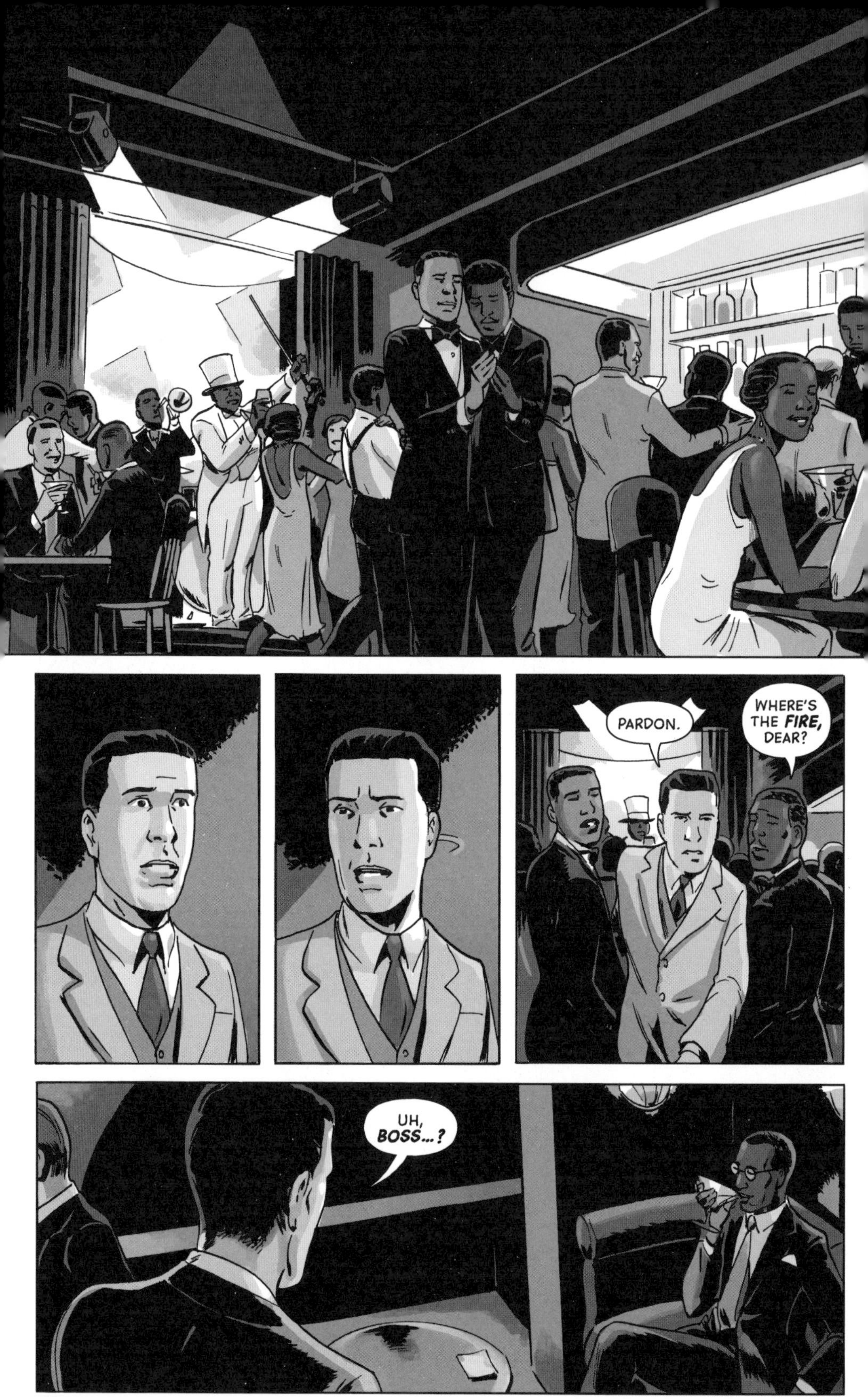
PARDON.
WHERE'S THE FIRE, DEAR?
UH, BOSS...?

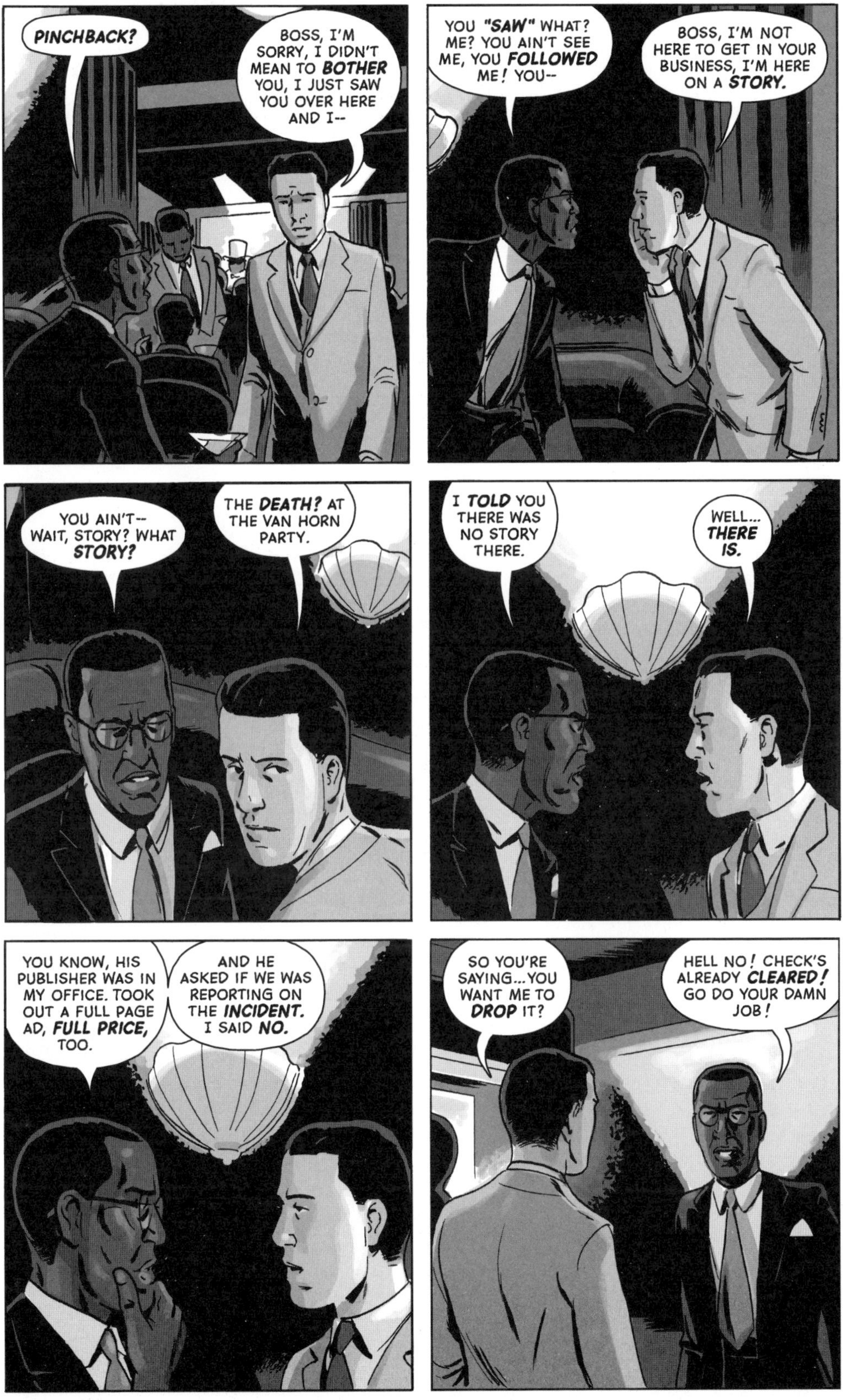
PINCHBACK?
BOSS, I'M SORRY, I DIDN'T MEAN TO BOTHER YOU, I JUST SAW YOU OVER HERE AND I--
YOU "SAW" WHAT? ME? YOU AIN'T SEE ME, YOU FOLLOWED ME! YOU--
BOSS, I'M NOT HERE TO GET IN YOUR BUSINESS, I'M HERE ON A STORY.
YOU AIN'T-- WAIT, STORY? WHAT STORY?
THE DEATH? AT THE VAN HORN PARTY.
I TOLD YOU THERE WAS NO STORY THERE.
WELL... THERE IS.
YOU KNOW, HIS PUBLISHER WAS IN MY OFFICE. TOOK OUT A FULL PAGE AD, FULL PRICE, TOO.
AND HE ASKED IF WE WAS REPORTING ON THE INCIDENT. I SAID NO.
SO YOU'RE SAYING... YOU WANT ME TO DROP IT?
HELL NO! CHECK'S ALREADY CLEARED! GO DO YOUR DAMN JOB!

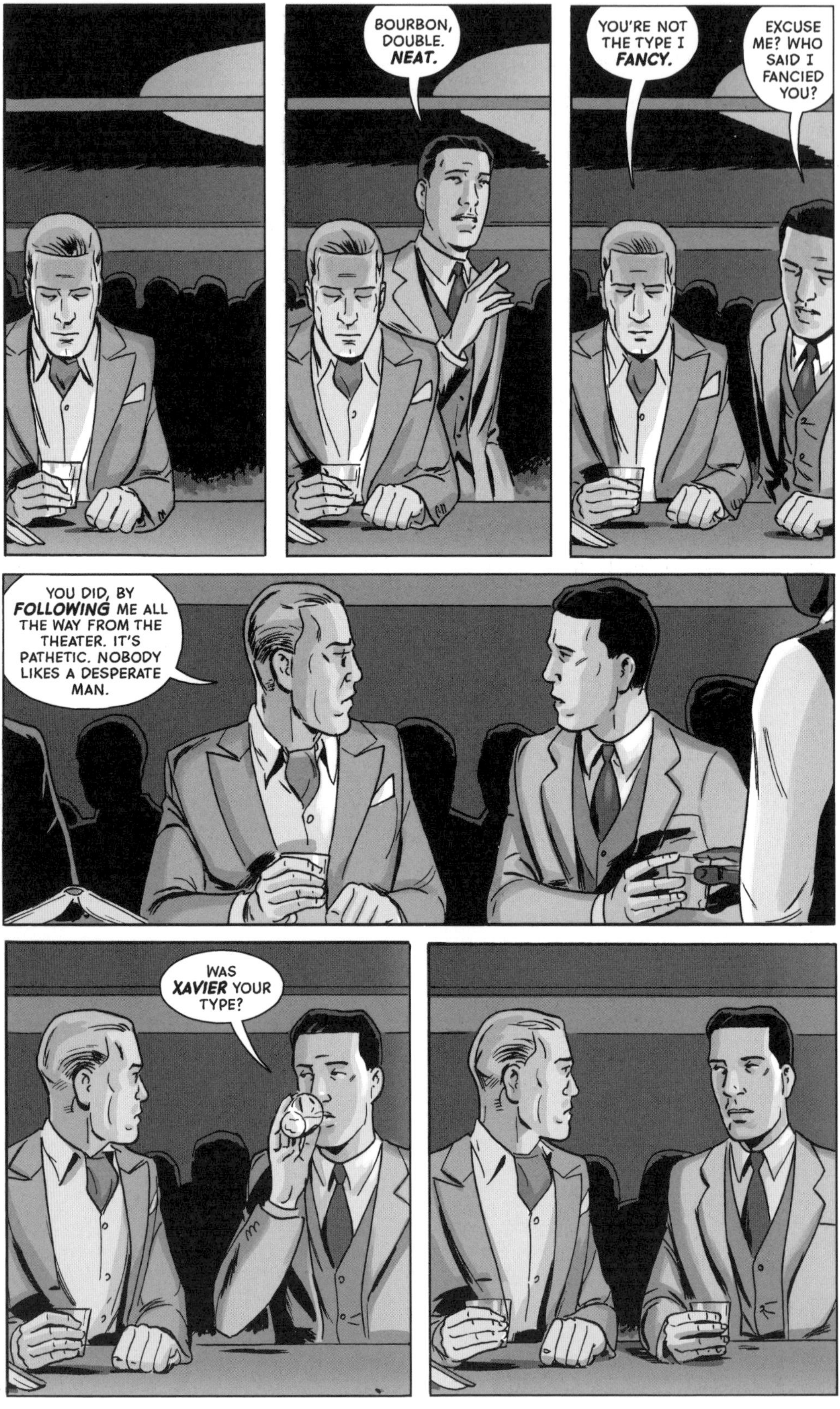
BOURBON, DOUBLE. NEAT.
YOU'RE NOT THE TYPE I FANCY.
EXCUSE ME? WHO SAID I FANCIED YOU?
YOU DID, BY FOLLOWING ME ALL THE WAY FROM THE THEATER. IT'S PATHETIC. NOBODY LIKES A DESPERATE MAN.
WAS XAVIER YOUR TYPE?

YES, HE WAS. AND I THOUGHT IT WENT **BOTH** WAYS, BEFORE I REALIZED HE WAS JUST **USING** ME.

SO...YOU TWO HAD A LOVERS' **QUARREL.** IS THAT WHY YOU HATED HIM?

HATED HIM? I **ADORED** HIM. HE WAS THE INDIFFERENT ONE. HE LED **ME** ON.

GOT ME TO BRING HIS **HUSSY** IN FOR AN AUDITION AFTER OUR LAST "MAGGIE" TOOK OFF FOR CALIFORNIA.

BETTE?

THAT IS THE HUSSY OF WHICH I SPEAK!

SAW YOU **SNIFFING** AROUND HER DRESSING ROOM, TOO. YOU WERE WARNED. SHE'LL **RUIN** YOU LIKE SHE DID XAVIER!

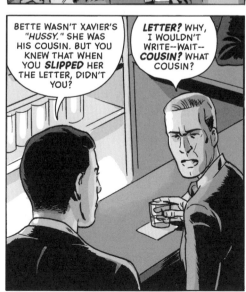

BETTE WASN'T XAVIER'S "HUSSY." SHE WAS HIS COUSIN. BUT YOU KNEW THAT WHEN YOU **SLIPPED** HER THE LETTER, DIDN'T YOU?

LETTER? WHY, I WOULDN'T WRITE--WAIT--**COUSIN?** WHAT COUSIN?

YOU THREATENED TO EXPOSE HER FOR BEING **COLORED,** YOU--

THEY WERE **JUST** COUSINS? THAT'S WHY HE--WHY HE WAS **ALWAYS** WITH HER? WHY HE WOULDN'T SAY...

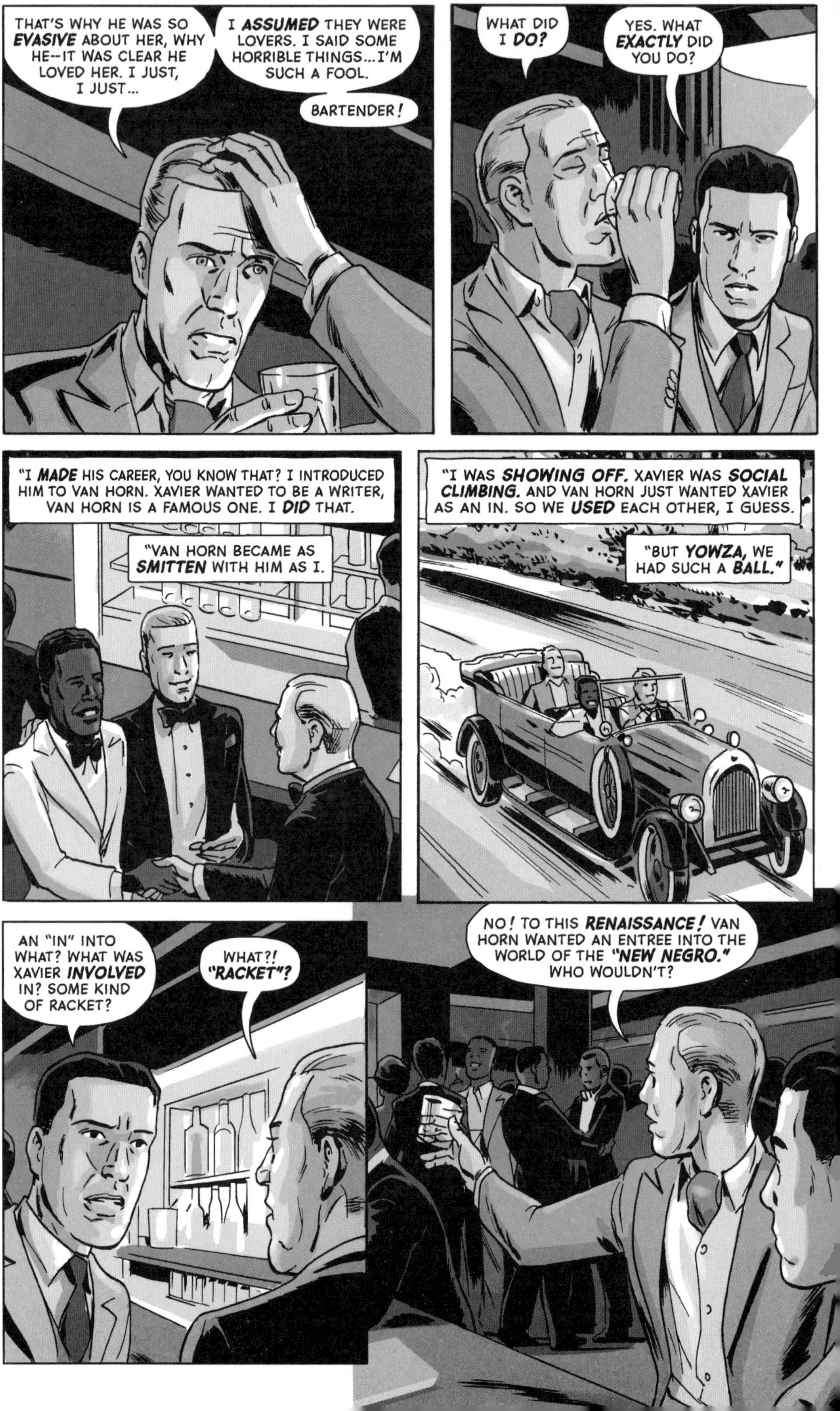
THAT'S WHY HE WAS SO EVASIVE ABOUT HER, WHY HE--IT WAS CLEAR HE LOVED HER. I JUST, I JUST...
I ASSUMED THEY WERE LOVERS. I SAID SOME HORRIBLE THINGS...I'M SUCH A FOOL.
BARTENDER!
WHAT DID I DO?
YES. WHAT EXACTLY DID YOU DO?
"I MADE HIS CAREER, YOU KNOW THAT? I INTRODUCED HIM TO VAN HORN. XAVIER WANTED TO BE A WRITER, VAN HORN IS A FAMOUS ONE. I DID THAT.
"VAN HORN BECAME AS SMITTEN WITH HIM AS I.
"I WAS SHOWING OFF. XAVIER WAS SOCIAL CLIMBING. AND VAN HORN JUST WANTED XAVIER AS AN IN. SO WE USED EACH OTHER, I GUESS.
"BUT YOWZA, WE HAD SUCH A BALL."
AN "IN" INTO WHAT? WHAT WAS XAVIER INVOLVED IN? SOME KIND OF RACKET?
WHAT?! "RACKET"?
NO! TO THIS RENAISSANCE! VAN HORN WANTED AN ENTREE INTO THE WORLD OF THE "NEW NEGRO." WHO WOULDN'T?

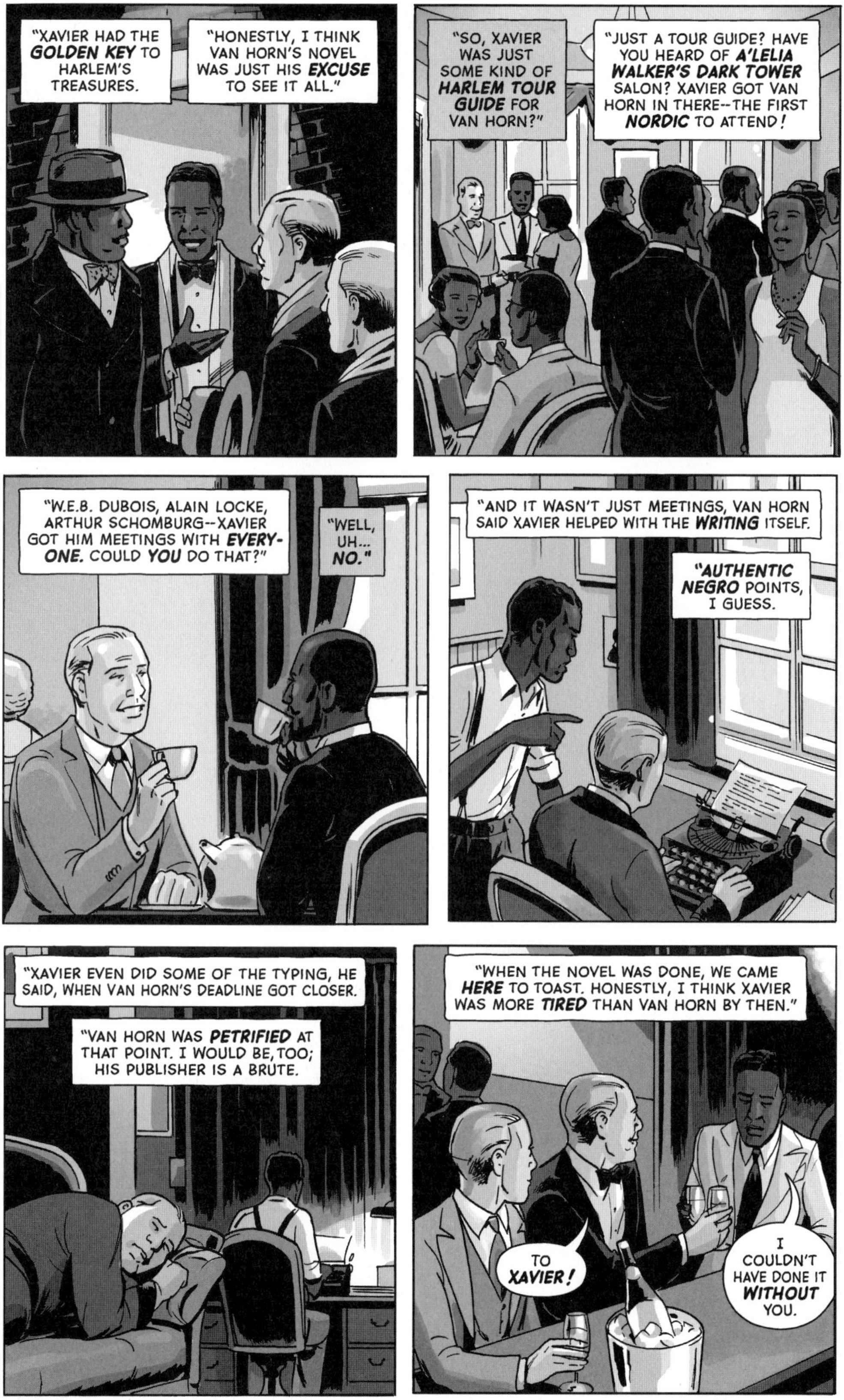
"XAVIER HAD THE GOLDEN KEY TO HARLEM'S TREASURES.
"HONESTLY, I THINK VAN HORN'S NOVEL WAS JUST HIS EXCUSE TO SEE IT ALL."
"SO, XAVIER WAS JUST SOME KIND OF HARLEM TOUR GUIDE FOR VAN HORN?"
"JUST A TOUR GUIDE? HAVE YOU HEARD OF A'LELIA WALKER'S DARK TOWER SALON? XAVIER GOT VAN HORN IN THERE--THE FIRST NORDIC TO ATTEND!
"W.E.B. DUBOIS, ALAIN LOCKE, ARTHUR SCHOMBURG--XAVIER GOT HIM MEETINGS WITH EVERY-ONE. COULD YOU DO THAT?"
"WELL, UH... NO."
"AND IT WASN'T JUST MEETINGS, VAN HORN SAID XAVIER HELPED WITH THE WRITING ITSELF.
"AUTHENTIC NEGRO POINTS, I GUESS.
"XAVIER EVEN DID SOME OF THE TYPING, HE SAID, WHEN VAN HORN'S DEADLINE GOT CLOSER.
"VAN HORN WAS PETRIFIED AT THAT POINT. I WOULD BE, TOO; HIS PUBLISHER IS A BRUTE.
"WHEN THE NOVEL WAS DONE, WE CAME HERE TO TOAST. HONESTLY, I THINK XAVIER WAS MORE TIRED THAN VAN HORN BY THEN."
TO XAVIER!
I COULDN'T HAVE DONE IT WITHOUT YOU.

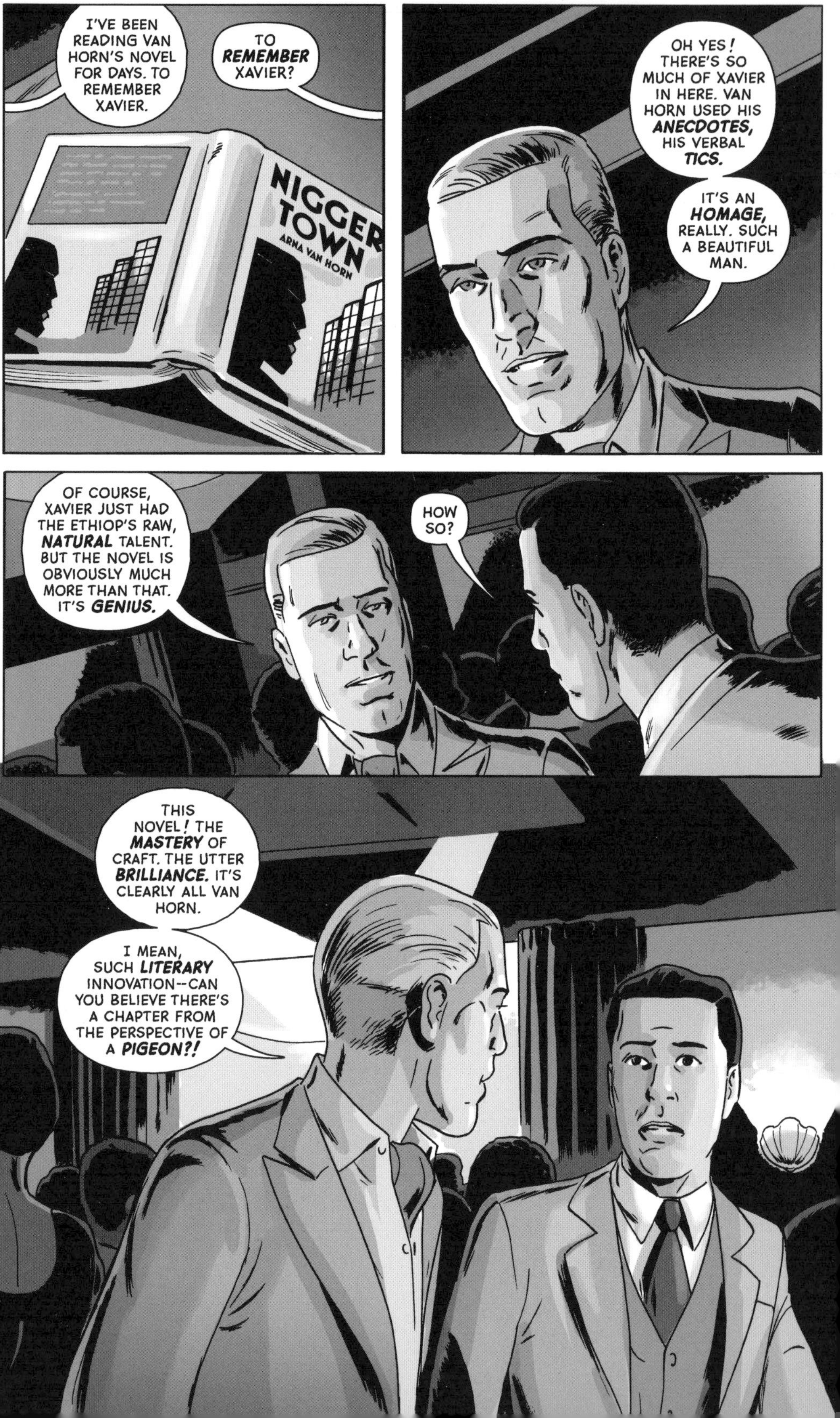

I'VE BEEN READING VAN HORN'S NOVEL FOR DAYS. TO REMEMBER XAVIER.
TO **REMEMBER** XAVIER?
NIGGER TOWN
ARNA VAN HORN
OH YES! THERE'S SO MUCH OF XAVIER IN HERE. VAN HORN USED HIS **ANECDOTES,** HIS VERBAL **TICS.**
IT'S AN **HOMAGE,** REALLY. SUCH A BEAUTIFUL MAN.
OF COURSE, XAVIER JUST HAD THE ETHIOP'S RAW, **NATURAL** TALENT. BUT THE NOVEL IS OBVIOUSLY MUCH MORE THAN THAT. IT'S **GENIUS.**
HOW SO?
THIS NOVEL! THE **MASTERY** OF CRAFT. THE UTTER **BRILLIANCE.** IT'S CLEARLY ALL VAN HORN.
I MEAN, SUCH **LITERARY** INNOVATION--CAN YOU BELIEVE THERE'S A CHAPTER FROM THE PERSPECTIVE OF A **PIGEON?!**

CHAPTER V

"BYLINE"

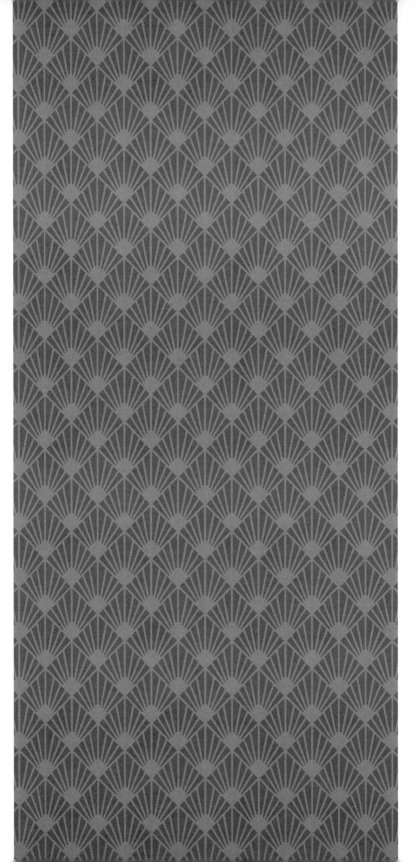

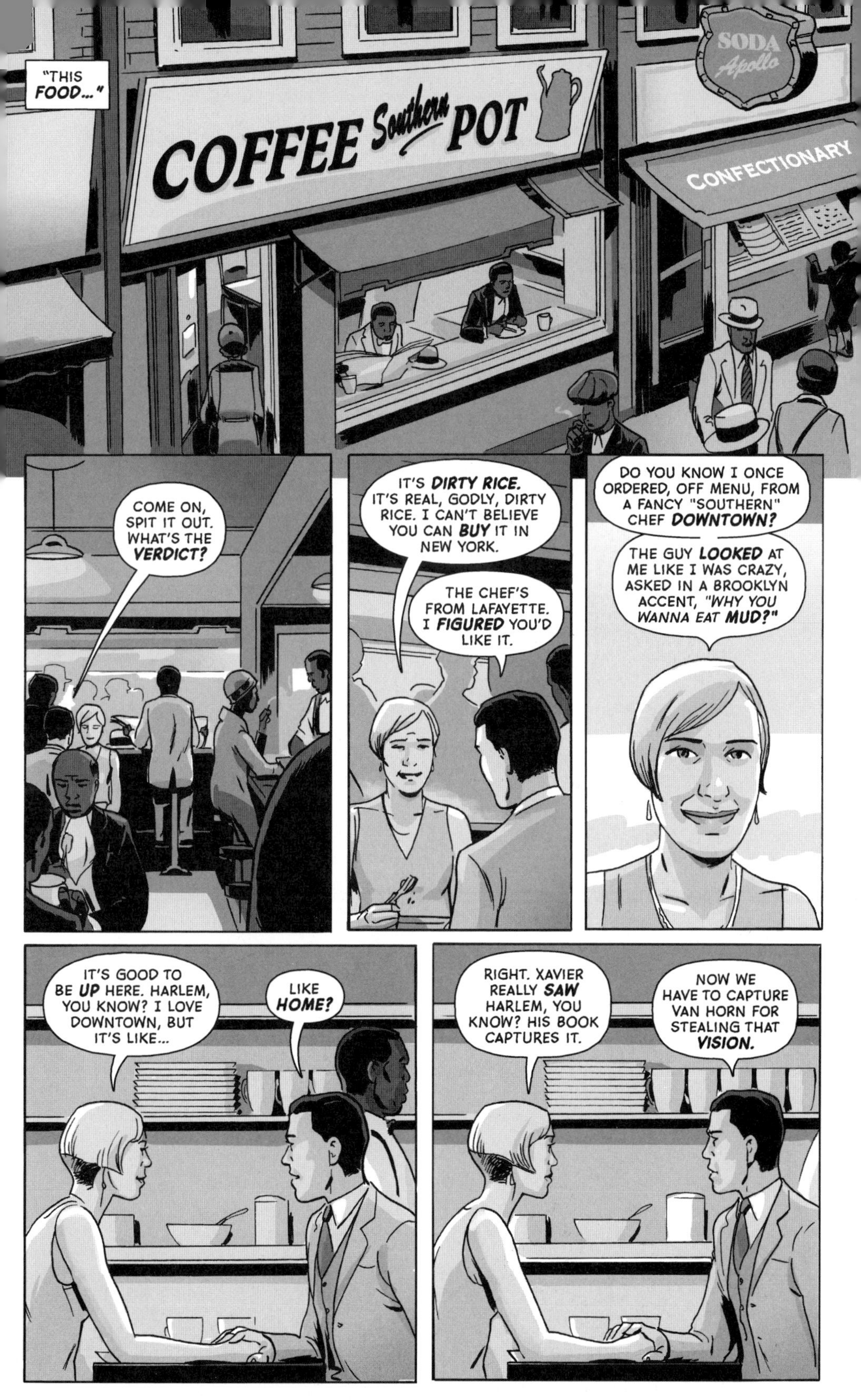
"THIS FOOD..."
COFFEE Southern POT
SODA Apollo
CONFECTIONARY
COME ON, SPIT IT OUT. WHAT'S THE VERDICT?
IT'S DIRTY RICE. IT'S REAL, GODLY, DIRTY RICE. I CAN'T BELIEVE YOU CAN BUY IT IN NEW YORK.
THE CHEF'S FROM LAFAYETTE. I FIGURED YOU'D LIKE IT.
DO YOU KNOW I ONCE ORDERED, OFF MENU, FROM A FANCY "SOUTHERN" CHEF DOWNTOWN?
THE GUY LOOKED AT ME LIKE I WAS CRAZY, ASKED IN A BROOKLYN ACCENT, "WHY YOU WANNA EAT MUD?"
IT'S GOOD TO BE UP HERE. HARLEM, YOU KNOW? I LOVE DOWNTOWN, BUT IT'S LIKE...
LIKE HOME?
RIGHT. XAVIER REALLY SAW HARLEM, YOU KNOW? HIS BOOK CAPTURES IT.
NOW WE HAVE TO CAPTURE VAN HORN FOR STEALING THAT VISION.

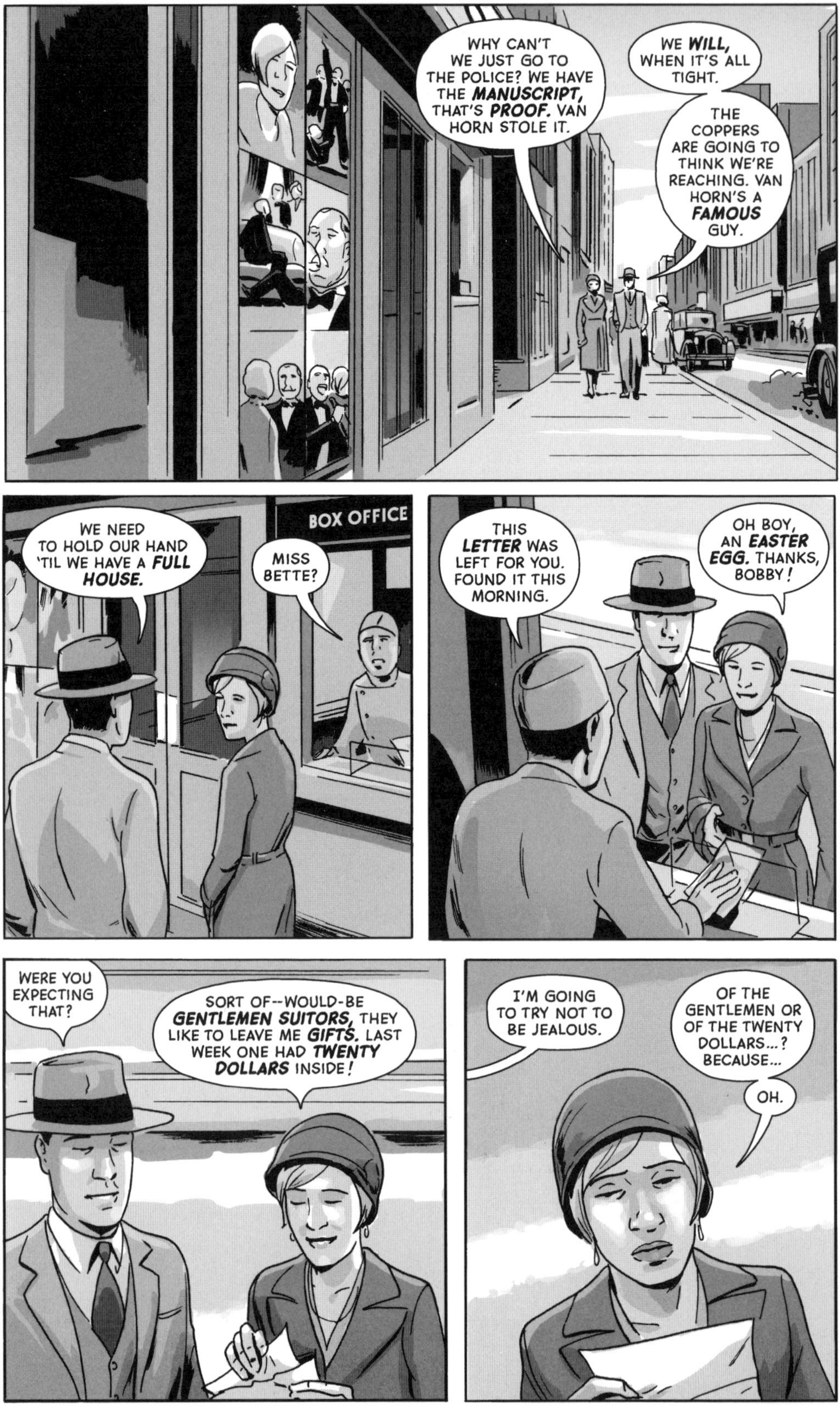
WHY CAN'T WE JUST GO TO THE POLICE? WE HAVE THE MANUSCRIPT, THAT'S PROOF. VAN HORN STOLE IT.
WE WILL, WHEN IT'S ALL TIGHT.
THE COPPERS ARE GOING TO THINK WE'RE REACHING. VAN HORN'S A FAMOUS GUY.
WE NEED TO HOLD OUR HAND 'TIL WE HAVE A FULL HOUSE.
BOX OFFICE
MISS BETTE?
THIS LETTER WAS LEFT FOR YOU. FOUND IT THIS MORNING.
OH BOY, AN EASTER EGG. THANKS, BOBBY!
WERE YOU EXPECTING THAT?
SORT OF--WOULD-BE GENTLEMEN SUITORS, THEY LIKE TO LEAVE ME GIFTS. LAST WEEK ONE HAD TWENTY DOLLARS INSIDE!
I'M GOING TO TRY NOT TO BE JEALOUS.
OF THE GENTLEMEN OR OF THE TWENTY DOLLARS...? BECAUSE...
OH.

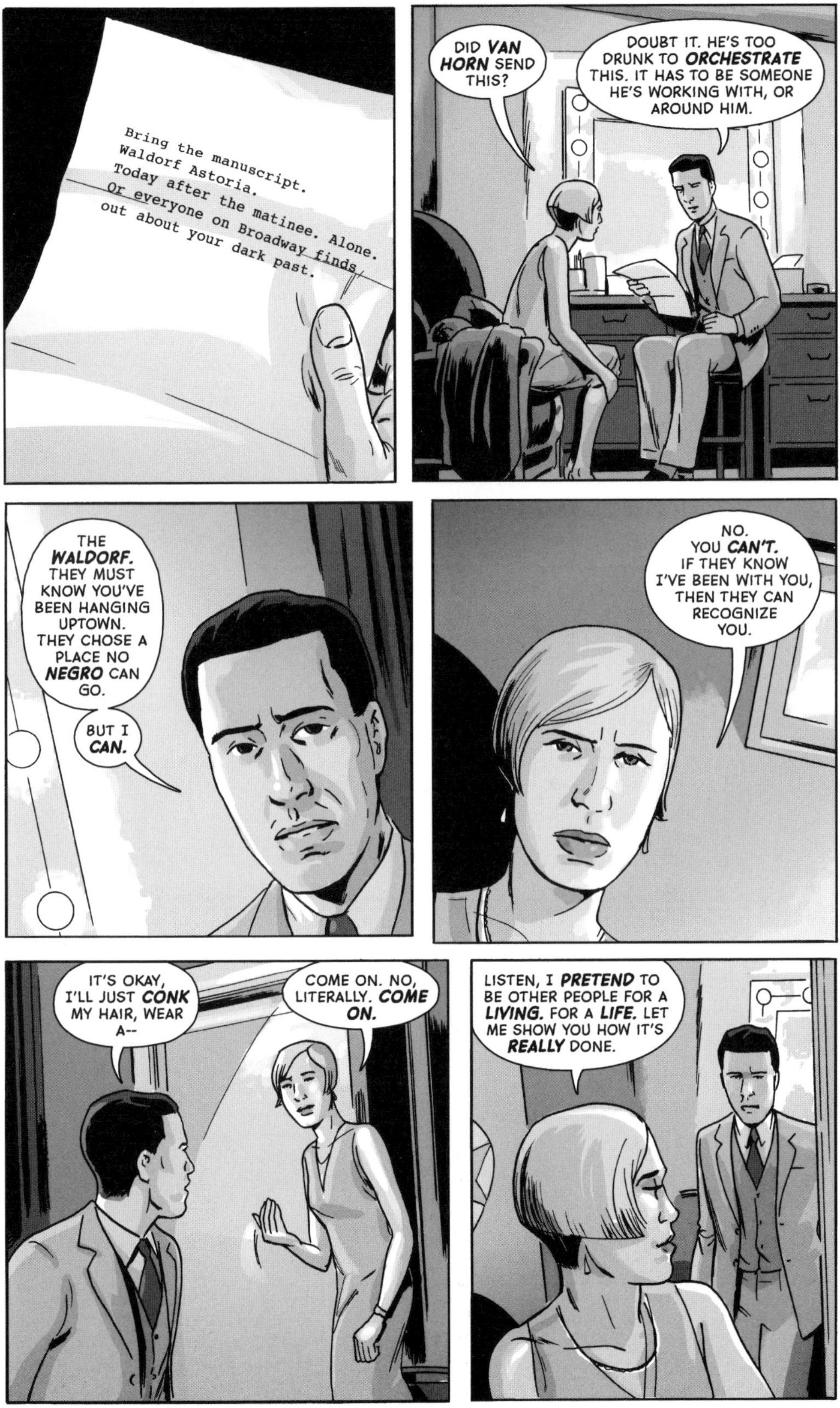
Bring the manuscript.
Waldorf Astoria.
Today after the matinee. Alone.
Or everyone on Broadway finds out about your dark past.
DID VAN HORN SEND THIS?
DOUBT IT. HE'S TOO DRUNK TO ORCHESTRATE THIS. IT HAS TO BE SOMEONE HE'S WORKING WITH, OR AROUND HIM.
THE WALDORF. THEY MUST KNOW YOU'VE BEEN HANGING UPTOWN. THEY CHOSE A PLACE NO NEGRO CAN GO.
BUT I CAN.
NO. YOU CAN'T. IF THEY KNOW I'VE BEEN WITH YOU, THEN THEY CAN RECOGNIZE YOU.
IT'S OKAY, I'LL JUST CONK MY HAIR, WEAR A--
COME ON. NO, LITERALLY. COME ON.
LISTEN, I PRETEND TO BE OTHER PEOPLE FOR A LIVING. FOR A LIFE. LET ME SHOW YOU HOW IT'S REALLY DONE.

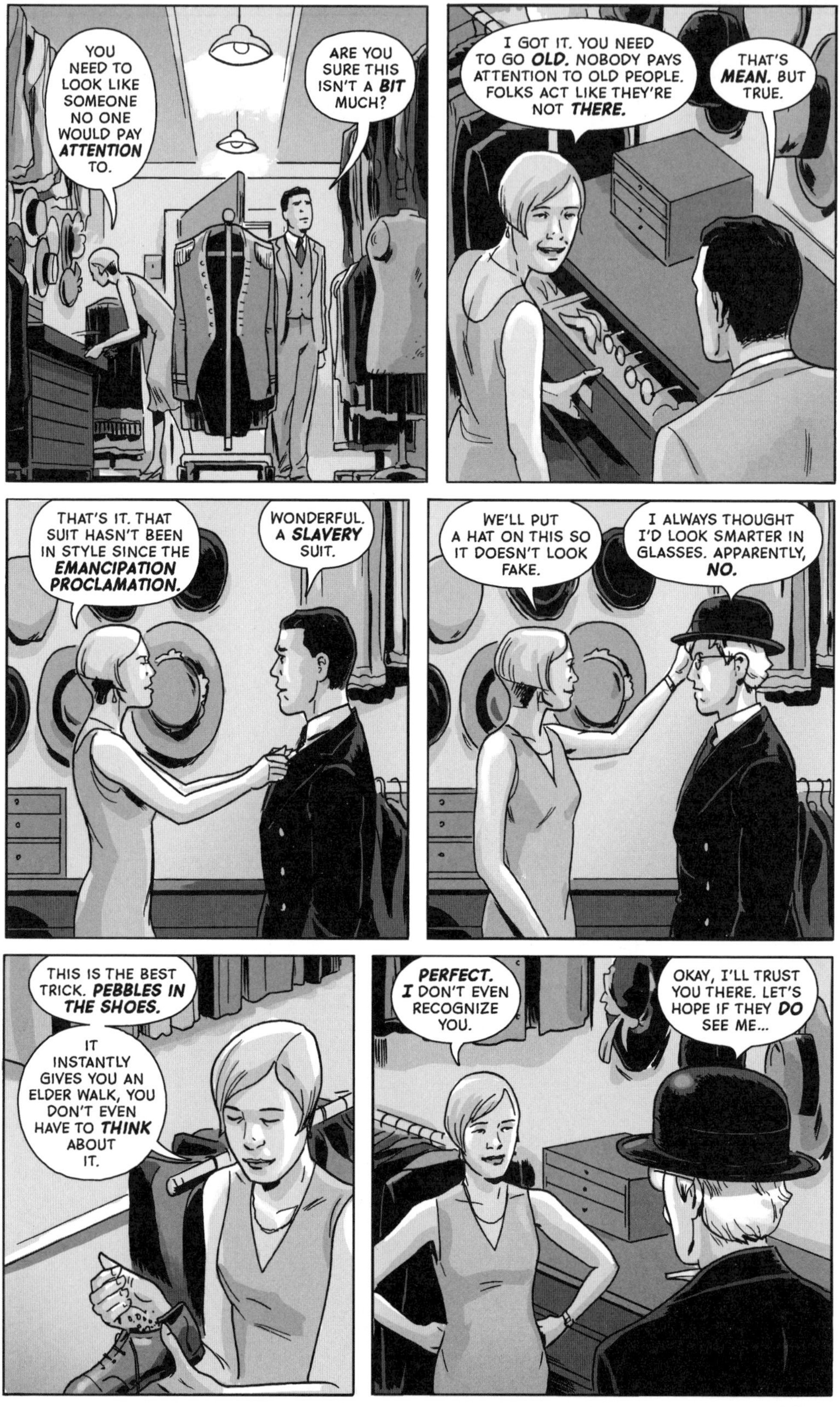
YOU NEED TO LOOK LIKE SOMEONE NO ONE WOULD PAY ATTENTION TO.
ARE YOU SURE THIS ISN'T A BIT MUCH?
I GOT IT. YOU NEED TO GO OLD. NOBODY PAYS ATTENTION TO OLD PEOPLE. FOLKS ACT LIKE THEY'RE NOT THERE.
THAT'S MEAN. BUT TRUE.
THAT'S IT. THAT SUIT HASN'T BEEN IN STYLE SINCE THE EMANCIPATION PROCLAMATION.
WONDERFUL. A SLAVERY SUIT.
WE'LL PUT A HAT ON THIS SO IT DOESN'T LOOK FAKE.
I ALWAYS THOUGHT I'D LOOK SMARTER IN GLASSES. APPARENTLY, NO.
THIS IS THE BEST TRICK. PEBBLES IN THE SHOES.
IT INSTANTLY GIVES YOU AN ELDER WALK, YOU DON'T EVEN HAVE TO THINK ABOUT IT.
PERFECT. I DON'T EVEN RECOGNIZE YOU.
OKAY, I'LL TRUST YOU THERE. LET'S HOPE IF THEY DO SEE ME...

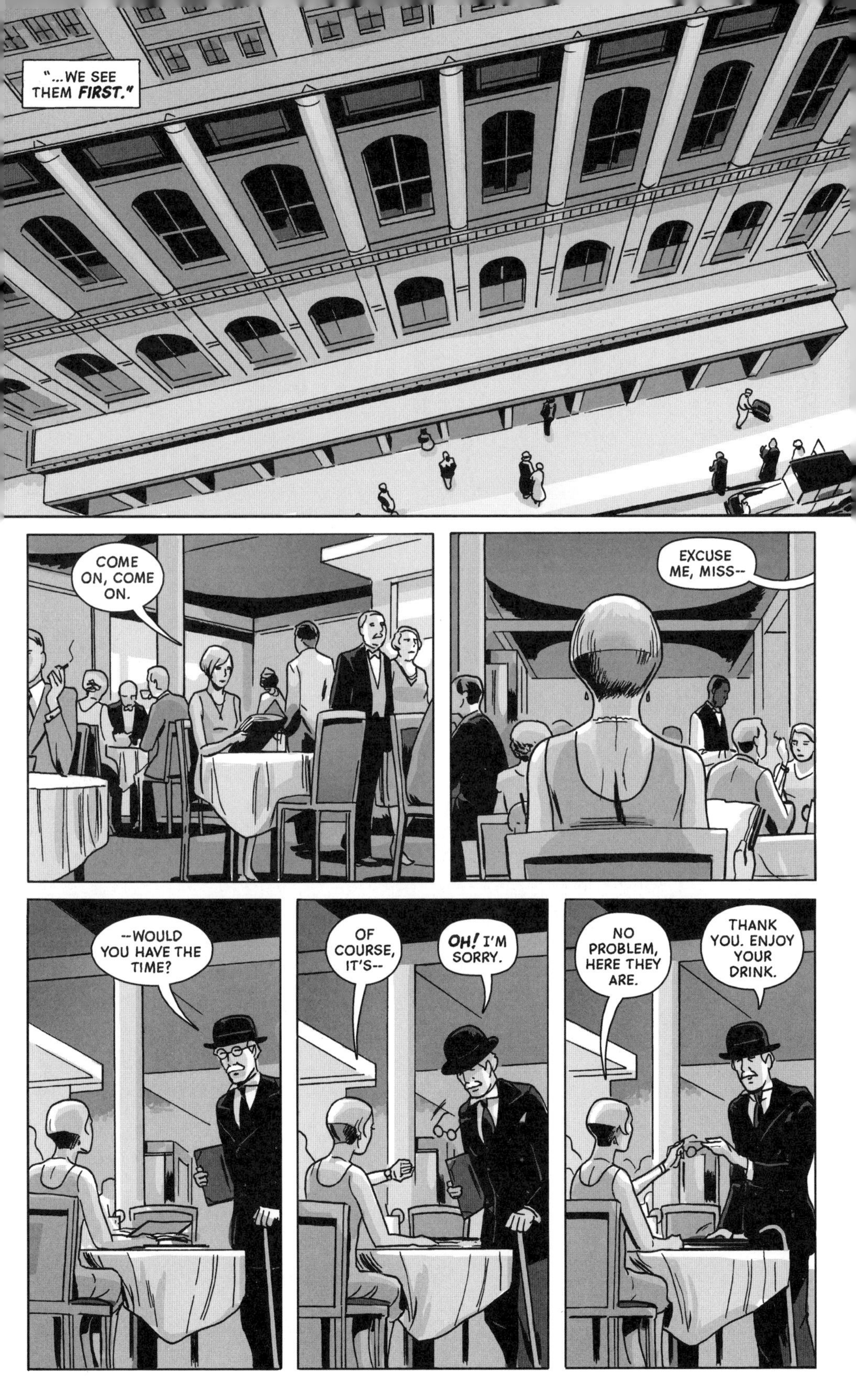
"...WE SEE THEM FIRST."
COME ON, COME ON.
EXCUSE ME, MISS--
--WOULD YOU HAVE THE TIME?
OF COURSE, IT'S--
OH! I'M SORRY.
NO PROBLEM, HERE THEY ARE.
THANK YOU. ENJOY YOUR DRINK.

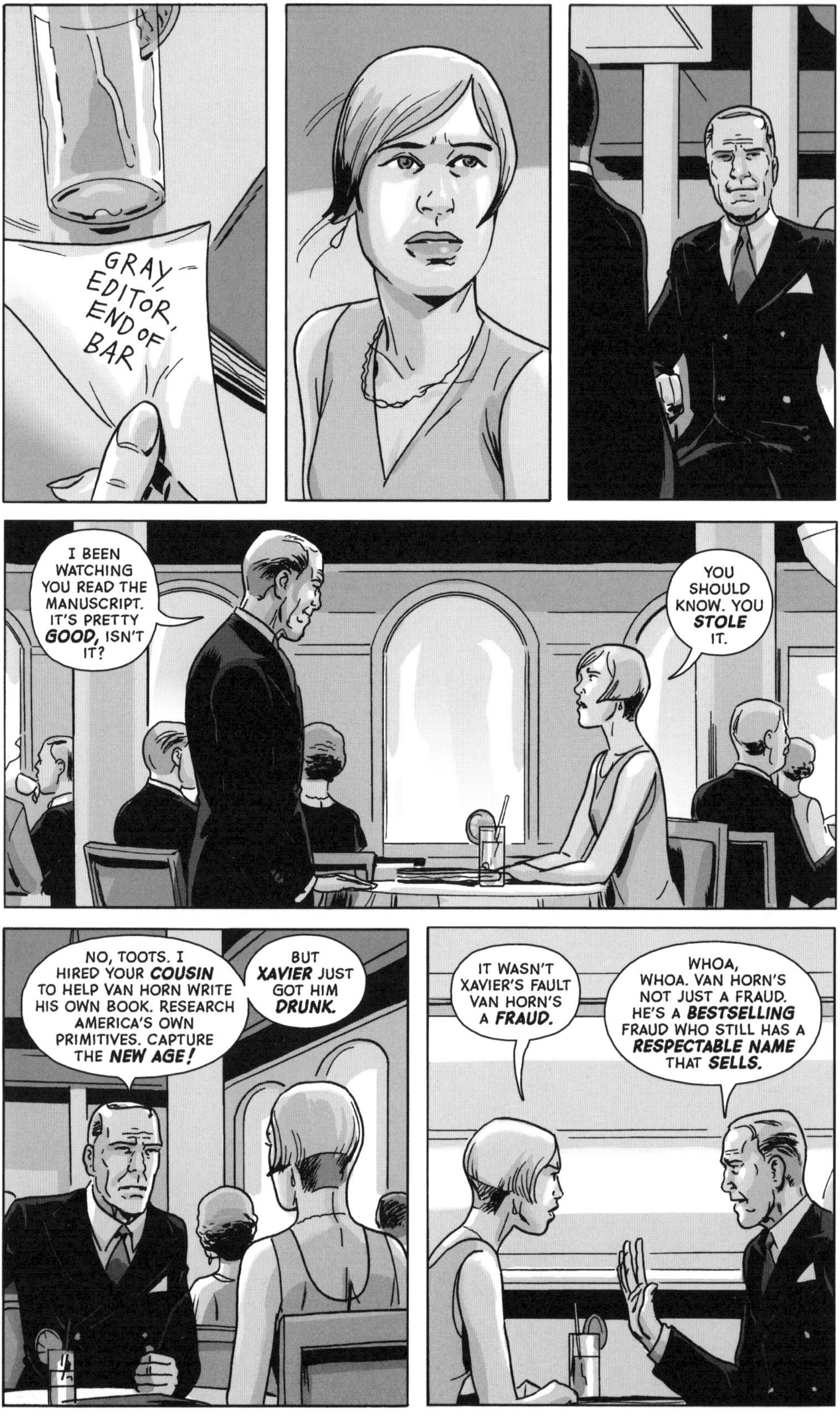
GRAY, EDITOR, END OF BAR
I BEEN WATCHING YOU READ THE MANUSCRIPT. IT'S PRETTY GOOD, ISN'T IT?
YOU SHOULD KNOW. YOU STOLE IT.
NO, TOOTS. I HIRED YOUR COUSIN TO HELP VAN HORN WRITE HIS OWN BOOK. RESEARCH AMERICA'S OWN PRIMITIVES. CAPTURE THE NEW AGE!
BUT XAVIER JUST GOT HIM DRUNK.
IT WASN'T XAVIER'S FAULT VAN HORN'S A FRAUD.
WHOA, WHOA. VAN HORN'S NOT JUST A FRAUD. HE'S A BESTSELLING FRAUD WHO STILL HAS A RESPECTABLE NAME THAT SELLS.

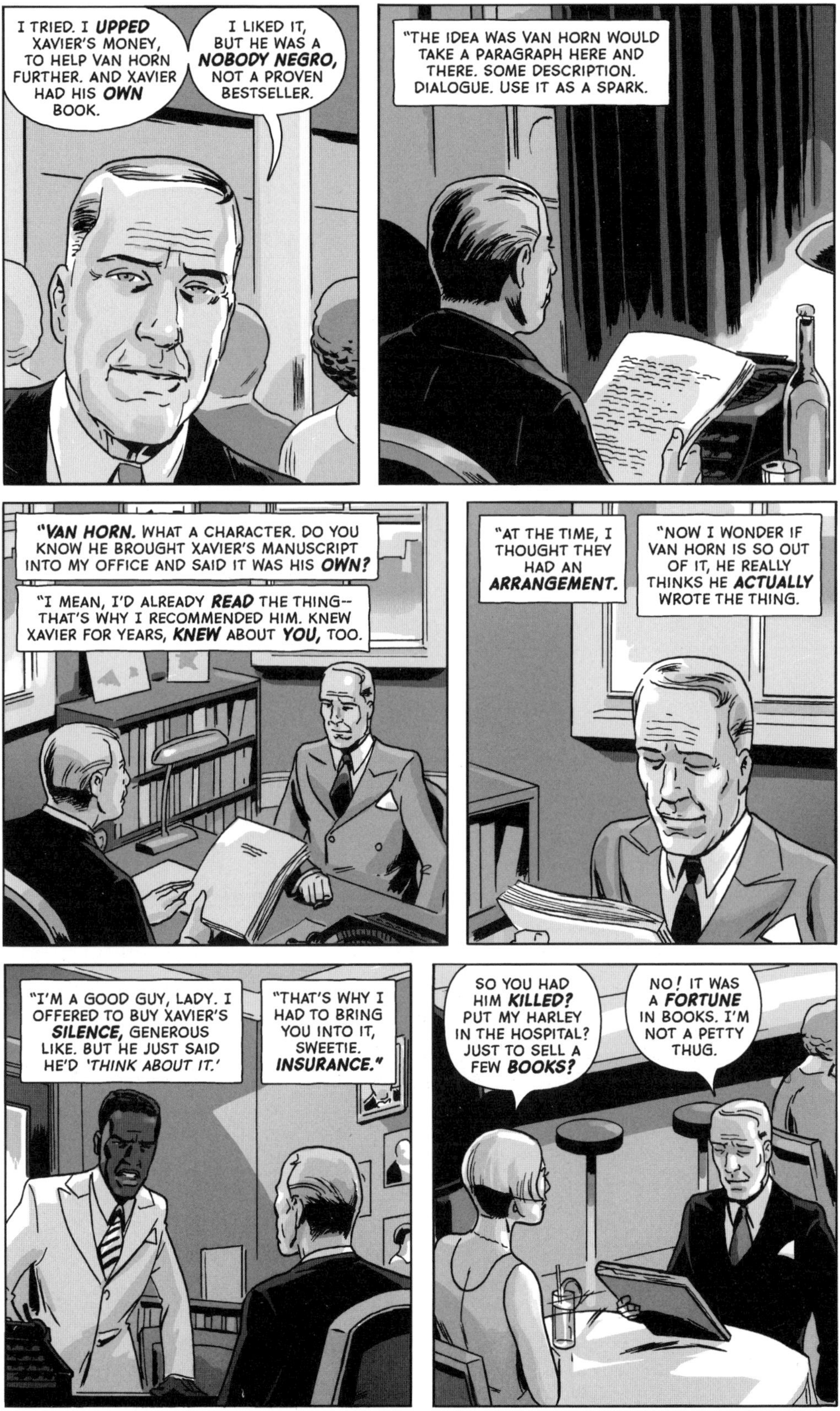
I TRIED. I UPPED XAVIER'S MONEY, TO HELP VAN HORN FURTHER. AND XAVIER HAD HIS OWN BOOK.
I LIKED IT, BUT HE WAS A NOBODY NEGRO, NOT A PROVEN BESTSELLER.
"THE IDEA WAS VAN HORN WOULD TAKE A PARAGRAPH HERE AND THERE. SOME DESCRIPTION. DIALOGUE. USE IT AS A SPARK.
"VAN HORN. WHAT A CHARACTER. DO YOU KNOW HE BROUGHT XAVIER'S MANUSCRIPT INTO MY OFFICE AND SAID IT WAS HIS OWN?
"I MEAN, I'D ALREADY READ THE THING--THAT'S WHY I RECOMMENDED HIM. KNEW XAVIER FOR YEARS, KNEW ABOUT YOU, TOO.
"AT THE TIME, I THOUGHT THEY HAD AN ARRANGEMENT.
"NOW I WONDER IF VAN HORN IS SO OUT OF IT, HE REALLY THINKS HE ACTUALLY WROTE THE THING.
"I'M A GOOD GUY, LADY. I OFFERED TO BUY XAVIER'S SILENCE, GENEROUS LIKE. BUT HE JUST SAID HE'D 'THINK ABOUT IT.'
"THAT'S WHY I HAD TO BRING YOU INTO IT, SWEETIE. INSURANCE."
SO YOU HAD HIM KILLED? PUT MY HARLEY IN THE HOSPITAL? JUST TO SELL A FEW BOOKS?
NO! IT WAS A FORTUNE IN BOOKS. I'M NOT A PETTY THUG.

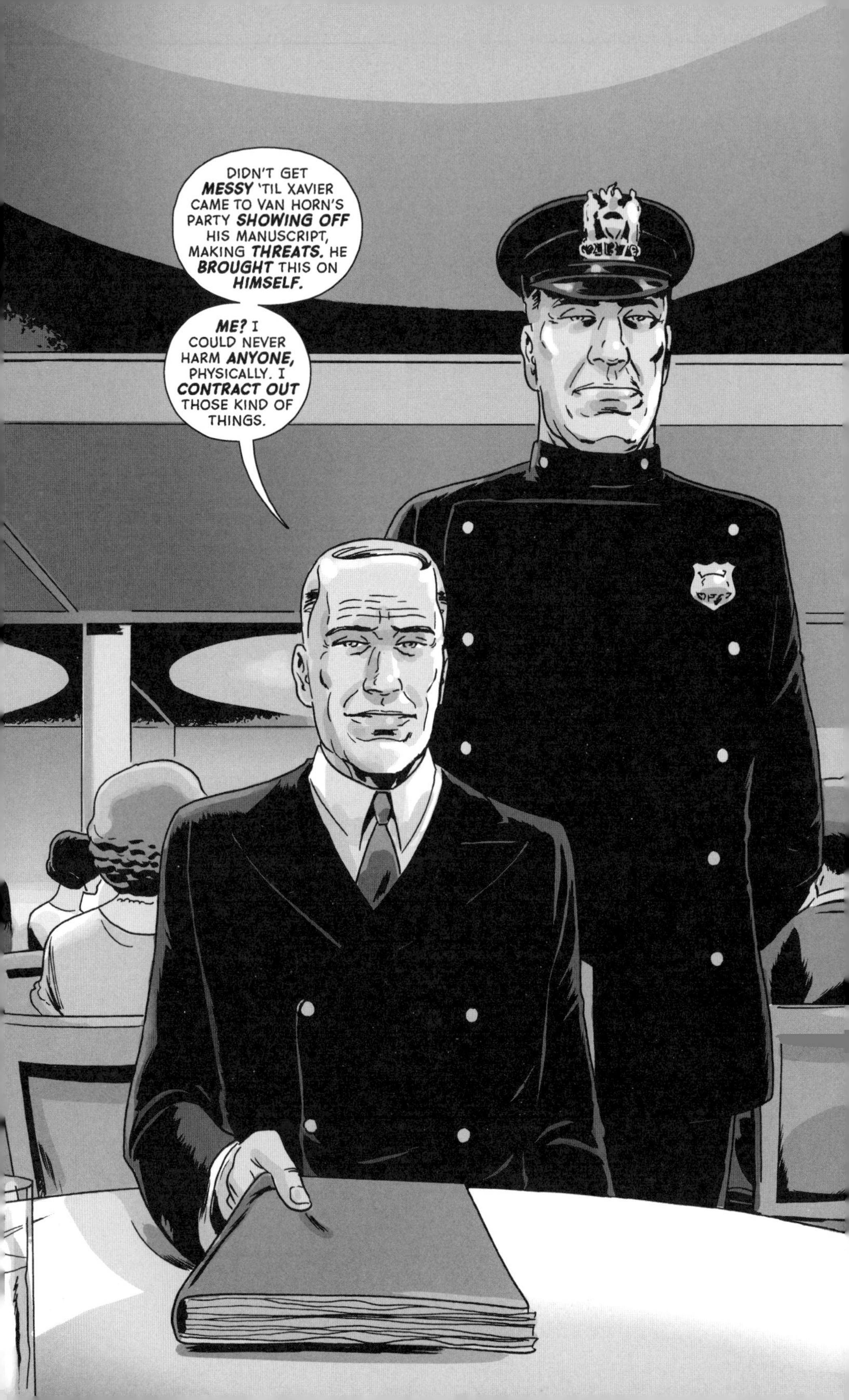
DIDN'T GET **MESSY** 'TIL XAVIER CAME TO VAN HORN'S PARTY **SHOWING OFF** HIS MANUSCRIPT, MAKING **THREATS.** HE **BROUGHT** THIS ON **HIMSELF.**
ME? I COULD NEVER HARM **ANYONE,** PHYSICALLY. I **CONTRACT OUT** THOSE KIND OF THINGS.

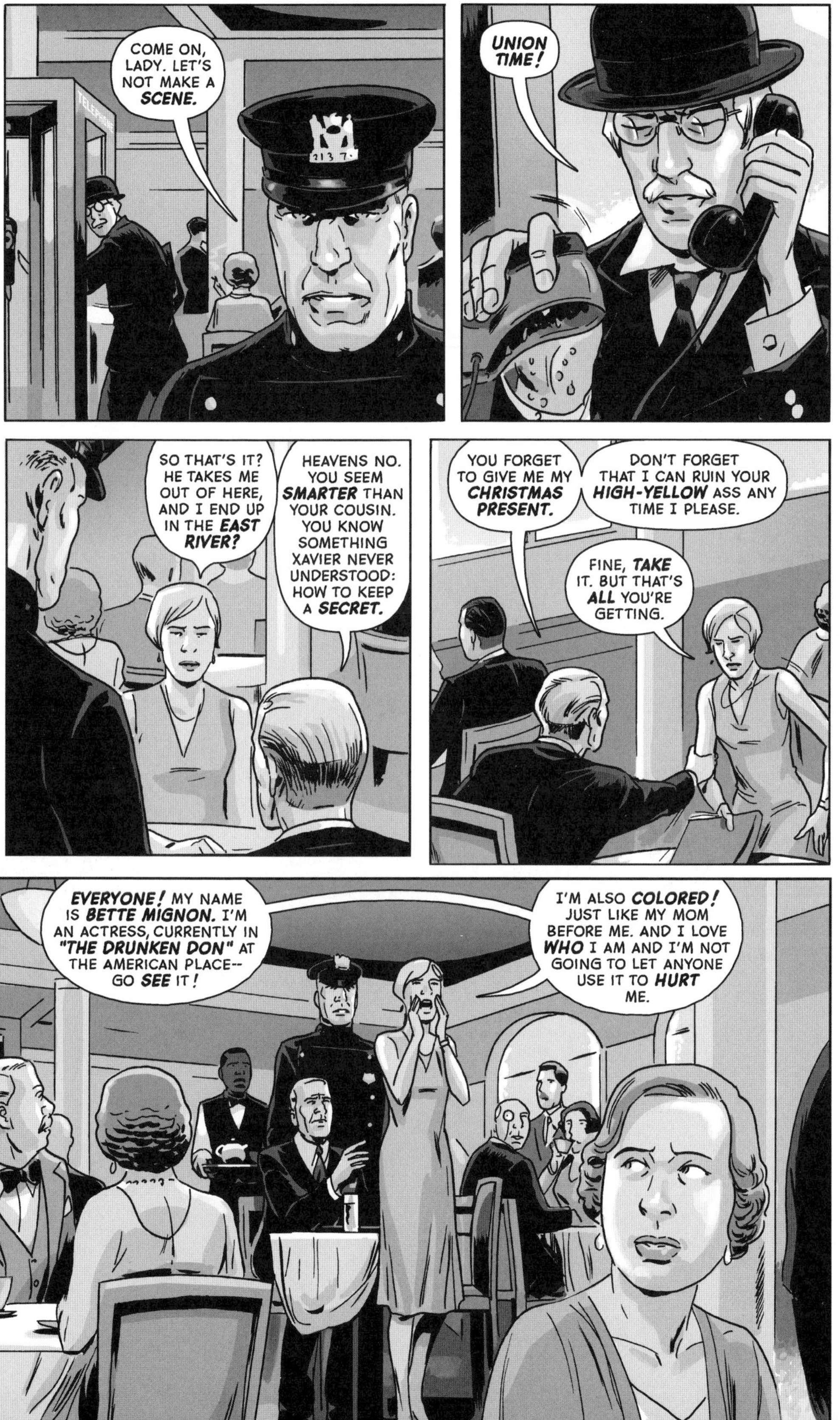
COME ON, LADY. LET'S NOT MAKE A SCENE.
UNION TIME!
SO THAT'S IT? HE TAKES ME OUT OF HERE, AND I END UP IN THE EAST RIVER?
HEAVENS NO. YOU SEEM SMARTER THAN YOUR COUSIN. YOU KNOW SOMETHING XAVIER NEVER UNDERSTOOD: HOW TO KEEP A SECRET.
YOU FORGET TO GIVE ME MY CHRISTMAS PRESENT.
DON'T FORGET THAT I CAN RUIN YOUR HIGH-YELLOW ASS ANY TIME I PLEASE.
FINE, TAKE IT. BUT THAT'S ALL YOU'RE GETTING.
EVERYONE! MY NAME IS BETTE MIGNON. I'M AN ACTRESS, CURRENTLY IN "THE DRUNKEN DON" AT THE AMERICAN PLACE-- GO SEE IT!
I'M ALSO COLORED! JUST LIKE MY MOM BEFORE ME. AND I LOVE WHO I AM AND I'M NOT GOING TO LET ANYONE USE IT TO HURT ME.

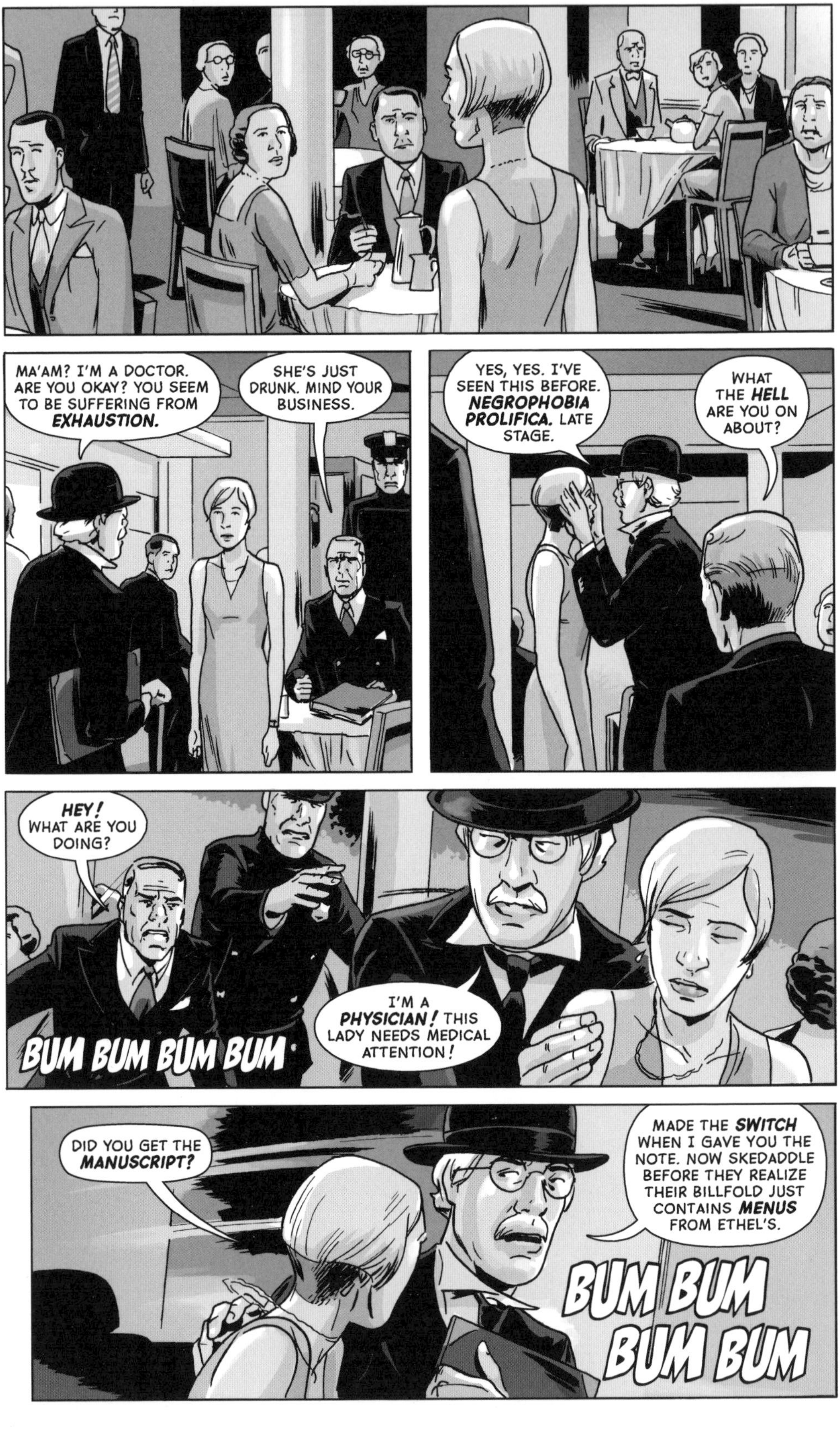
MA'AM? I'M A DOCTOR. ARE YOU OKAY? YOU SEEM TO BE SUFFERING FROM EXHAUSTION.
SHE'S JUST DRUNK. MIND YOUR BUSINESS.
YES, YES. I'VE SEEN THIS BEFORE. NEGROPHOBIA PROLIFICA. LATE STAGE.
WHAT THE HELL ARE YOU ON ABOUT?
HEY! WHAT ARE YOU DOING?
I'M A PHYSICIAN! THIS LADY NEEDS MEDICAL ATTENTION!
BUM BUM BUM BUM
DID YOU GET THE MANUSCRIPT?
MADE THE SWITCH WHEN I GAVE YOU THE NOTE. NOW SKEDADDLE BEFORE THEY REALIZE THEIR BILLFOLD JUST CONTAINS MENUS FROM ETHEL'S.
BUM BUM BUM BUM

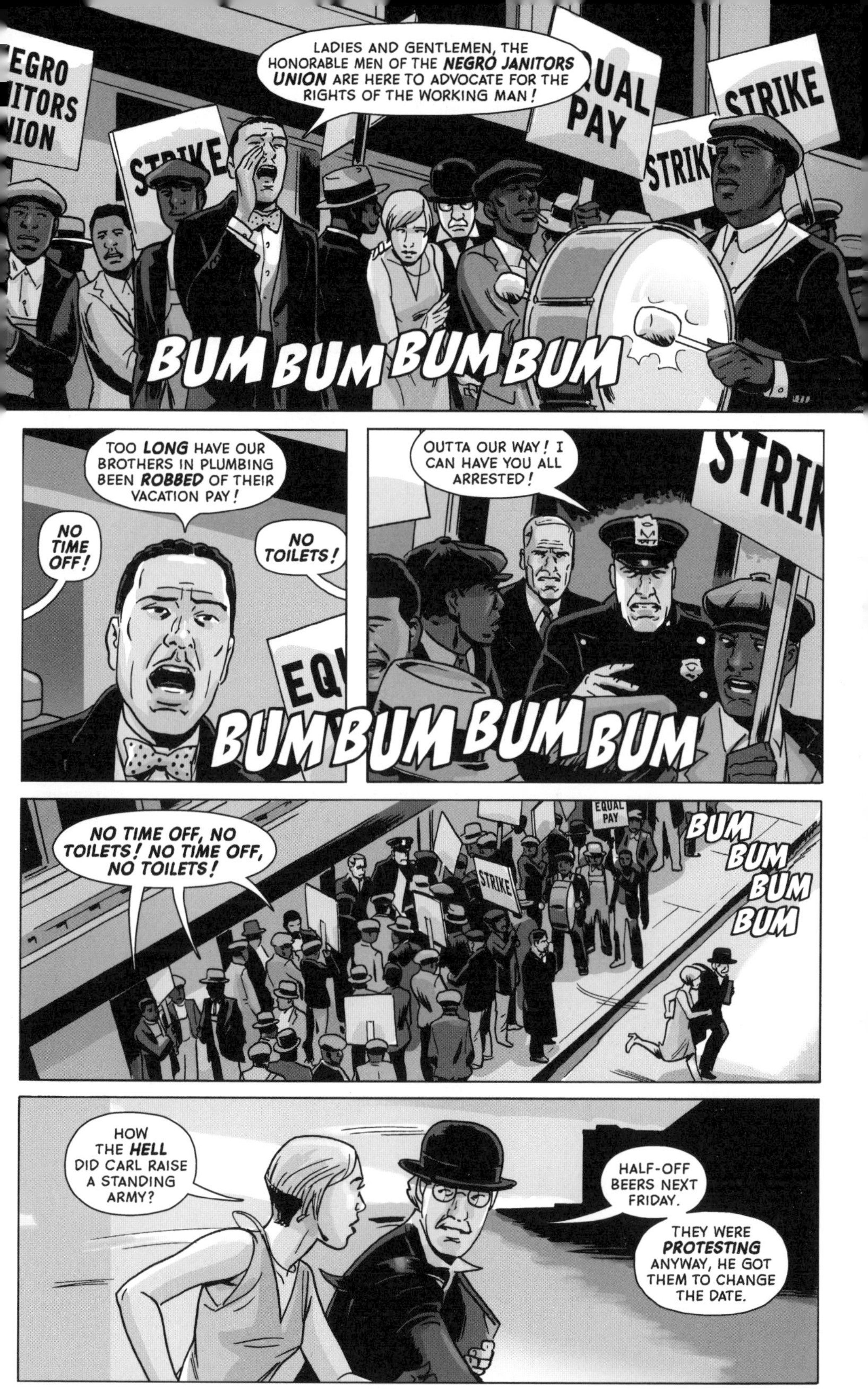
NEGRO JANITORS UNION
STRIKE
LADIES AND GENTLEMEN, THE HONORABLE MEN OF THE NEGRO JANITORS UNION ARE HERE TO ADVOCATE FOR THE RIGHTS OF THE WORKING MAN!
EQUAL PAY
STRIKE
STRIKE
BUM BUM BUM BUM
TOO LONG HAVE OUR BROTHERS IN PLUMBING BEEN ROBBED OF THEIR VACATION PAY!
NO TIME OFF!
NO TOILETS!
OUTTA OUR WAY! I CAN HAVE YOU ALL ARRESTED!
BUM BUM BUM BUM
NO TIME OFF, NO TOILETS! NO TIME OFF, NO TOILETS!
EQUAL PAY
STRIKE
BUM BUM BUM BUM
HOW THE HELL DID CARL RAISE A STANDING ARMY?
HALF-OFF BEERS NEXT FRIDAY.
THEY WERE PROTESTING ANYWAY, HE GOT THEM TO CHANGE THE DATE.

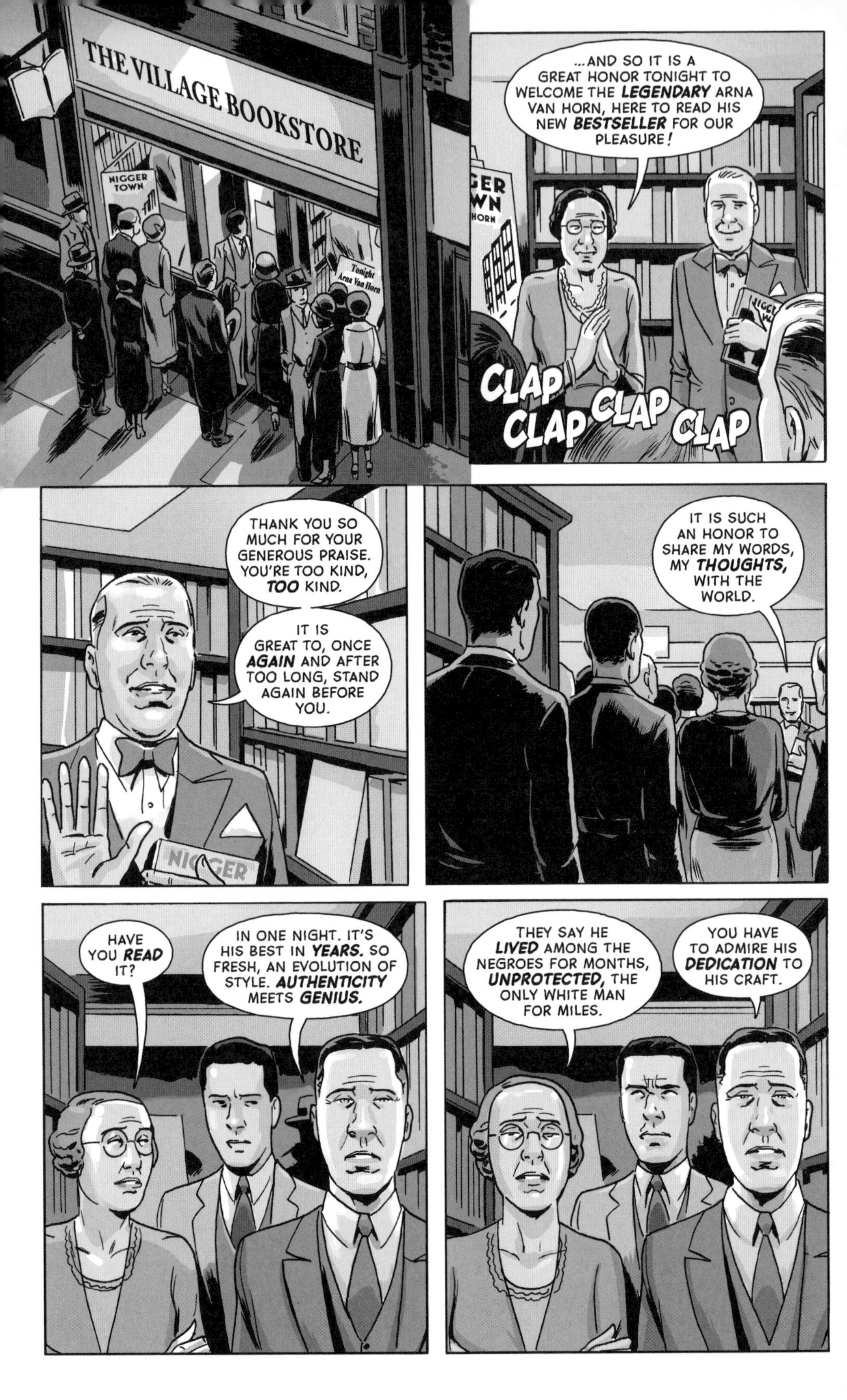
THE VILLAGE BOOKSTORE
NIGGER TOWN
Tonight Arna Van Horn
...AND SO IT IS A GREAT HONOR TONIGHT TO WELCOME THE LEGENDARY ARNA VAN HORN, HERE TO READ HIS NEW BESTSELLER FOR OUR PLEASURE!
CLAP CLAP CLAP CLAP
THANK YOU SO MUCH FOR YOUR GENEROUS PRAISE. YOU'RE TOO KIND, TOO KIND.
IT IS GREAT TO, ONCE AGAIN AND AFTER TOO LONG, STAND AGAIN BEFORE YOU.
IT IS SUCH AN HONOR TO SHARE MY WORDS, MY THOUGHTS, WITH THE WORLD.
HAVE YOU READ IT?
IN ONE NIGHT. IT'S HIS BEST IN YEARS. SO FRESH, AN EVOLUTION OF STYLE. AUTHENTICITY MEETS GENIUS.
THEY SAY HE LIVED AMONG THE NEGROES FOR MONTHS, UNPROTECTED, THE ONLY WHITE MAN FOR MILES.
YOU HAVE TO ADMIRE HIS DEDICATION TO HIS CRAFT.

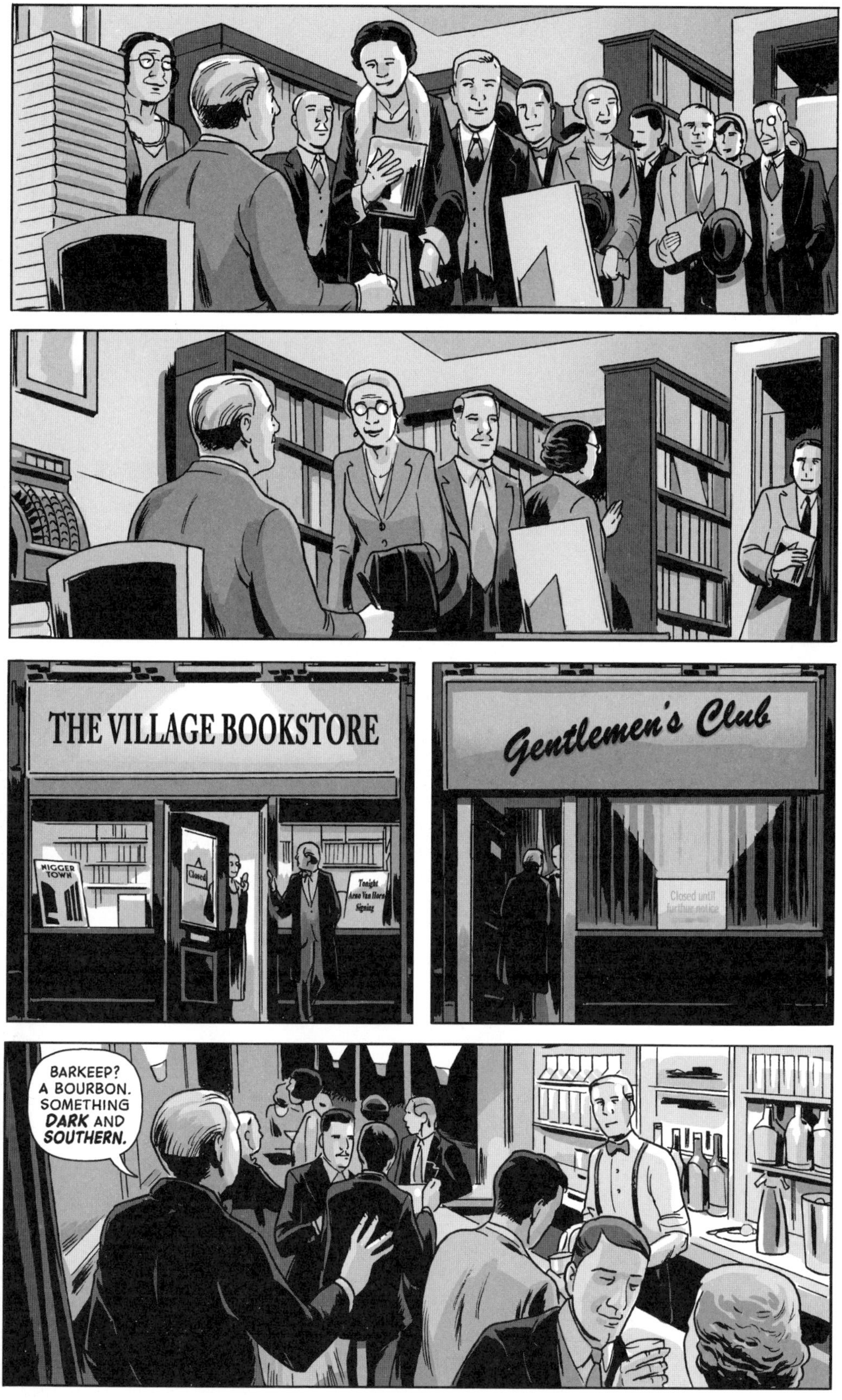
THE VILLAGE BOOKSTORE
NIGGER TOWN
Closed
Tonight Arno Van Horn Signing
Gentlemen's Club
Closed until furthur notice
BARKEEP? A BOURBON. SOMETHING **DARK** AND **SOUTHERN.**

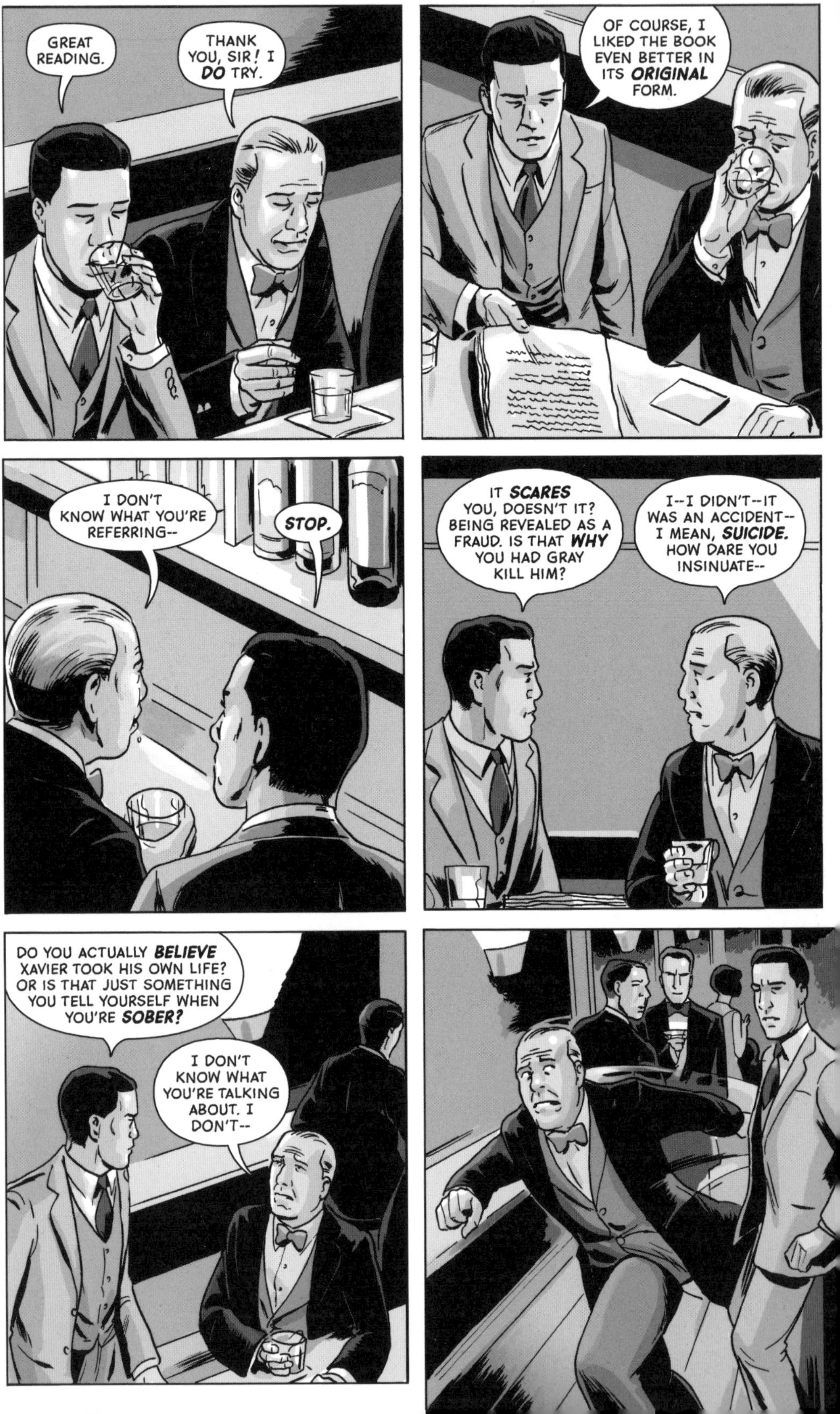
GREAT READING.
THANK YOU, SIR! I DO TRY.
OF COURSE, I LIKED THE BOOK EVEN BETTER IN ITS ORIGINAL FORM.
I DON'T KNOW WHAT YOU'RE REFERRING--
STOP.
IT SCARES YOU, DOESN'T IT? BEING REVEALED AS A FRAUD. IS THAT WHY YOU HAD GRAY KILL HIM?
I--I DIDN'T--IT WAS AN ACCIDENT-- I MEAN, SUICIDE. HOW DARE YOU INSINUATE--
DO YOU ACTUALLY BELIEVE XAVIER TOOK HIS OWN LIFE? OR IS THAT JUST SOMETHING YOU TELL YOURSELF WHEN YOU'RE SOBER?
I DON'T KNOW WHAT YOU'RE TALKING ABOUT. I DON'T--

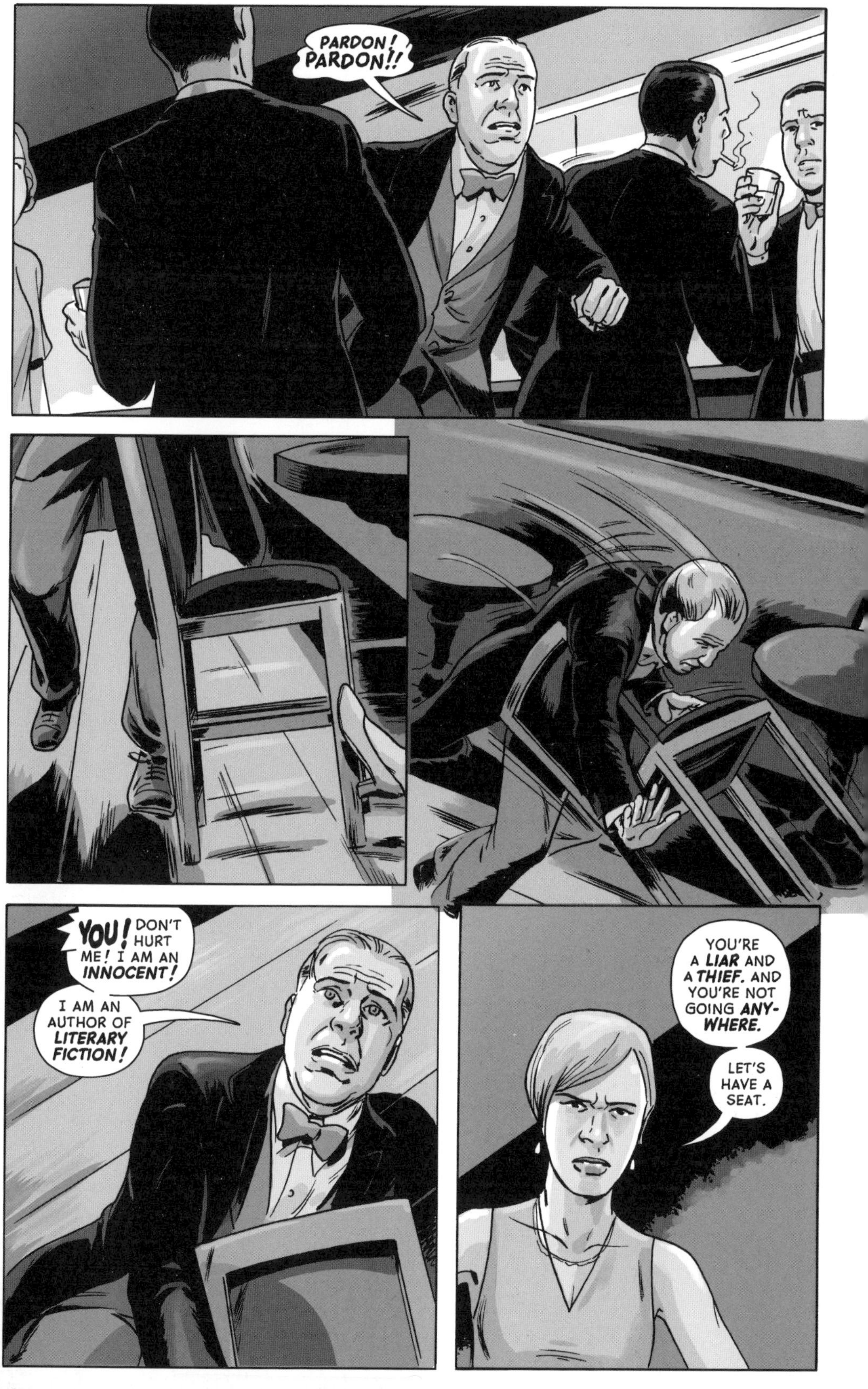
PARDON! PARDON!!
YOU! DON'T HURT ME! I AM AN INNOCENT!
I AM AN AUTHOR OF LITERARY FICTION!
YOU'RE A LIAR AND A THIEF. AND YOU'RE NOT GOING ANYWHERE.
LET'S HAVE A SEAT.

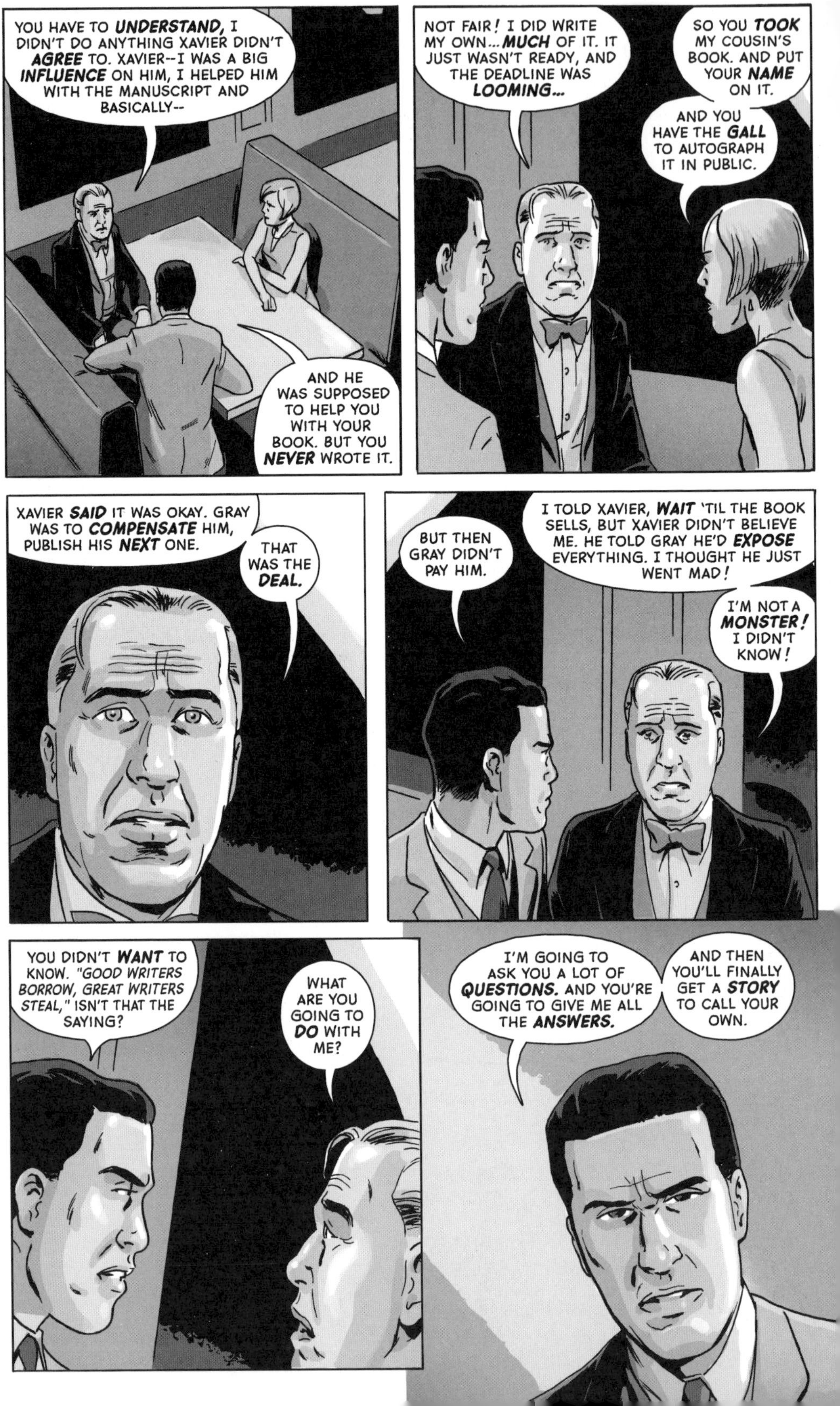

YOU HAVE TO **UNDERSTAND,** I DIDN'T DO ANYTHING XAVIER DIDN'T **AGREE** TO. XAVIER--I WAS A BIG **INFLUENCE** ON HIM, I HELPED HIM WITH THE MANUSCRIPT AND BASICALLY--
AND HE WAS SUPPOSED TO HELP YOU WITH YOUR BOOK. BUT YOU **NEVER** WROTE IT.
NOT FAIR! I DID WRITE MY OWN... **MUCH** OF IT. IT JUST WASN'T READY, AND THE DEADLINE WAS **LOOMING...**
SO YOU **TOOK** MY COUSIN'S BOOK. AND PUT YOUR **NAME** ON IT.
AND YOU HAVE THE **GALL** TO AUTOGRAPH IT IN PUBLIC.
XAVIER **SAID** IT WAS OKAY. GRAY WAS TO **COMPENSATE** HIM, PUBLISH HIS **NEXT** ONE.
THAT WAS THE **DEAL.**
BUT THEN GRAY DIDN'T PAY HIM.
I TOLD XAVIER, **WAIT** 'TIL THE BOOK SELLS, BUT XAVIER DIDN'T BELIEVE ME. HE TOLD GRAY HE'D **EXPOSE** EVERYTHING. I THOUGHT HE JUST WENT MAD!
I'M NOT A **MONSTER!** I DIDN'T KNOW!
YOU DIDN'T **WANT** TO KNOW. *"GOOD WRITERS BORROW, GREAT WRITERS STEAL,"* ISN'T THAT THE SAYING?
WHAT ARE YOU GOING TO **DO** WITH ME?
I'M GOING TO ASK YOU A LOT OF **QUESTIONS.** AND YOU'RE GOING TO GIVE ME ALL THE **ANSWERS.**
AND THEN YOU'LL FINALLY GET A **STORY** TO CALL YOUR OWN.

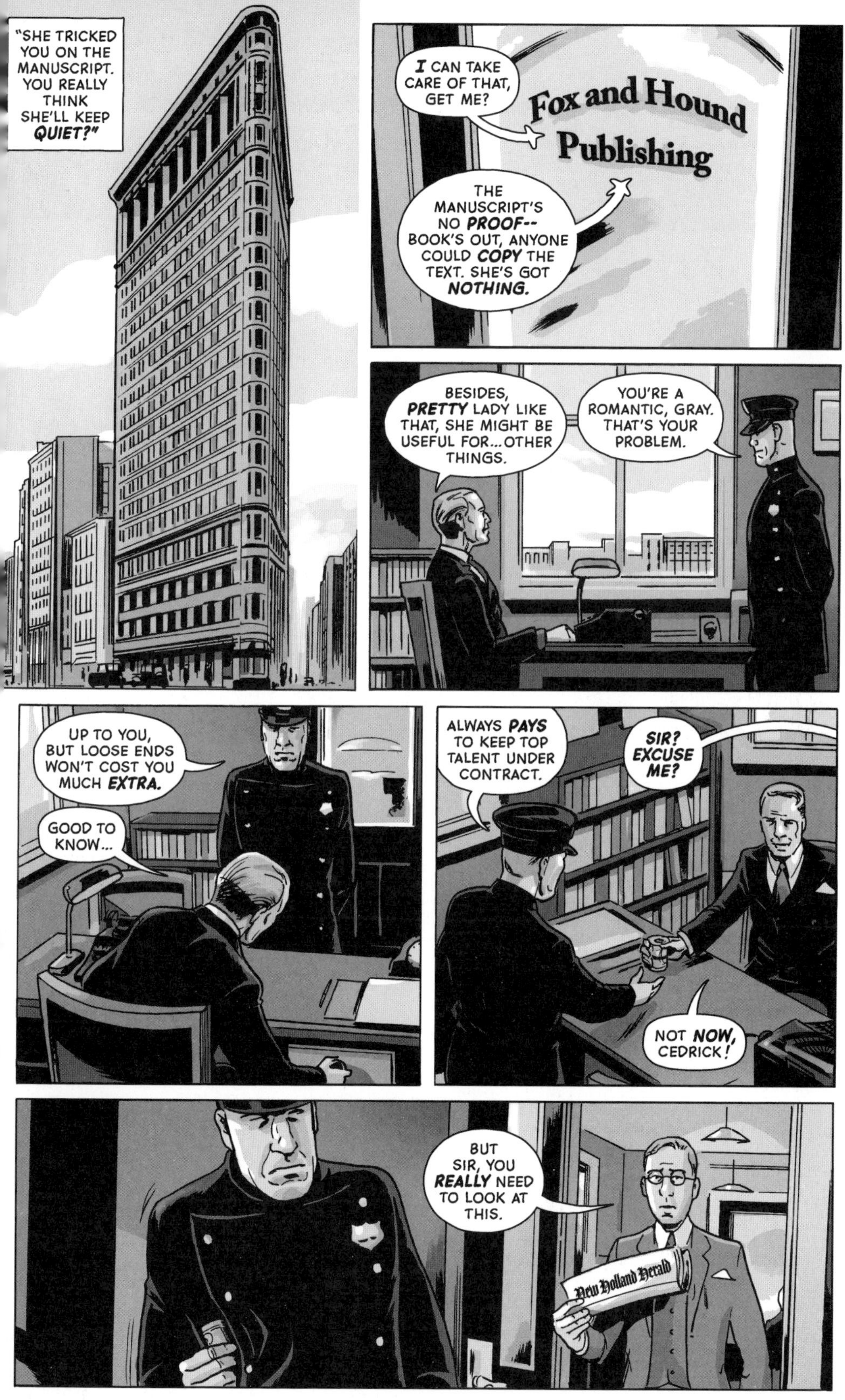
"SHE TRICKED YOU ON THE MANUSCRIPT. YOU REALLY THINK SHE'LL KEEP QUIET?"
I CAN TAKE CARE OF THAT, GET ME?
Fox and Hound Publishing
THE MANUSCRIPT'S NO PROOF-- BOOK'S OUT, ANYONE COULD COPY THE TEXT. SHE'S GOT NOTHING.
BESIDES, PRETTY LADY LIKE THAT, SHE MIGHT BE USEFUL FOR...OTHER THINGS.
YOU'RE A ROMANTIC, GRAY. THAT'S YOUR PROBLEM.
UP TO YOU, BUT LOOSE ENDS WON'T COST YOU MUCH EXTRA.
GOOD TO KNOW...
ALWAYS PAYS TO KEEP TOP TALENT UNDER CONTRACT.
SIR? EXCUSE ME?
NOT NOW, CEDRICK!
BUT SIR, YOU REALLY NEED TO LOOK AT THIS.
New Holland Herald

...THAT **GODDAMN** GHOST-FACED NI--

New Holland Herald
MURDER BY THE BOOK

Christopher Gray, Publisher

Arna Van Horn "I'm not a monster." By Zane Pinchback

Harlem, NY, Celebrated

In a stunning turn of events, the death of Xavier Mignon at the book party of noted author Ama Van Horn, once reported as a suicide, has been revealed to be a murder resulting from a blackmail scheme bringing the authorship of the novel into question

Following an undercover investigation by one of our own journalists, it...

WHAT DOES IT SAY?! AM I IN THERE?

IT'S-- IT'S JUST A **DARKIE RAG**. IT AIN'T THE **TIMES!** NO RESPECTABLE PEOPLE WILL BELIEVE THIS.

I GOTTA GET OUT OF HERE.

NO. YOU'RE NOT **RUNNING** ANY-WHERE. THESE PEOPLE ARE KNOWN LIARS AND CRIMINALS.

WE ARE THE **ESTABLISHMENT. WE** MAKE THE RULES.

KEEP IT TOGETHER! WE **DON'T** BACK DOWN, WE GO **HARD!**

THIS IS **SLANDER!** VAN HORN IS WEAK, A DRUNK, A PROFESSIONAL FABULIST-- **EVERY-BODY** KNOWS THAT!

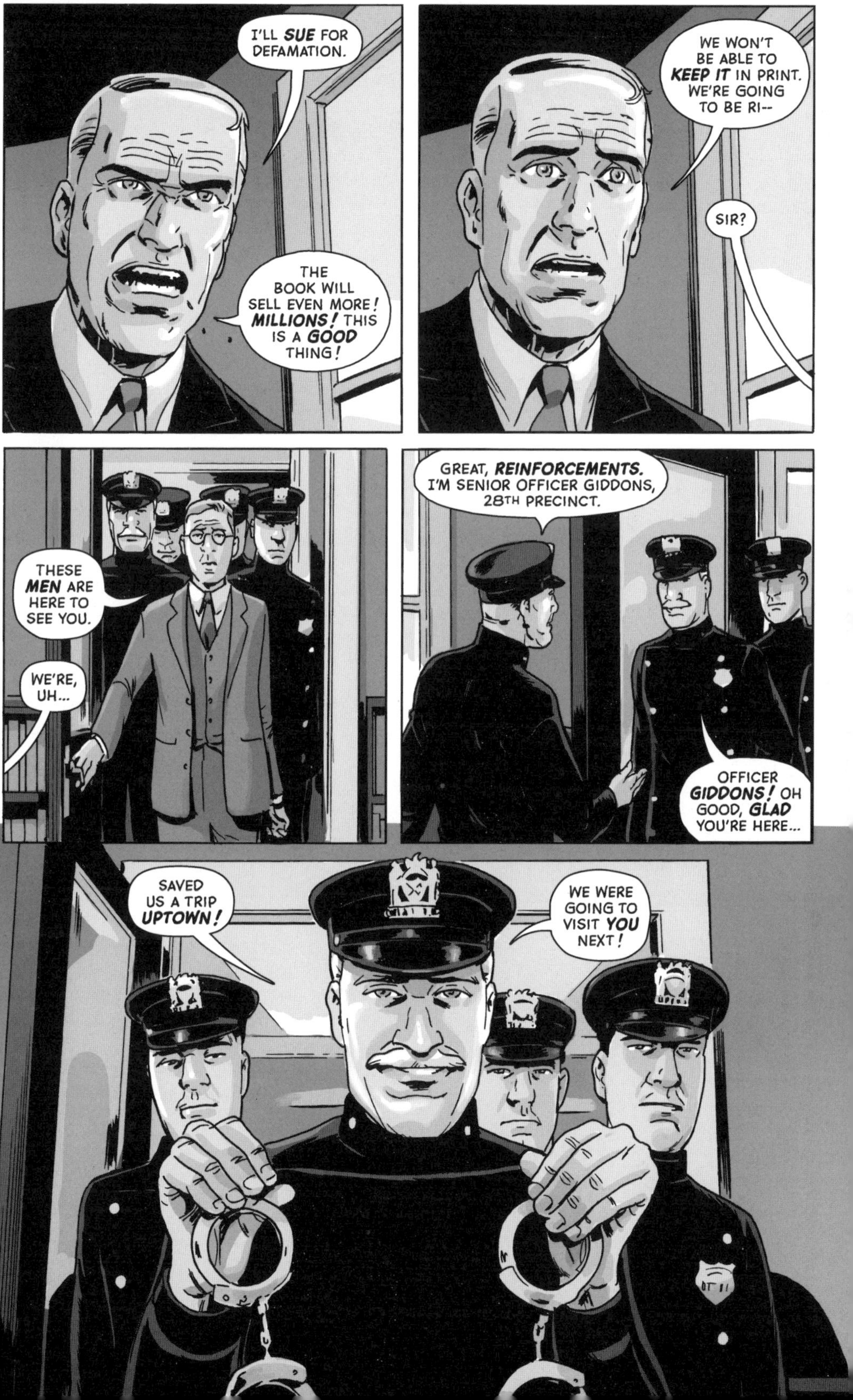
I'LL SUE FOR DEFAMATION.
THE BOOK WILL SELL EVEN MORE! MILLIONS! THIS IS A GOOD THING!
WE WON'T BE ABLE TO KEEP IT IN PRINT. WE'RE GOING TO BE RI--
SIR?
THESE MEN ARE HERE TO SEE YOU.
WE'RE, UH...
GREAT, REINFORCEMENTS. I'M SENIOR OFFICER GIDDONS, 28TH PRECINCT.
OFFICER GIDDONS! OH GOOD, GLAD YOU'RE HERE...
SAVED US A TRIP UPTOWN!
WE WERE GOING TO VISIT YOU NEXT!

THREE
MONTHS
LATER...

HURTIG & SEAMON'S
NEW BURLESQUE THEATRE

TONIGHT! BETTE MIGNON

New Holland Herald

TAX FRAUD, EMBEZZLEMENT,
MURDER

Disgraced publisher, Christopher Gray, found guilty of murder, tax fraud and embezzlement at Manhattan's court yester...

New Holland Herald

TAX FRAUD, EMBEZZLEMENT,
MURDER

HURTIG & SEAMON'S
NEW BURLESQUE THEATRE
present
BETTE MIGNON:
UP FROM BROADWAY!

From
Tabloids to
Top Billing!
All-Colored
Review/
Variety Show

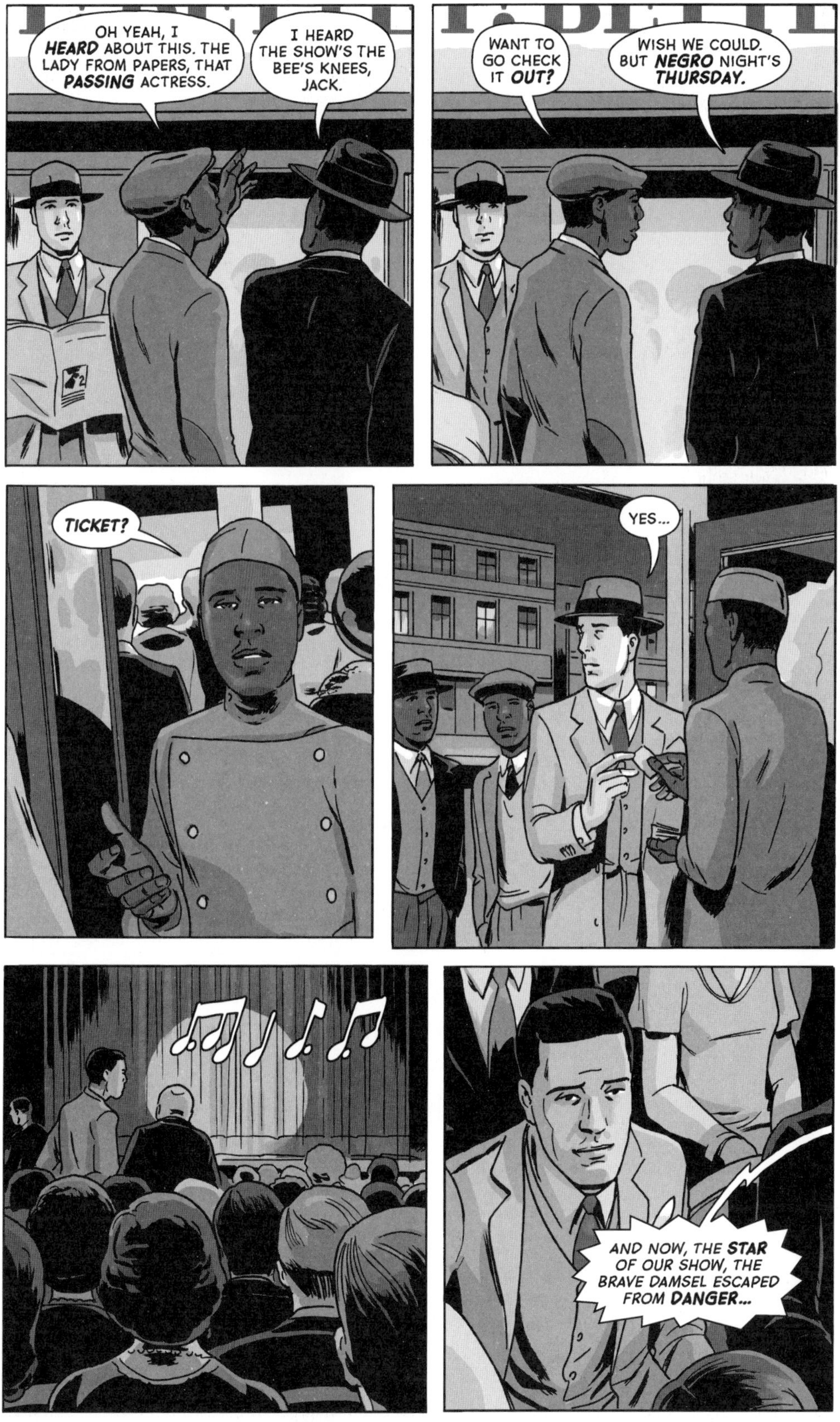
OH YEAH, I HEARD ABOUT THIS. THE LADY FROM PAPERS, THAT PASSING ACTRESS.
I HEARD THE SHOW'S THE BEE'S KNEES, JACK.
WANT TO GO CHECK IT OUT?
WISH WE COULD. BUT NEGRO NIGHT'S THURSDAY.
TICKET?
YES...
AND NOW, THE STAR OF OUR SHOW, THE BRAVE DAMSEL ESCAPED FROM DANGER...

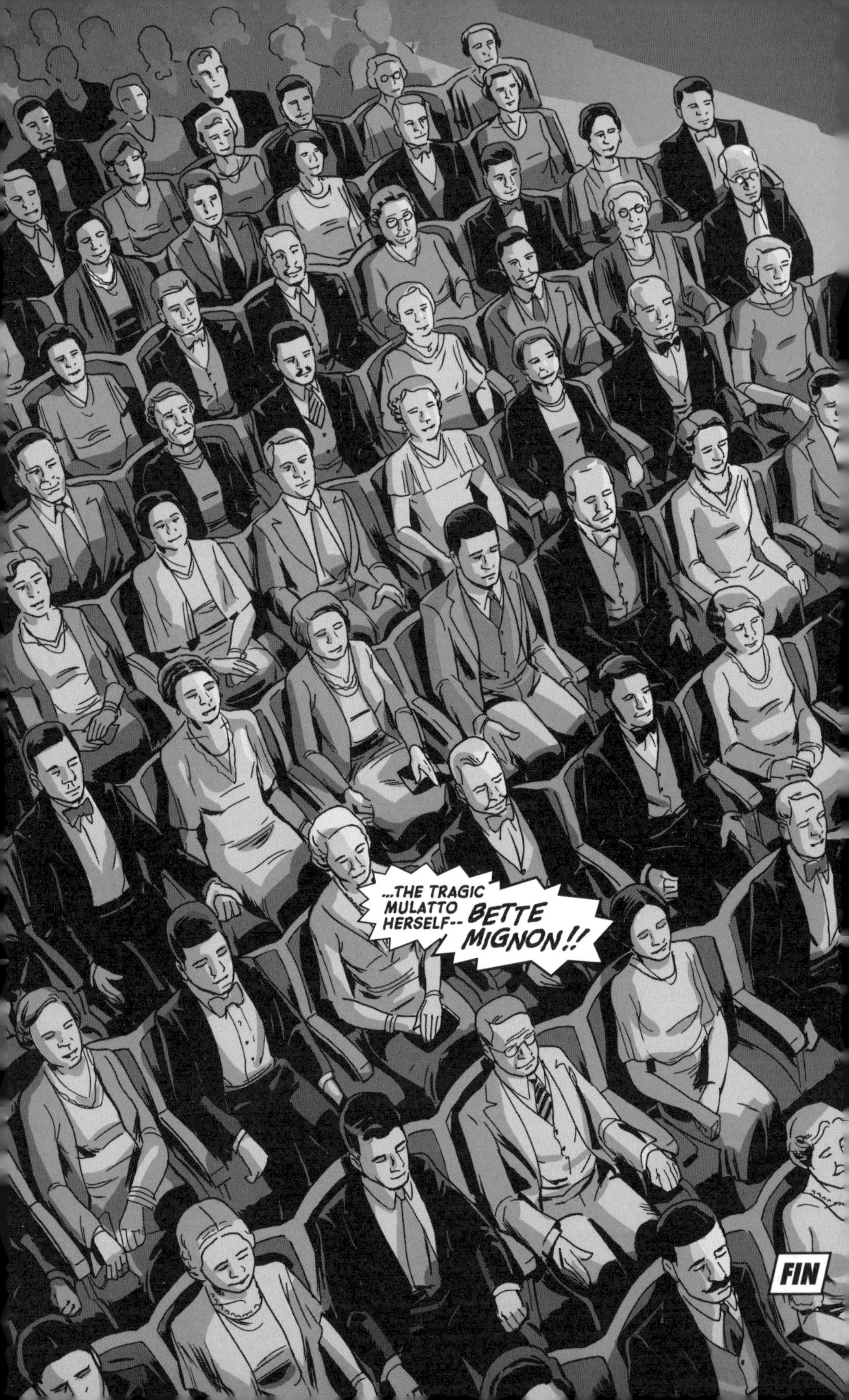
...THE TRAGIC MULATTO HERSELF-- BETTE MIGNON!!
FIN

When we did the first graphic novel for *Incognegro*,

it was the easiest major project I'd worked on in my life. The script sort of erupted in just a month, the editing was light (particularly for a writer prone to typos like myself), every pencil panel Warren Pleece did was on point (I literally made one change: reducing the number of horses on a buggy). The whole project took about eight months of work, start to finish, and that totally amazes me now. I mean, it once took me *eight years* to write one novel, so eight months seems absurd. But I like to think the process was so smooth because it was the right story, at the right time, done by the right people, editors Jon Vankin and Karen Berger included.

And luckily, the world seemed to agree. The first *Incognegro* graphic novel became my first book to be reviewed in *The New York Times*, and in the time since it's been adapted by countless high schools and colleges and been seen on the shelves of bookstores around the world.

And then it went out of print. The teachers of those classes who used it kept emailing me over the years for new copies, like they were a recipe I refused to cook up anymore. So hey, guys: sorry for the wait, here you go. Not only is the original graphic novel in print, but here we are, back with a brand-new storyline: *Incognegro: Renaissance*.

You can't understand *Incognegro*'s lead, Zane Pinchback, without looking at the Harlem Renaissance. His DNA shows his connection to the great writers of that time, people like Nella Larson, Langston Hughes, and particularly Wallace Thurman. *Incognegro: Renaissance*'s instigating event, the death of a failed writer drowning in a bathtub at a party and leaving only a ruined manuscript behind, was inspired by a scene in one of my favorite novels, Wallace Thurman's *Infants of the Spring*. It's actually sadly funny in the novel, but I always wanted vengeance for that poor guy. So here we are.

When *Incognegro: A Graphic Mystery* first appeared in 2008, Warren Pleece and I were younger and also, like, waaay hotter. Despite our physical decay over the last decade, I like to think we've grown as artists. Zane Pinchback has certainly aged well—and I write that with no small amount of sadness. Unfortunately, the voices of xenophobia in general and white supremacy in particular seem, as I write this in 2018, to have become louder since the first book was published. Not that those voices weren't there before, but that what was largely whispered has, for the moment, become emboldened to roar. But it's *for* that very reason that I take particular pleasure in presenting another tale in the Zane Pinchback storyline to you. My hope is that *Incognegro: Renaissance* not only entertains, but also reminds the reader that we have been here before, and there were real people who, like Zane, faced overwhelming odds, and chose to push back against them to make a better world.

— *Mat Johnson*

When Zane and Carl arrive at Arna Van Horn's book party, Xavier greets them and says, "Don't let all the white folks scare you, they're all negro-lovers—at least for tonight."

> *What do you think he means by this?*
> *What does his comment seem to suggest about the state of society in regards to race relations at the time?*

Zane explains to Xavier that he could never "pass" for white in his day-to-day life because he loves who he is and isn't a "traitor." "You can't have a career about telling the truth based on a lie," he states.

> *What does this tell you about Zane?*
> *What are some of the challenges a person of mixed-race heritage might have to face in society? What might it mean for their sense of personal identity?*

Xavier criticizes Van Horn for having unoriginal ideas. "That's what they do now, white artists. They come to Harlem, and they steal. Composers sit in the audiences of jazz clubs and take notes. Painters copy African masks, then pretend to invent abstractism."

> *Have you observed cultural appropriation in the arts? If so, what forms did it take?*
> *How does the appropriation of a culture harm the identity of people belonging to that culture?*

During Van Horn and Xavier's confrontation, Xavier implies that the only reason Van Horn's book was published is because he is a white author, and that black authors aren't afforded the same opportunities.

> *Why is it important for people of color and other minority groups to have space for telling their own stories?*
> *How can white people and other dominant groups help create those spaces without appropriating them?*

The police, and even Van Horn, are quick to classify Xavier's death as a suicide rather than a murder, even without investigating.

> *How might racial stereotypes have impacted the assumptions the police made about Xavier and the manner of his death?*
> *Do you think racial bias impacts the way crimes are treated today? How?*

Once Zane reveals which newspaper he works for, Mr. Gray states that they "only talk to the *real* press." But then Van Horn immediately claims that he's "a warrior for the dark masses."

> *How does this incident expose Van Horn and how he uses his connections and influence?*
> *In which areas of society would his behavior probably elevate him, and which groups would most likely feel less supported by his actions?*

Questions & Topics for Discussion

In issue #2, Carl makes Zane over to appear even whiter. This includes coaching him on his mannerisms and gait.

After seeing himself with his altered appearance, does Zane's resolve/attitude toward going "incognegro" evolve? If so, how?
What advantages or disadvantages might Zane encounter while "incognegro"?

In Issue #3, Bette openly reveals her "incognegro" status to Zane. However, by that point in the story she'd already hinted at it, and even openly admitted that Xavier had been her family.

Given these observations, why do you think Zane was still so taken aback by her admission of going "incognegro"?
What social and personal issues make the decision whether or not to "pass" for white so important to these characters?

Bette acknowledges that both she and Xavier faced particularly pronounced dangers—she as a white-passing woman of color and Xavier as a gay man—in New York.

How did Bette's and Xavier's identities make their lifestyles more dangerous than Zane's?
What kind of prejudice do women and LGBT+ people still face, and how does that differ from racial discrimination?

Throughout the series, Zane expresses guilt for "indulging in a privilege denied our people," while Bette states that she "makes her own guilt."

What do you think Bette means by this, and how does her attitude differ from Zane's philosophy?
Is Zane able to reconcile his sense of self and personal identity with this guilt he feels? Why or why not?

Bette and Zane both pay a price for the ways they choose to present themselves to the world around them.

What does Bette sacrifice in order to "pass" for a white woman with more privileges than a woman of color?
What does Zane sacrifice by choosing to embrace his Black heritage even though he can "pass" for white?

Reflect on the book's subtitle: "Renaissance."

What is the definition of a renaissance, and how does it relate to the events of the story?
The subtitle also refers to the Harlem Renaissance of the 1920s. Why was that time period referred to as a "renaissance," and where do we see the qualities of a renaissance depicted in the story?

Mat Johnson is the author of the novels *Loving Day*, *Pym*, *Drop*, and *Hunting in Harlem*, the nonfiction novella *The Great Negro Plot*, and the graphic novels *Incognegro* and *Dark Rain*.

He is a recipient of the American Book Award, the United States Artist James Baldwin Fellowship, The Hurston/Wright Legacy Award, the John Dos Passos Prize for Literature, and is a regular contributor on NPR's Fresh Air. Mat Johnson is a Professor at the University of Oregon.

Meera Bowman Johnson

A.Figgs

Warren Pleece is a comic book artist mostly known for his work on DC Comics' Vertigo imprint for titles such as *Deadenders*, *Hellblazer*, and *Incognegro*. As well as having worked for the magazine *2000AD*, Titan Comics' *Doctor Who* series, and for numerous publishers including Jonathan Cape, Macmillan, and Simon and Shuster, he is also co-creator of a comic magazine, *Velocity*, the graphic novels, *The Great Unwashed* and *Montague Terrace*, and the web series, *Alby Figgs*.

This volume collects issues #1–#5
of *Incognegro: Renaissance*.

Published by Dark Horse Books
A division of Dark Horse Comics, Inc.
10956 SE Main Street, Milwaukie, OR 97222

DarkHorse.com
ComicShopLocator.com

First Hardcover Edition: October 2018
ISBN: 978-1-50670-563-7

Printed in China
10 9 8 7 6 5 4 3 2 1

Library of Congress Cataloging-in-Publication data is available.

THE BOOK THAT STARTED IT ALL...

INCOGNEGRO

A GRAPHIC MYSTERY

By Mat Johnson & Warren Pleece

IN A TIME WHEN LOOKS COULD KILL, THERE WAS ONLY ONE WAY TO SURVIVE...

In the first half of the 20th century lynchings were commonplace throughout the American South. To most of the press, this epidemic of racial murder wasn't even news. But a few courageous reporters from the North risked their lives to expose these atrocities. They were light-skinned African-American men who could "pass" for white. They called this dangerous assignment "going incognegro."

Zane Pinchback, a reporter for the New York-based New Holland Herald, escapes with his life after his latest "incognegro" story goes bad. But when he returns to the sanctuary of Harlem, he's sent on a new story—the arrest of his own brother, charged with the brutal murder of a white woman in Mississippi.

This Special Tenth-Anniversary Edition features enhanced art, with a new afterword by the author and character sketches from the artist.

"Mat Johnson doesn't just push the boundaries of race, he blows them up."
—ESSENCE

BERGER BOOKS

Available now at all fine bookstores & Amazon.